John Wolf retired as a highly decorated soldier, having served over 35 years in the Army. Throughout his varied and changing career, he served in several countries, including Saudi Arabia, Kuwait, Iraq, Oman, Jordan, Afghanistan, Canada, USA, France, Germany, Denmark, Northern Ireland and Cyprus.

The Reality of War is the first book in the series which chronicles some of the experiences he faced whilst serving his country.

This book is dedicated to all those who served out there and especially those who gave the ultimate sacrifice.

John Wolf

THE REALITY OF WAR

A Soldier's Diary of the Gulf War

AUSTIN MACAULEY PUBLISHERS™

LONDON · CAMBRIDGE · NEW YORK · SHARJAH

A CIP catalogue record for this title is available from the British Library.

ISBN 9781786933911 (Paperback)
ISBN 9781786933928 (Hardback)
ISBN 9781786933935 (E-Book)

www.austinmacauley.com

First Published (2019)
Austin Macauley Publishers Ltd
25 Canada Square
Canary Wharf
London
E14 5LQ

Introduction

Most people only think or dream about how a war plays out and how they would react in it. The reality is somewhat startling.

I wrote this diary for a few reasons, some I will elaborate on below, but the main one was to allow people who have never been exposed to war to read about what a young soldier experienced and felt when sent into a major combat operation for the first time. I wanted it to be a truly open and honest account, rightly or wrongly, of exactly what went on each and every day, how people were treated and how they coped with it. I was determined not to write it worrying about how someone else would feel reading the diary later on. I was simply just going to record as many facts as possible, as and when they presented themselves.

Until 8th Jan, 1991, when Lorraine (an American female soldier) sent me a blank book through the post, I had nothing to write on that I could safely hide. Therefore, when I first started to write this diary, I had to try and recall a lot from others and my memory of when we first got out to the Gulf. After that, I wrote each day, mainly during a quiet period when I was manning the radios in the twilight hours. After a time, I started allowing other soldiers to read and contribute to it. Although some of the officers in our troop objected to what I was putting in it, some for reasons such as embarrassment, others simply because it was just not the done thing to say anything derogatory about the military or an officer at all, nobody contested events that were recorded or how I got hold of the information. What was written down was exactly what went on or, in some cases, what the lower ranks in the command element were informed went on, either from our immediate bosses or those directly above them.

After the war, I did not research the conflict to try and better understand what had transpired. If I had, it might have cleared things up or given me an understanding as to what and why things had happened. It might have even justified some of it. The fact was: it would not have changed what had happened and how we were treated or felt at the time, which was the whole point of writing the diary in the first place. For that reason alone, I have deliberately left the diary part of this book untouched and only expanded upon things for clarity or to explain military terms. It is written as if you were there (today in time). This then allows you, the reader, to live each and every day as we did. You will be amazed at what actually goes on. It will hopefully give you an insight and understanding of what it's really like when you get sent to war, because it involves a lot more struggles than just fighting the enemy, and this diary exposes all of them. This was no military exercise, film, TV show or PlayStation game; there was no reset button to use if it all went badly wrong. This was real and people died before, during and after the war.

Learning from history is very important, especially for those in the military world, but you need all the facts. Not only does history give you evidence and education, it allows you to digest a situation and then apply thought and logic to it without any pressures. This can give you hindsight and the ability to correct and learn from others' mistakes rather than committing the same ones again and learning the hard way. Regiments keep Regimental diaries for a record of the unit's history. The stories entered into them are written by officers after being stringently vetted by other, more senior, officers within the same unit, something that a personal diary is not subjected to. You will be very hard pushed to find anything negative in them. When comparing Regimental diaries of units that fought together in the same battles, whilst the timeline might remain consistent, events of who did what and when vastly differ in order to claim bragging rights. Writing like this then becomes another version of history. It's distorted and does not reflect the truth of exactly what went on because details have been deliberately omitted or misrepresented.

There are quite a few books today that have been written about conflicts, either by military personnel looking back on their experiences, or by someone else researching it. Having actually been involved in some of these conflicts, and in some cases personally known the author, it is very easy to see where most of the negativity has been removed and where stories have been wildly exaggerated, embellished or simply just made up in order to 'sell' the books. Again, it is distorting the facts and the truth. In most cases it's trying to paint a rosy picture. Personal diaries record the facts as and when they are happening and capture the good and the bad times. They become a living record years after the conflict is over, and in some cases all but forgotten about.

Despite many famous quotes and examples about leadership, there are still far more bosses than leaders in the Army. In the military, leaders will actively encourage the careers of the people under their command. They will get to know and understand their soldiers, especially their strengths and weaknesses. They will then utilise them in the best way possible after explaining why things need to be done and then allow them to get on with it. This type of command, called 'Mission Command', will give them a fighting force that is so much more potent because the guys actually want to do it. They will feel valued and appreciated, so morale will be high and the work rate will go up. Bosses are only interested in their own career and will simply just bark out orders, using people as and when they need to. Being like this with intelligent soldiers is detrimental, and it will ultimately lead to one outcome: they will eventually feel undervalued, underappreciated and they will leave. High-ranking officers in the military recognised this years ago and termed it 'Toxic Command'. After the war, a lot of professional, really switched on soldiers left the Regiment. Yes, there were many reasons why, but I know from individuals who had confided in me that the sole reason they left was what went on out in the Gulf and the way they were treated. I, myself, solely based on how I had been treated by certain individuals, went from a slightly brainwashed, keen-as-hell soldier wanting to join the Special Air Service (SAS) to wanting to leave the Army within a space of three months. War is not just about being the best soldier you can be and killing the enemy. How you live and how you are treated can have a direct impact on other things such as morale, fatigue, how you fight, and ultimately the end state of your Regiment months after it's all over. These are the things that an individual's diary can express so well, giving a human context to the events that transpired, something that is often forgotten and not recorded in history books.

Whilst the military teach and insist that soldiers capture and learn as many lessons as possible from previous exercises or operations, the reality is somewhat twisted, with some lessons either not being captured at all or simply swept under the carpet and, hence, being repeated again and again. The MOD and many officers, both serving and those who have left, are far more worried about reputation than character. It's a strange stance, considering character drives a reputation. It's also very dangerous because someone always calls our bluff and people get killed when we get exposed and show lacking. The Army, especially, favours and listens to rank over qualifications and/or experience. Some bosses appear not to be interested if someone can or cannot do their job correctly, if they do or do not have the right equipment, training or qualifications. Rather than listening and then sorting the issues out in order to make everyone and everything so much more professional, credible, effective and efficient, they are more concerned about their own career, so they just keep the boss above them happy by getting the job done and shutting up the people who point issues out. This diary captures many examples of the issues mentioned above and they were still going on when I left the Army!

I have waited for many years to publish these books because I was still serving and very mindful of the consequences. That said, I am still quite sure that the books will be frowned upon by most Military bosses because they say it as it is rather than distorting things or covering them up. Procedures, tactics, training, equipment and how the Army does its business today have vastly changed; however, some things have not. When reading the next books, you will be able to compare the facts for yourself. This first book is just my story about the Gulf War, and I will explain later how I went about obtaining the information contained within it.

Throughout the diary when I'm talking about 'we' or 'us', I'm generally referring to the lower ranks which are those ranks below that of Sergeant. I have deliberately not used the names of certain individuals, especially those that were in command. Their names are not relevant, only their actions. I have at times simply grouped and referred to those in command as 'They', 'The top' or the 'Chain of Command'.

At the back of this book is some helpful information for the reader. There is a glossary with some explanations of military terms and abbreviations, the rank structure within the Regiment at the time and how the military use the 24-hour clock.

Chapter 1

An Insight About the Regiment and Myself Before the Gulf War

My father was in the military and as such we moved around the world a lot. When he was stationed in Germany in the seventies, I ended up going to a British boarding school for four years just outside a town called Hamm. It was called Windsor Boys School. Even though the regime was almost military like and learning was forced upon you, I really enjoyed my time there. Not only did I meet lots of new friends and play practically every sport going, but for me, it was away from home. Being the middle child of the family, I always felt like the black sheep. My sister was Daddy's little girl and my brother was a right Mummy's boy.

In the military, at the time, drinking was an accepted culture and you were actively encouraged to take part. All sport and social activities involved drinking. In Germany, it was very cheap and plentiful. My father, I would have to say, drank a lot, which I guess at the time with them all doing it, didn't appear on the surface to be too out of the normal. However, sometimes he got violent when he had too much to drink, especially after drinking whiskey, and at times, this led to him hitting my mother. Another perceived culture of the Army at the time was that wives and children were classed as baggage; the Army was only interested in the soldier. So, when events like this happened, it was covered up by the Regiment, especially if rank was involved. For me it was unacceptable and as I got older I started to challenge my farther. I took a few knocks, but all that did was toughen me up and make me more resolved to keep having a go. Then came the day when I put him on his arse; however, what happened next blew my mind. My mother had a go at me for doing it, even though I protested that all I was doing was protecting her. I couldn't get my head around it. Unlike my brother and sister, who just kept out of it, I was not prepared to watch my father hit my mother, but protecting her just resulted in all of the anger coming my way from both parents. I needed to leave home at the earliest opportunity.

We moved back to the UK in 1980, where I finished off my last years of school. I left with nine 'O' Levels, six of them being 'A' grades. I was offered an apprenticeship with British Aerospace as a design technician just up the road from where we were living; they said I was only one of six school leavers in the whole of the UK who had managed not only to draw the test design correctly but also actually complete it. They had asked for and been sent my schoolwork, and they liked what they saw. If I accepted the offer, it would mean living at home even longer until I managed to get my life sorted and a place of my own, something my parents were not willing to help me with. My father was a strict believer that you had to stand on your own two feet in order to get on in the world.

I wanted to leave home and fast; therefore, I turned down the offer and decided to pop into the Army careers office in Bournemouth. They told me if I passed all the tests, I could be starting in as little as three months. I jumped at the opportunity and signed up. They still had the old tradition, but instead of taking the king's shilling, it was now a five-pound note. I told my parents I was staying with a friend and instead, went to a selection centre at Sutton Coldfield for a few days. The written tests, I have to say, were very easy for me and I passed them all with top grades. The one and a half mile run that we had to complete as a physical fitness test, I found hardly broke me into a sweat. Well, I was running or cycling ten miles every other day just to get out the house. We all got shown a video on the variety of jobs available in the Army. We were then asked to write down in order of preference from one to ten where we would like to go and what did we think best suited us for a job. I had uncles in the SAS and the Parachute Regiment (Paras). The SAS was where I wanted to end up in my Army career, but I knew you had to do a minimum of five years in a regular unit before you could apply for selection. I put the Paras as my first choice and the Royal Marines as my second; Royal Armoured Corps (RAC) was my seventh choice. We then had individual interviews with an officer, who went through each of the selections. He worked his way down my list giving me an excuse of exactly why they would not suit me. I was fit enough for the Marines and Paras but given the fact I was intelligent, he said I wouldn't like it. The next two were the other way around. I had the intelligence but they were mainly desk jobs and given all the sport and fitness I was doing, again I wouldn't like it. He eventually got to the RAC, where he now said he wasn't too sure about my commitment given how low down on my list it was. He also thought they were totally full and that there were no vacancies left, but he would go and check on my behalf. I was beginning to think I would not be getting into the Army, even though I had passed all the tests; maybe I wasn't as good as I thought I was. I felt ashamed and the fear of failure was creeping in. He returned after what seemed like an age and said there was one vacancy left. He was still unsure whether to give it to me, but then he asked, "Would you like to have the very last vacancy for the RAC?" Of course, I bloody well wanted it.

I left the room really pleased with myself and met two others in the corridor who were ahead of me. They asked me if I got the last RAC vacancy. I was impressed they knew that and enquired how. They also had been given the 'very last' RAC vacancy. 12 of us on that selection day had all been sold the same story and had all managed to be given the 'very last' vacancy for the RAC. The careers guy was an Army officer and had played a cameo role, but I couldn't get over the fact he had blatantly lied to us all. How were you supposed to trust people in charge of you if they could lie so easily? This was a lesson worth noting and for me to be wary of. I later found out, as with everything in the Army, they tackle the immediate problem first rather than looking at the bigger picture. You were sent to where they needed the manpower the most at the time, not what was best suited for you. Ironically, if they looked at and utilised your skills, intelligence, motivation, drive and commitment, not only would it benefit the individual, but ultimately, it would benefit the Army in both the short and the long term.

When I got home, I told my parents I had joined up. My father was indifferent and said I would never make it since I didn't have the ability or the right attitude. He said it would show because I wouldn't even get past selection. I told him I had already passed it and that they had accepted me; my mother blew a fit and blamed my father for me throwing my life away.

I joined the Army in 1982, starting off in the Junior Leaders Regiment (JLR) based in Bovington, Dorset. The structure and training of the Regiment was based off the Royal Military Academy Sandhurst for Army officers. The concept of JLR was to produce leaders for the future. Amongst other things, it was trained and drilled into you about being professional at all times, physically fit, to always win, and to try and be the best at everything you did. Question what does not make sense, think logically then act, don't just blindly obey for the sake of it. This was constantly reinforced by all the training staff, who kept telling us that men who excelled in these areas always got promoted in the Regiments. Men who did not fell by the wayside, which was fine and not seen as a failure, since the Army needed highly trained skilled soldiers. This type of training would ensure that future leaders were men that were looked up to and followed. The Army was evolving and they wanted intelligent soldiers from now on, not robots. They were going to mould us into that perfect soldier, as I was sure they had always done throughout time. For want of better words, it was brainwashing at its best and it worked very well.

Young soldiers who were selected for the RAC, The Royal Military Police (RMP) and Army Air Corps (AAC) started off here as boy soldiers straight from school. We spent 18 months doing training as opposed to our non-JLR counterparts (RAC) who only completed eight weeks basic training in Catterick up north. Catterick was for guys joining at any point in their lives up to the maximum entry age, which at the time, I believe, was 28 years old. This meant you had a blend of people of all different ages and backgrounds. There was always banter and a lot of resentment from the guys who had been through Catterick about the guys from the JLR. Clearly, it did not take the brains of an Archbishop to see that one of us, given the amount of training we had, would be better placed and far more qualified for the regular Army units. This obviously produced resentment in the units when it came to promotion time.

JLR was just like a boarding school to me. Set out in four terms where you stayed there during the term and were let home afterwards with a wad of cash, most of which, if you were like me, went straight to your parents. Each term you progressed to higher recognition and more intense training. There was even a promotion system in place, where you got given extra privileges if you got promoted. Term one you were not allowed to do anything or go anywhere unsupervised. You got paid five pound a week; the rest was saved and given to you at the end of the term. Each week trying to get this money was something to behold, as I am sure every person who has been through the training system will remember. You had to march in, salute and state your number, rank and name. If they liked what they saw, you were given the money, if not, back out, form up at the back of the queue and try again. Sometimes I'd laugh, other times I'd almost be crying in frustration marching in and out every two minutes. Once a week you got marched to the NAAFI (Navy, Army, Air Force Institution) a shop on camp, where you could spend your five pounds on things like toiletries or sweets. As the terms went on, you got given more money and were even allowed out of camp.

Training included the normal military stuff like learning how to be a soldier, fitness and drill. It also included classroom education subjects like Maths, English, Science, German and Military Studies (MS). In MS you'd learn all about military history and past battles, how we won and lost them, and how to improve the next time; in other words, lessons to be learnt. Interestingly, it was very noticeable to see that some of the same mistakes were being made over and over again in battles. This struck me as lessons not being learnt, only repeated by different people who were in charge at the time. We also did trade training. For the RAC guys, it meant that by the time you left you were qualified as a tank driver, signaller and gunner. That way you were a more rounded soldier for your new unit to employ since they could utilise you in quite a few roles, unlike the guys from Catterick, who only came out as tank drivers.

The downside to JLR training, which you only really found out when you got to your new Regiment, was the reality of all the brainwashing. Not only did you contend with the guys from Catterick and their views of soldiers coming from JLR, but unfortunately, a lot of guys in the Regiments were still stuck in the old ways. It was going to take quite a few years for the changes to filter in and be accepted, something that has no doubt always happened in the military when changes are made. They had to start somewhere but until everyone got on board and accepted the new changes, there were always going to be problems and clashes. The old guard firmly believed in the old ways; why would they think anything different? This was how they had been taught in the military and as far as they were concerned, it had worked for them, so why was a change needed? They did not believe people should question them when they told you to do something, especially if you were a lower rank than them. It was not accepted that this was simply the way you had been trained, it was viewed that you were a 'gobby' person. When someone told you to jump, the only question you were allowed to ask was how high? Conforming like this would get you accepted into the fold and ultimately viewed favourably when promotion time came around. The other major point that struck the guys coming from JLR was that promotion appeared not to be based on things like merit, fitness, being good at your job, man management, loyalty, leadership, etc. It was mainly focused on time served in the Regiment and your face fitting. This was no doubt born out of how the Cavalry officer got promoted, which then filtered into the system for everyone else. Accepting this system and way of life, rather than the indoctrinated one I had been taught in training, was something that bit me in the ass after a few years in the Regiment; it resulted in a Squadron transfer and a hold up of my promotion.

At the time, a lot of soldiers coming from JLR didn't last long or left the Army soon after their time bar was up. When you left training, you signed a form to say you would serve for a period of time (called a time bar); it was either for three, six or nine years. As an incentive, you got paid a little bit extra for serving longer. The guys leaving fuelled an ongoing argument to close down JLR. It being said that Catterick worked fine and everyone should be going through there; not only would it save time and money, but it would ultimately produce more manpower far quicker. Trade training could be done in the Regiments when they arrived. Soldiers from Catterick already proved this could be done. That and a few other arguments eventually led to the closure of JLR; anything that saved money in the military always seemed to come out on top. Years later, the closing down of JLR was deeply regretted by many and calls for it to reopen were proposed but soon rejected. One thing you learn very quickly in the military is that when a decision has been made involving a very high-ranking officer, it is seldom ever reversed.

I personally did struggle in the first term at JLR; I think this was what my father was on about, my attitude and reluctance to follow orders. I am sure I wasn't the first or would be the last teenager to struggle with this concept straight from school. At the end of term one, I was told in no uncertain terms to get my act together or I would be getting kicked out. I was excelling in everything but being let down by this. I was even told that I would have been promoted by now, but due to this underlying issue, it was turned down. Like everything in life, I saw this as a direct challenge and I was determined to prove them, and my father, wrong. I switched on and started to focus on everything I was doing to ensure things were done perfectly first-time round. Everything I did or competed in I wanted to come first; nothing and no one was going to beat me. If I couldn't do something or did not come first in it, I would keep practising until I did. If nothing else, it got me very fit and highly motivated in areas I would no doubt have dropped very quickly if I was not in the military. As a result, I managed to get promoted three times up to the rank of Junior Sergeant during my stay there.

One of many highlights for me was when we broke the record for the assault course at JLR in term two, something that had stood for many years. For that I was picked for a team that took on the Royal Marine recruits at Lympstone on their own assault course; we beat them. For those that don't know what a military assault course is, as a team you run a distance, along the way there will be obstacles that you either have to get over, up, down, through, around or under. An assault course can also be run carrying weights or equipment, for example a log (telegraph pole). It serves quite a few disciplines such as teamwork, fitness, motivation, etc.

For coming second, the Royal Marine recruits got the added pleasure of going over their assault course again and again. I don't think their instructors were best pleased at all. We, on the other hand, were treated to fish and chips and a few beers. It didn't sound like much, but since alcohol was banned in JLR for terms one to three, this was a godsend. The treat, I later found out, was not because we had won but because our instructors had won quite a lot of money making bets on us. Had we lost, I dread to think what would have happened to us. I'm sure running over the assault course again would have been the least of our problems.

In term four, we all had to apply for our choice of Regiment that we would like to serve in once leaving JLR. It was not guaranteed so we had to put three Regiments down. I was in A Squadron at the time and two out of the four senior instructors in the Squadron were both from the same Regiment as my father and knew him really well. As such, throughout the term they pushed me to apply to join it, saying it was a family Regiment and as such they would look after me. They kept asking me why would I want to take a chance on going to an unknown Regiment, where life for me could be bad, when they had already sent word back about how well I was doing. They reassured me that I was guaranteed a place because my father was still serving in it.

After completing JLR in late 1983, I joined my Regiment, 16th/5th The Queens Royal Lancers, who were stationed in Tidworth, Hampshire. The Regiment at the time was a Reconnaissance (Recce) unit and equipped with Combat Vehicle Reconnaissance (Tracked) or CVR (T) for short. The CVR (T) was designed to be light and agile so it could be air portable; hence, it was small and made mainly out of aluminium alloy to keep the weight down. It actually ended up having less ground pressure than a man per square feet. On open days, the regiment always showed a CVR (T) being balanced on 10-pint glasses to prove it, not bad for an 8-tonne vehicle. There were seven variants of the CVR (T) and each one had a unique role. Each was classed as an Armoured Fighting Vehicle (AFV), even though some had limited to no weapons at all, and they all shared the same basic automotive components, e.g. engine, suspension, tracks, etc. Aptly named, the Scorpion and Scimitar had a turret with a main gun (76mm and 30mm) and a 7.62mm machine gun. The Sultan was the Command and control Vehicle, commonly called a CV, with the Samaritan being the ambulance. The Spartan carried infantry soldiers and the Striker carried the anti-tank Swingfire missiles. The recovery vehicle was called the Samson.

I was posted to A Squadron, which was out in Beirut at the time. Due to my age and the fact that there were bullets flying around everywhere, not to mention the US and French Embassies/Barracks had just been bombed a few days ago, I was sent across the water to B Squadron, who were doing a six-month tour as peacekeepers with the United Nations (UN) in Cyprus. Guess they didn't think it would make great reading in the papers someone getting killed just weeks out of training.

Once there, I was placed in 4th troop, where I just kept my mouth shut and watched what was going on. Unlike JLR where it was drilled into us to act and be a team at all times regardless of rank, this was not the case in the Regiment. It was very evident that the rank structure not only came with a pecking order and certain privileges, and rightly so, but also a distinct divide with exclusive social groups which created an unhealthy environment of a 'them and us' status.

Up to the rank of Corporal, you were all classed as the lower ranks. These were basically all the workers who ate, slept and worked together. At the rank of Corporal, which by the way came with a nice pay rise, you had a hell of a lot of responsibility put on your plate and depending on the personality depended on how they spoke and treated the people below them. As the saying goes, it is the Corporals that run the Army, not the officers, because they are the ones that know the guys inside out because they live and breathe with them. Unlike most other Regiments in the Army, our Corporals had their own Mess (bar). Next came the Senior Non-Commissioned Officers (SNCOs) who were Sergeants and Staff Sergeants. These were akin to managers/dads. At this rank you were deemed to have shown your worth so you were elevated in status. The SNCOs had their own separate Mess which comprised of accommodation, cookhouse and a bar which they shared with the Warrant Officers. The Warrant Officers were above the SNCOs and were scary people. They were another 'click' and basically could do as they pleased. Each Squadron had a Warrant Officer who was the Squadron Sergeant Major (SSM). They basically ran the Squadron on the behalf of the officer in charge of it. Above them all sat the Regimental Sergeant Major (RSM). He was 'God' to everyone and you did not want to cross his path, ever. Then came the officers. In the Regiment there was a massive social divide between them and everyone else and it was constantly pointed out to remind you of your social standing, and your place within the unit. Being friendly, what was called 'Mixing', between the ranks was totally forbidden. It really was a 'them' and 'us'. Examples will become apparent throughout the book. At the back of the book the rank structure within the Regiment is explained in detail.

The good thing about being in Cyprus was that we were on our own as a troop of 12 guys in an outstation. The troop was made up of one officer, one Sergeant, three Corporals and the rest of us were lower ranks. Minus the officer, everyone else was required to pull their weight to live and work together, so I was cut a lot of slack as the 'new guy' because they needed me as a team member. Despite being given plenty of shit, and a few individuals making it very clear to me that my father had rubbed them up the wrong way, it was constantly pointed out to me during the tour about how easy I had it compared to other new guys, something I did not fully comprehend until later on after returning back to the UK, when I witnessed the behaviour first-hand that was dished out to new guys. It was seen, and accepted, by most as some sort of tradition/initiation; you were treated like shit until it was deemed you were good enough to be part of the team, and it would normally last a minimum of six months. One group of lads in B Squadron took it upon themselves to dish a beating out to all the new guys; the excuse used was that it happened to everyone who was new to remind you to keep your mouth shut and not to be gobby.

One night when it was the turn of Jonno, Cliff and I, a friend had pre-warned me it was coming. I sleep very lightly anyway, I always have done; the slightest of noises and I am awake. I heard them coming so immediately jumped out of bed and grabbed a broken chair leg that I had put under the bed. The door opened and the lights went on; there were four of them, all big lads. It made me mad as hell, not only could I not stand bullies, but it was the fact it was four guys doing this to blokes asleep in bed at night. I told them the first guy to come near me was going to get severely hurt, and I didn't give a shit if they kicked my head in. Now I knew who they were, every day I saw them, no matter where we were or what we were doing, or who they were with, I would go for them and it wouldn't stop. They would then have the added problem of trying to explain exactly why I had an issue with them. They thought I was crazy and left the room to go and get the other two. That was the first and last time I had dealings with that lot, although two held grudges towards me for a very long time and ensured my name was always mud within the Squadron. When I spoke to other guys in the Squadron later on, they told me these guys had always done it and got away with it. It had been reported before, but it was completely ignored. The person who reported it subsequently had a life of misery until they eventually left. 'Grassing' people up was just unacceptable, no matter what the reason.

Whilst out in Cyprus, I was 'introduced' to alcohol. We were down in the Austrian sector at the time and ended up getting invited for drinks at one of their outposts. When I was asked what I would like to drink, I replied Coke. The question got repeated and my reply was the same. My troop Corporal (Cpl) Jack N, thought I was being funny until I explained I didn't touch the stuff at all. I was committed to training and fitness. I didn't mention about my father having a massive influence on me as well, mainly because he was still serving. Jack got a bottle of bourbon, and I was encouraged by all to help him drink it. Needless to say, they all had a good laugh later on watching me puking it all back up. I felt like crap for two days afterwards, heat and a hangover from hell do not go very well together. My suffering didn't deter the guys from ensuring I was given plenty of other opportunities to drink again. Like I said, alcohol was part and parcel of everyday life in the Army at the time and in Cyprus it was dirt-cheap. I adopted a regime of going for a run first thing in the morning to sweat all the alcohol out if I drank the night before. It seemed to work for me and quickly removed my hangover.

I got my first taste of politics and the military during this tour. One night, Cpl John T (SAS Tomo) and I got called back to our main operating base in Nicosia Airport. We received a brief from the Squadron boss about a substantial truck bomb threat against the UK Embassy, that just happened to be located in the UN protective zone. Being there meant British troops could not protect it because they were not allowed inside the UN zone and UN troops could not protect it because it did not belong to the UN. The Greek checkpoints before entering the UN zone were not willing to get involved, and should a car or truck run at them, they said they would simply let it through, no doubt driven by the long history over the British occupation in Cyprus. The plan, therefore, was to use a few guys either end of the roads that lead into the Embassy. The Canadians would guard one side, us the other. Being UN troops, we could not fire unless fired upon and nobody was allowed to have loaded weapons full stop. Should someone drive a car or truck towards the Embassy, we were to block it by driving our Ferret scout car into its path. The intelligence said the threat was very real and the players were believed to be after the British because of our involvement in Beirut. The attack was likely to be very similar to the ones carried out over there on the US and French Embassies.

So, basically, without actually saying it, they wanted us to ram a car/truck bomb with our vehicle to stop it getting to the Embassy because our hands were tied by politics, rules and regulations. I pointed out that I was not exactly happy with this plan and was firmly told to shut up. The Canadians, on the other hand, also stated they were not happy and said they were going to use an Armoured Personnel Carrier (APC) parked between the walled barriers on the road checkpoint. They were also going to mount a loaded 50-calibre machine gun on top and bollocks to the politics.

Four of us did this task, six hours on, six off for three weeks solid. One day we had a scare when a speeding car was let through the Greek checkpoint. On seeing us in the middle of the road it skidded to a halt 100 metres away. After a long pause, Tomo told me to load the main machine gun and if the guy took him out, to promise him I would get the bastard. I promised him and then loaded up. Once I was set and ready, Tomo went up to the car and approached the driver. Turned out to be a lost, drunk taxi driver. Tomo instructed him how to get back out.

A Squadron, the following year, were given a six-month cooling off tour in Cyprus for their efforts in Beirut. They asked for six guys from B Squadron to go with them to help show them the ropes, one per troop. Because I was single and A Squadron was my original intended Squadron, I was 'invited' to go. I really didn't mind, as I loved the place. So, I spent another six months in Cyprus, this time with 5th troop. The troop had some great guys in it and was run by a troop Sergeant (Sgt), Paul C, they did not have an officer in it. He was very keen on fitness and had even attempted SAS selection. He found out I had been a cross-country runner before joining up so entered me for every race on the island. I utilised it all as part of my overall fitness plan and even managed to win a few. As a troop, we entered into every march and shoot competition on the island. There were nine other nations serving out in Cyprus at the time, and each hosted a unique competition of their own, normally held within their controlled sector of the island. They would also enter several teams into the other competitions, so there were always lots of teams to compete against. One of the marches which was hosted by the Danish contingency was aptly called the Dancon March. It involved carrying 35 pounds 25 miles up Troodos Mountains on day one. This was followed by drinking lots of beer and meeting soldiers from all the other nations serving out there. You then got up the next day and did it all over again.

Whilst stationed in Cyprus, the troop adopted a policy of working eight days on followed by four days off to do whatever we liked. A Land Rover was made available to the guys who had the time off to explore the island. I loved exploring new places and meeting new people, so I took full advantage of the time off and even manage a trip across to Egypt to see the pyramids. I also managed to get a freefall parachuting and a BSAC sport diver course done. Anything to do with sport and the troop Sgt was 100 percent behind you. Overall, I would have to say the guys in A Squadron accepted and treated me far better than those in B Squadron, not only did I have a brilliant time but I made quite a few new friends. The troop Sgt asked command if I could stay in his troop on return, but it got turned down.

On returning to the UK I went back to B Squadron and became specialised in signals (radios and communications), weapons, tactics, mine warfare and demolitions. I was now in their 5th troop, or what we all commonly referred to as Boot troop. This was a troop of guys that were normally your fittest and very keen soldiers. They were all trained in infantry tactics, including all weapons, hence the name Boot troop. The exact make-up of the Regiment and its Squadrons is explained at the back of the book under military structure at the time.

This was the Cold War era and as such all training was based upon the Warsaw Pact attacking NATO and how we would cope and defend ourselves before slowing them down, stopping them and then ultimately forcing them back. We never practised NATO attacking them. As a Recce Regiment, we could be used to fulfil two main roles depending on what the Divisional Commander wanted at the time. We regularly practised both roles on small and large-scale exercises. Most of the large ones involved going overseas to countries like Germany, Norway, Turkey or Denmark to give us the real estate to play on. We would start at one end of the country and play until we got to the other end. It was just brilliant being given complete freedom in a country to drive unrestricted anywhere we wanted to at any time. It was a sight to behold seeing so much military hardware from the various nations driving across country, through fields, towns and villages, something we never did in the UK.

One of our roles was to operate deep behind enemy lines acting as the eyes and ears of the Division. A Division was made up of two or more Battlegroups, (I will expand on these later on when talking about my time in Canada). The idea was that we would be on our own right up on the front line, with all the Division miles away dug in ready for a fight. Staying completely hidden, we would allow the Warsaw Pact to roll right over and past us. Our job was to report to the Division exactly what was coming, numbers, formations, equipment, etc. and its direction. We needed the main fighting forces to go past us and then we would hit the command groups and logistics that would follow them up. The other role was to actually withdraw in contact with the enemy. The idea was to get them to follow us, or channel them into killing grounds that the Division had prepared. Throughout the withdrawal we would be constantly engaging the enemy and then running; shoot and scoot as we called it. The aim was to try and slow them down a bit in order to buy the Division more time to get prepared. At a certain point, very close to our main forces, we would come across the Battlegroups Recce troop. Here we would do a handover then completely withdraw, regroup and await further orders from higher.

Whatever the role we performed, stealth and cunningness were our main weapons of choice, given the lightly armoured vehicles we used, that and plenty of training to stay alive and be self-sufficient before returning to our own front lines, assuming you survived that long. Hence, it was important that guys in the troops got trained and became specialists in a minimum of three fields/disciplines. Where possible you had at least two guys per troop trained in each discipline in case your specialist got killed or captured. It was always perceived (and played at) that after five days, the Warsaw Pact would have been stopped and either be in full retreat, and/or trying to negotiate some sort of deal to end it. There were no other scenarios practised, we never ever lost.

The staying hidden and operating effectively was always practised on Regimental exercises and Boot troop was used to great effect here. Our job was to try and find our own troops, day or night. If they were doing their jobs correctly and covertly, we would not find them, and the only guys who suffered were us lot, walking about all day and night. The troops always got praised from the top lot for us not finding them. If, however, we found them, which was normally due to them making noise or having poor light discipline at night, it was free rein what we could do to them as it was deemed nothing compared to what would happen if they were found during a war. The punishment for being discovered went from attacking them (with blank ammunition, flares and thunder flashes), to nicking bits of kit, letting down the tank tracks, to physically capturing one of their men. The letting down of tracks was the favourite one, followed by a full-on attack. The tracks on our tanks had to be taut for it to drive correctly; pumping grease into a track tensioner does this. It's a bit of hard work and is all done by hand. Attacks at night cause massive confusion, especially when you are firing flares, designed to go up into the air, directly at the guys. During the attack, if they got into their tanks and tried to drive off in all the confusion, what we called bugging-out drills, it inevitably threw the track off the wheels due to it being too slack. This now meant a whole lot of work for the guys to get it back on and then pump up the tensioner with grease, assuming they had some. There is nothing worse than track bashing at night in the rain.

One of my most memorable nights, and not for the right reasons I might add, was when we managed to sneak undetected into a troop hide and get the sentry. That's the person who stays awake and alerts the rest of the guys if the enemy approach. It took us hours on our bellies in the pouring rain to sneak right into the hide. One of the guys managed to get behind him, place a knife to his throat and whisper, "You're now dead, hand the weapon over, sit down and shut the fuck up." He handed the rifle to the guy and sat down, followed by shouting at the top of his voice, "Stand to, stand to!" He might have said more were it not for a rifle butt to the face. At the time, I was more pissed off that he didn't play the game fair and square; it also spoilt what was going to be an epic planned attack.

No matter what we did when we found a troop, the result was the same: the troop would have to bug out as per their drills. That meant pack everything up, move location and start all over again. Moving involved that little extra physical exercise of trench digging again at the next location. It would normally take about six hours minimum at night to build an observation trench quietly and correctly. As you can imagine, in the big scheme of things, Boot troops were being used to train the guys to be very professional for their own sake, but in reality, it messed them about no end and they hated it, and us.

The second role of the Regiment, to withdraw in contact, was when Boot troop really came into its very own. Boot troop training was based on slowing/delaying or channelling the enemy into killing grounds using demolitions, traps, mines, air and/or artillery support and good old infantry tactics. Depending on if we were trying to channel them or just slow them down, as our own guys passed through our positions, we would have set traps and demolitions that we could now either set off as the last friendly vehicle passed us, or use it against the first enemy vehicle. If we managed to channel the enemy into killing grounds that we had prepared ourselves, not only did we have anti-tank weapons with us that we were all trained on how to use, but we were also trained in calling in artillery and/or air support, depending on what was available at the time. We trained using a different artillery mission compared to the rest of the Army guys. We had trained laser target operators (myself being one) so we could use artillery to hit a target far faster than the conventional method, which was taught to everyone else. The Artillery, for some reason, didn't want anyone to use this method, only us and their own guys.

The thing that was never practised on exercises was the actual handover between the Battlegroups Recce and us. We just never trained together. On our Regimental exercises, we just had a notional point where we would conduct this make-believe handover. Instead of conducting a handover, it was used for a break in the exercise, where the Regiment could draw a line in the sand and reset the guys ready for the next lot of tasks in order to get the maximum benefit out of the time we had available. The Recce they did was different to what we did, mainly because they had the Battlegroup right behind them for protection and so never strayed too far. The differences in how the Battlegroup Recce operated was highlighted to us when our new Commanding Officer (CO) came from an Armoured Corps Regiment equipped with Main Battle Tanks (MBT). Normally, your CO was an officer who had served in your Regiment for years, but on very rare occasions, you ended up with someone coming in from a different Regiment. The new CO wanted us all to change how we operated to how it was done in his old mob, since he believed that was how Recce should be done. There was, shall I say, lots of interesting arguments and people getting sacked left right and centre during his time in the Regiment. He was affectionately called the 'pink pig', although if memory serves me right, this was more to do with his looks and the fact the guys just needed an excuse to vent frustration. God help you if he ever heard those words.

The rolling countryside of Germany provided great killing grounds for MBTs, especially modern ones that could fire up to four kilometres. You only had to study a few battles of WWII to figure that out. Knowing what we knew, especially about capabilities and how we were training, most of the guys who had a reality caption knew damned well that if we went to war with the Warsaw Pact, by the time we got back to our own lines having done our war-time role, the Regiment would exist in name only. It was a concept a lot of the top people either failed to realise, denied or simply just ignored; it was just one big game to them, and this was further reinforced because we always won the battles we played on exercises. The opposition force were never allowed to win because they were always instructed how to play. They were not allowed to use their initiative or come off-script as that might disrupt the overall outcome/aim of the exercise. One of the many things I took away from JLR was that the enemy always had a vote; therefore, don't follow the book blindly, have a plan and remain flexible. Chances are your plan was going to change and you needed to be able to adapt rapidly; better still, anticipate as many of the 'what ifs' before they happen so you can stay one step ahead, a bit like a chess game. As we say in the military, no plan survives first contact.

I really enjoyed my time in Boot troop, not only did my thirst for knowledge grow but I made some new friends. However, things were about to change. I mentioned previously about the brainwashing of JLR soldiers. Seeing people in positions that went totally against the grain of what you had been indoctrinated on soon led to a conflict of interest, that and rubbing people up the wrong way, very, very quickly. Of the seven guys who I hung around with in the Squadron, four were hounded out of the Regiment by what today would be akin to bullying and abuse of rank, something that would not be tolerated in the military today. It mainly came from one individual who was the newly appointed Squadron Sergeant Major (SSM). In those days, there was no such thing as bullying, harassment, discrimination etc. If anyone 'grassed', their life was made a living hell and nobody trusted them. You were simply expected to man up and accept life as it was; otherwise, you were seen as being weak, there were no women in the 'teeth arms' full stop. The 'teeth arms' were those combat units that did the fighting on the front line.

On taking over as the new SSM of B Squadron, he actually got all seven of us into his office and told us he was going to make it his personal mission to get rid of us. He didn't agree with how the old SSM had allowed us to get away with things, and he certainly didn't like our attitudes or our way of life. He informed us all that he was going to keep putting us on charges until we either left the Regiment ourselves or were eventually thrown out of the Army. A charge is when you are punished for a crime. First charge and you were up in front of your own Officer Commanding (OC) the Squadron, unless it was serious or for a second offence, then your OC would send you in front of the CO of the Regiment. Obviously, the punishment would be greater coming from the CO. To be a good soldier, you were expected to just accept the charge, take the punishment and move on. In some of the Squadrons, it was deemed not the norm if you got promoted all the way up to the rank of SSM and had not been in serious trouble at some point in your career. Unlike all the other SSMs, our new SSM was squeaky clean.

It soon became my turn to be his main focus of attention, and the next guy for him to get rid of. Having had me charged twice already and done the OC and the CO part, he soon had me up on yet another charge of insubordination and insolence. This was a charge that at the time covered anything from sighing to looking at someone in a manner they did not like, to blatantly saying NO and refusing to do something they had just ordered you to do. If someone wanted you charged but they feared it might not sound correct when read out, or there was a chance it might be turned down, then this was the charge to use. It was a catch-all charge which you did not have to explain, and it ensured that the system/Army always won. Because this was going to be my third charge for the same offence, this now meant the punishment would have to be a jail sentence.

The Regimental Sergeant Major (RSM), who not only had come into the Army via the JLR system but also knew my parents very well, had a word with me. He told me that going to jail, which would be the outcome of this charge if I accepted it, would not be a good career move for me, regardless of what I had heard or believed. He said he was starting to see a pattern from my SSM with regards to recent individuals that had been thrown out of the Regiment, and given the fact there were quite a few other people in the unit that had also raised concerns about the SSM, he was going to take a very keen interest in his activities from now on. However, in the meantime, he wanted to know what my decision was before we marched into the CO's office. I informed him I would take his advice and refuse the charge.

I was marched in and back out of the CO's office at the speed of light, leaving one very annoyed CO. How dare I refuse a charge? The RSM told me to wait in his office while he had a word with the CO. Any other day or person, you would have been marched straight into the RSM's office from the CO's, had your head ripped off (or re-educated as they called it), then marched straight back into the CO's office, where you *would* have accepted the charge, which by the way now incurred extra punishment because you had the audacity to refuse it first time around. Going against the flow of how things were done meant you were a troublemaker, so in good old military traditional fashion, you needed taking down a peg or two to get you in line and on board with everyone else. 'The System' as it was commonly referred to.

The RSM returned and said to me that if I now accepted the charge, I would be transferred to another Squadron tonight and the punishment would not be jail but something like five days Restriction of Privileges (ROPs). He said the CO, rightly or wrongly, given his position, must back his SSM's up. That is how it always has been and always will be. This was a good deal for me and I should seriously take it. ROPs were designed to mess you around. You had parades in different uniforms, one before and after work, and one at 2230 at night. You would incur extra ROP days if your kit wasn't up to the required standard, to a point where you were simply jailed. Between your evening inspections, you turned up to the guardroom and worked, doing any jobs that they, or anyone else in the Regiment, had or could find you. It could be absolutely anything from sweeping the roads, picking up leaves all night long, polishing brass, bulling other people's boots, or helping out in the cookhouse peeling spuds and washing pots and pans. At weekends, you worked all day long.

I was once more marched into the CO's office at the speed of light. I accepted since it meant I could get out of the Squadron and away from the SSM. The CO awarded me 14 days ROPs and a transfer to C Squadron. It was still better than going to jail.

Whenever you were charged by the CO, you had to report back to your SSM, who would normally rip your head off for embarrassing the Squadron before putting you in front of your own OC, who would do likewise. It was just another way of ensuring you got the message that everyone was now watching you. On returning to the SSM to inform him of my punishment, after the bollocking, with a smirk on his face, he told me that once I had finished my ROPs, he would be after me again. The smug look on his face incensed me, so I took great delight in telling him that it would be a little difficult since I was no longer in his Squadron anymore and therefore, he was not my SSM. He was furious, and after giving me another bollocking for me being so smug, he rang the RSM and attempted to get it changed whilst he made me stand there at attention. The RSM must have put him right, because he blew another fit at me before telling me to get the hell out of his office. I never went back in front of the OC at all.

I reported to my new SSM in C Squadron the next morning. C Squadron at the time was part of the Allied Command Europe Mobile Force (AMF), so trips to Norway and Turkey came each year for the Squadron.

I instantly took to the SSM because I was actually spoken to like a human being for once, that and he told me he also had a bit of a dislike towards the other SSM. He informed me that he had received a telephone call from him all about me. He couldn't believe someone could be that bad; therefore, he was going to give me a chance. I was on a six-month probation period, and if I messed up just once, God help me. I went into 3rd troop and again, the troop Sgt (Ralph R) gave me pretty much the same speech. It was totally fine with me, and I respected where they were both coming from; after all, they had no idea who I was. I was just so grateful of the chance to have a fresh start again and prove to them just how good a soldier I really was.

Six months later the SSM called me in for my progress report/chat. He told me everyone was extremely happy with my performance so far even to the point that the troop Sgt wanted me promoted to Lance Corporal (L/Cpl). Whilst he agreed with him, he said this, of course, could not be allowed to happen because quite a few people knew what had transpired in my old Squadron; if I were to be promoted it would raise questions about the integrity of the other SSM and certain individuals in B Squadron. It would all get ugly; therefore, to keep everyone happy, when we moved to Germany next year, I would be getting promoted and posted to Canada for two years out of the way.

You might say I was lucky, but the truth was, I was not vindicated and my promotion had suffered because of it. My cards and reputation were marked with guys of that old-school mindset in B Squadron, and I would cross them again sooner or later.

Chapter 2
BATUS

In 1986 we moved as a Regiment to Herford in Germany. I was promoted and posted to Canada to work at The British Army Training Unit Suffield (BATUS) for two years. When I arrived, I noticed that I was the only soldier from my unit serving out there. I found this very surprising given the set-up of the place and the type of training that went on. Out in BATUS was every bit of equipment in the British Army's inventory at the time: MBTs, APCs, helicopters, artillery guns, you name it, it was there. All this equipment and kit was used on a training area which happened to be the size of Wales back home. I never even knew the place existed until I was posted there. The main reason being, Divisions did not train there and thus neither did their Recce Regiments. The sole purpose of BATUS was to put Battlegroups through their paces and test them. It was where I learnt all about the Combined Arms Battlegroup and armoured warfare.

A Battlegroup was either Armoured, in which case it was made up of two tank Regiments and one Infantry Regiment, or it was Mechanised, in which case it had two Infantry Regiments and only one tank Regiment. Amongst many others, an Engineer unit, air and Artillery always supported the Battlegroup. The Battlegroup had its own Recce, normally consisting of eight vehicles; if it was an Armoured Battlegroup they were CVR (T)s. Seven exercises, called Medicine Mans (Med Mans), were run each year to put the guys through their paces as a Battlegroup. About 2000 guys at a time were flown in to take part in each Med Man, which itself was split into two parts. The first part involved live firing and was therefore called Live Ex. The second was dry, meaning no live ammunition was used at all by anyone; it was known as TES Ex, which was short for Test Exercise but also just happened to be the abbreviation for the fitted simulation system. A Med Man was overseen by call sign Niner and his range safety and control staff. Niner was a Brigadier, a one-star General, and if he didn't like or approve of something, you soon got the message. Everyone who had ever heard his voice on the radio net knew exactly what was coming next.

Live Ex started off low key, with individual units getting to grips with their own firing systems and procedures. This quickly built up to full-size Battlegroup attacks across the vast Alberta Prairie. It was awesome to watch some of the battles when the live firing started. Fast jets were also used and called in to drop live bombs. Most impressive to me was the Giant Viper, a very long tube, about 500 metres in length, filled with explosives. This was designed and used to clear a path through a minefield so vehicles could get through it. It would be fired into the air across the minefield, where it would slowly settle with the aid of parachutes. Once on the ground, it was detonated. One of my many jobs was to drive down to the vehicle firing it in an armoured scout car (called a Ferret) and ensure no tanks tried to cross the minefield before it had safely gone off. When it went off, you knew it: the noise was deafening and the shockwave that followed was equally impressive. If I remember rightly, it left a trench half a metre down by a metre and a half wide; the shock wave in theory would also set off any dug in mines nearby. The idea was the tanks would cross the minefield by sticking one of their tracks into that trench, guaranteed that there would be no mines left in it, and drive through. If somehow the other track was unfortunate to hit a mine that had not been detonated by the shock wave, the next tank behind would simply just push the first one along until it cleared the minefield. Once through, you now had a clear lane for all vehicles in the Battlegroup to use.

Once Live Ex was complete after two weeks, everyone and every vehicle was then fitted with a system called Tactical Effects Simulation (TES) ready for TES Ex. This was basically like one big laser game. If you got hit, a light would start flashing and your system would cease to function until the safety staff (us lot) reset you. Like the Live Ex, TES Ex would start off low key, with elements doing their own troop training that quickly built up to Regimental training. Before you knew it, you were all fighting as a Battlegroup against an Opposition Force (OPFOR). Unknown to the Battlegroups, OPFOR were instructed exactly how to play to enable the new commanders in the Battlegroup to learn templates from the doctrine books. Therefore, the Battlegroup always won every battle, which was fine if the overall aim was just to learn doctrine and a template. However, some commanders actually believed they won the battle because they were great tacticians, even to the point of making fun of the OPFOR and commenting on just how bad their tactics were, and that was the sole reason they got their asses handed to them. To further fuel the arguments and install doctrine, Battlegroups were told OPFOR would be using Soviet-style tactics; thus when they lost, and they always did, our tactics and doctrine looked perfect. Many soldiers stated that to really test the Battlegroups you needed to allow the OPFOR to have freedom of rein and to use their own initiative. It never happened in my time out there.

After a battle, a debrief would take place at Exercise Control (Ex Con). All the commanders had to go to Ex Con, which was a set-up on top of a hill out in the training area. They would all gather in the large theatre and go through exactly what happened. This was chaired by Niner, with his senior staff conducting the debrief on points they wanted to bring out. I always remember the time he ripped into a Captain (Capt) because he got his troop killed during TES Ex. The Capt insisted he had followed the training manual to the letter, so if his guys died, it was the fault of the manual, not him. The Brigadier hit the roof and, shall we just say, corrected the Capt in his error.

As much as it was great fun getting to drive big tanks at fast speeds with no restrictions and blowing the crap out of everything, there was at times a very high price paid by individuals at BATUS. It did shock me just how many guys had, and continued to, die out there. It had never entered my brain that we actually lost guys during training. Sure, I knew guys died, we had one die when

I was in JLR on a run, but those deaths always seemed to be played down as it was totally unlucky and a freak one-off thing. Out here in BATUS it was actually expected, and the exercise would only stop if more than nine guys got killed during it. I saw quite a few deaths during my two-year tour, some through sheer stupidity and others that were just so unlucky. I myself came very close on two occasions and that wasn't counting the times we actually got shot at with small arms, a term normally given to weapons under a certain calibre, namely those that could be carried by an individual.

The first was when we were parked up, all closed down with hatches locked and secured, at a bridge crossing point. The battle simulations (batt sims) started to go off, these being explosions to simulate an artillery bombardment by the enemy as the friendly forces crossed the bridge. All of a sudden, we heard a massive explosion and our vehicle was lifted into the air; I thought I had accidently driven into the batt sim area by mistake. Sand, dirt and smoke poured into the vehicle, quickly followed by oil and petrol. The fear of it igniting and us being burnt alive quickly entered my head. The vehicle then started to be shaken about something rotten, and there was a very loud noise of something grinding on top, the commander tried but couldn't get the top hatch open to have a look. I booted the driver's front hatch open and immediately received a face full of a batt sim going off. God knows how I didn't get injured from that. Next the whole turret came off our vehicle and we saw a very large tank track appear. A main battle tank had somehow driven on top of us. "STOP STOP STOP!" was called across the radio net. The exercise briefly stopped whilst my commander, who had broken his arm, was taken to hospital. The exercise then continued whilst I waited for another vehicle and a commander before carrying on.

The second time was when we were parked up next to a broken-down vehicle. Due to the guys being hyped up when they were attacking in the vehicles (Tanks and APCs), they would sometimes shoot before really looking at what they were shooting at, that or they just got bored of shooting at wooden targets. We had a few incidents of broken-down vehicles being engaged even though the troops had been pre-warned before they started the attack. One day a vehicle had broken down and it was pointed out that until the guys in the tanks cleared a ridge they would not see it; therefore, a bright idea was to get our Ferret to park next to it, since our Ferret was coloured white, you really couldn't miss it. The guys were all warned about us and given the grid with strict instructions NOT to engage either vehicle. Being as trusting as we were, having seen several incidents by now, the commander and I decided not to stay in the Ferret; a good job too, because the first tank to clear the ridge engaged the other vehicle, knocking ours over from the resulting explosion.

For me, as part of the range safety and control staff, it was hard work, but nowhere near as hard as what the guys on the Med Mans were being subjected to, albeit they were only there for just the one Med Man. I did 14, so got to play in the freezing cold and boiling hot temperatures. In Canada, where we were, the temperatures ranged from plus 35 degrees in the summer down to as low as minus 40 degrees in the winter. When it snowed, it really snowed. Winter brought ten feet of snow minimum. In the summer, not only did the temperature soar but so did all the bugs and midges that bite the hell out of you. After each Med Man, we got ten days off to explore. At first, I started visiting and exploring everywhere, either on my own or with a few mates, but I soon got involved with a Canadian girl called Michelle, so we ended up doing the things couples did. We hit it off and even got engaged. A lot of guys at the time did that; some even ended up marrying girls out there and leaving the Army. Others loved it so much in Canada, they just went absent without leave (AWOL). The RMPs were always chasing after guys. Most of the time they just waited it out, stating that it was just a matter of time before the guys were brought back to the base by the Canadian police, having fallen foul of the law somewhere.

I could have written a book about my time spent there and all the things I saw and experienced both on and off the base. I learnt so much about how the Combined Arms Battlegroup operated, its capabilities, both flaws and strengths. I also got to fire a variety of weapons during my time out there, something that I was really into. I would totally recommend this posting to any soldier, especially those serving in the Armoured Corps. It was, after all, what we joined for; boys and their toys. I could safely say it was an absolute highlight of my military career. I had a brilliant time, got to travel and see another part of the world and met and worked with some awesome guys from lots of different Regiments. It sold the Army to me and why I wanted to be in it. Towards the end of my posting, I asked the CO if I could extend for another two years. I had an interview with the Base Commander, who told me that he would love to have me stay and would personally write a letter to my CO requesting it. Unfortunately, this was rejected by my Regiment. For some reason, my Regiment was very reluctant to send guys in the first place to BATUS, let alone let them stay for a longer tour.

Michelle and I spoke about the future at length and decided the only real option was for us to get married and for me to leave the Army. We started searching for a job for me out in Canada. I went for an interview with the Royal Canadian Mounted Police (RCMP) in Edmonton. I did some tests and got accepted for a job with their Special Weapons and Tactics Team (SWATT). All I had to do was get married and apply for my visa and citizenship at the Canadian High Council (CHC) in Germany, and they would sort the rest out. On returning to the unit in Germany I arranged to have a medical and the interview at the CHC in Bonn during my leave. The person who interviewed me asked why I wanted to live in Canada and what would I be doing for a job. When I told him about the RCMP in Edmonton, he just couldn't do enough for me, turned out he was ex-RCMP himself. So, everything was now in place, I just needed to get married. Long and short of it, we never did it. I had a long look at the situation and asked myself a few soul-searching questions. Was I marrying Michelle because I loved her or was it just to get me into Canada? I had also still not achieved my life ambition of getting into the SAS. I couldn't get married knowing I had doubts and might be doing it all for the wrong reasons. I explained some of my reasons to Michelle, and she took it really well. We stayed friends and kind of agreed that if it was meant to be it would happen eventually.

On returning to the unit I was placed back into C Squadron and went into Squadron Headquarter (SHQ) troop due to my signals qualifications and my new-found knowledge of armoured warfare. As much as I wanted to get back into Boot troop, I found life in SHQ to be okay. I guess it was the change in role and the fact there were some really good guys in the troop; to be honest, the whole Squadron was great from the OC down. Whilst I had been away, there had been quite a few changes throughout the Regiment of all the top personalities. My new OC (like the time when I was in A Squadron) had this policy of work hard, play hard, so we really did play hard and yes it involved lots of drinking. Maj D was from the Scottish Dragoon Guards, and I have to say, even though he was a cavalry officer, he was completely different and a breath of fresh air in our Regiment. He really was a great bloke, down to earth and well-respected by all. The Squadron would do anything for him – what I call a leader of men. I won't write about his background, but let's just say he spoke fluent German and Russian, and this came in very handy for contacts. The Americans had a unit in Southern Germany that was fully equipped with Soviet equipment, from uniforms to rifles to tanks. They were known as Red Star Company, and their mission was to train and educate soldiers in Soviet equipment and tactics. Our OC, through his connections, arranged for us to regularly visit and train down there with them. I have loads of photos and memories of C Squadron using the Soviet kit. We learnt a great deal, and a lot of interesting facts about Soviet equipment and tactics; things that were not in any manuals.

I started to train again for the SAS. I was aiming to go for selection around 1990 as my mandatory five years serving in a regular unit would be up by then. Quite a few other guys in the Regiment wanted to train with me for various personal reasons, so we formed a core team to train together. It mainly comprised the following: John S who was working in the gymnasium at the time, Stevie B who became my best friend, Stu M who wanted to join the Marines, and Hodgy and Andy W, both of whom also wanted to go for SAS selection as well. It made sense for us to train together and push each other on. Every now and again, other guys from the Regiment would join the six of us for training or to enter into a competition. As a team, we entered every march and shoot competition going. A march and shoot competition normally involved a team of military guys carrying weights over a set distance and completing tasks at various stages. They were all different and each had its own unique challenges, e.g. the Swiss one was in the mountains carrying a 50-pound pack and covering 100 kilometres in a 24-hour period. Fulda, on the other hand, was a 20-mile run in the Black Forest doing set tasks every two miles; anything from building something, to sorting out a road traffic accident with casualties, to naming things you could or could not eat for survival.

We tried to get a few of our young officers involved, but since the training and competitions were run at weekends, we didn't get any takers. Besides our own Squadron bosses, we got the distinct impression the Regiment were not wholly supportive of us doing this and the exact reason why was unclear. Things started to be made difficult for us; for example, for any competitions that we wanted to compete in we were to make our own transport arrangements to get there and back, entrance fees were to come out of our own pockets and we were also not allowed to train during working hours. It did not deter us. The training came from entering the competitions themselves, as we did more and more, we got better and better and ultimately, we got fitter. Our overall aim was to win every competition or at least get into the top three places. After the first six months, we started to achieve this, sometimes even breaking records. We even got our mug shots in quite a few newspapers. When we started to return with trophies, especially one that was nearly three feet high, it soon got noticed and not for the right reasons either. Some trophies we could keep, but others had to be returned the following year; the idea being that you were allowed to hold onto them for a year, proudly showing others you were the winners, before having to return them, ready for everyone to compete for that prestige again. After being invited for a chat with the Adjutant, we were told that the Regiment would be taking any trophy that required returning and all trophies that they deemed large. They would be displayed in Regimental Headquarters (RHQ) for safekeeping and for visitors to look at. We would only be allowed to keep the little ones and any medals that we won. This did not sit well the team, especially considering we were paying out of our own pockets for the competitions. Most wanted to stop taking part in the competitions.

The OC and the SSM, both of whom actively encouraged us to compete in the competitions, told us that they not only believed it was good training for us but it was good publicity for the Regiment, especially when we won. Since the majority of the team came from C Squadron, they were willing to help out by making a deal with us. If we won a trophy and gave it to the Squadron, they would reimburse all our costs; however, if the Regiment took it, well that was up to us to try and negotiate a deal with them. Other team members who were not part of C Squadron were content for this to happen, so in an attempt to try and get some of our money back we started to give all the trophies to the Squadron. The display cabinet in the Squadron soon filled up and as such it wasn't very long before people in RHQ spotted it. Trophies soon disappeared and turned up in RHQ. As the team leader, I was invited for another one-way chat with the Adjutant about trying to go behind his back and how things were *going* to revert to how they were before. I did manage to keep one of the trophies from a competition that we did where we came second out of four hundred teams. I just never informed the unit that we entered a team!

After we had collected a trophy for winning a competition in Bavaria, a press team from the UK came and had a chat with us. We just thought it was an interview again for a local paper. They said they had heard and read about us lot in local papers and were doing a documentary in the UK. They wanted to film us training and then competing in the Nijmegen March. They told us that if we won it, they would pay for all our expenses and a little extra. Because it involved the press, it went straight to the CO, who wanted a chat with me as the team leader.

The CO thought it would be great publicity for the Regiment and so wanted us to do it. The downside (because there is always a downside) I had to step aside and allow two officers to run the team. It wasn't up for debate or negotiation; no officers, no march, it was that simple from him. Not really having any option, we set about getting the team prepared because the march was less than four months away. Although we were very physically fit by now, because this was going to be filmed and we wanted to win it, we set a training programme up to prepare us. Of the four officers who were basically told to train with us, not only did they sporadically turn up for training when they felt like it, but when they did, none could keep up. It was hardly surprising given all the competitions we had done previously, but it did annoy us because they were supposed to be leaders of men and set the example, they were supposed to be better than us, or at least put the effort in to try and be better than us. Whilst other team members said it was exactly what they expected, for me it wasn't. Their whole approach and attitude was not what I expected of an officer; it appeared that they just didn't seem to care as much about it as we did. For the Nijmegen March, you had to start and finish as a team, and the guys were simply not willing to slow down in order to allow them to keep up. They felt it would embarrass us all and ultimately, we would not win the competition 'carrying baggage', as one of the guys put it. The end result was that we were not allowed to take part. I was really disappointed that we had missed out on one of the best marching competitions in Europe. Things like this were fuelling a lack of respect towards the officers in the Regiment for me. From my limited experiences in the military so far, it seemed officers from other cap badges and units joined and wanted to be soldiers, but ours seemed only interested in playing at it.

Considering all officers in the Army went through Sandhurst, I found most of our cavalry officers to be a very unique breed. They just seemed to be full of themselves and thought they were better than everyone else, even to the point of disrespecting other military officers about money, background and education. Making fun (piss-taking) of others in the military is part and parcel of military life, it can be useful and help foster competitiveness, but this was none of that: it was just pure snobbery. This might have explained why I came across quite a few officers from different cap badges, rightly or wrongly, who did not like cavalry officers. Their whole way of life in the Regiment was completely different to ours; it seemed the focus for them was to socialise and network. Anyone who has served in a cavalry Regiment could tell you plenty of stories about their antics and how there appeared to be one rule for them and another for the lower ranks.

In our Regiment, troops would go months without ever seeing who their troop leader was; in most cases you only got to find out when an officer turned up for an exercise. After it was finished, you would be lucky if you ever saw them again; it was just the way it was in our unit. I did hear on my travels that other cavalry Regiments were exactly the same, if not worse; all seemed to have some unique culture/tradition to their officers. At one stage during my time in the Regiment, the CO banned baked beans, chips and tomato sauce in the officer's mess. He deemed them as food for poor people. When that rule was in force, some of the officers when they were on duty would ensure that the chips and baked beans for the blokes were cooked to the correct standard by eating a large plate of them in the cook house. As for the lower ranks, the general impression was that officers just saw and treated us all as servants. This was no doubt fuelled by the fact most of the men were forced to do at least a six-month stint in the officer's mess as waiters. Something else the Army careers' office failed to mention when I joined up as a soldier.

In 1990, the unit had a reshuffle. This was done every now and again to ensure that there was a balance of qualified personnel in each Squadron. I was told I would be going to Command troop in Headquarter (HQ) Squadron given the sterling job I had done in SHQ troop. The truth was they were short of qualified personnel, with nobody in the Regiment wanting to volunteer to go into that troop, and for very good reasons. Not only did it attract the stigma of not being a fighting troop with combat soldiers in it but when Command troop deployed, it became officer top heavy with all the command element from Regimental Headquarters (RHQ). As such, it would not be on the front-line in a battle but sitting back somewhere out of the way trying to control what was going on. Not only would it mean me leaving C Squadron but all the warry combat stuff would now stop and my role would change to constantly running around after officers and sitting on my ass all day and night doing radio stags. None of which I wanted to do or would help me towards my goal of joining the SAS.

In the Squadrons on exercise you always had time, or time was made available, for you all to get together, relax and have a laugh and a joke. This was normally done in the form of a maintenance day followed by a Squadron BBQ that night with plenty of food and beer. There was no such thing in Command troop; it was all taken very seriously and so just involved work. Tasks were constantly dished out by the officers, which would be fine if they were constructive, most were not – they were what we called 'bone tasks' e.g. folding piles of maps up for other people to use because it was deemed they were far too busy to fold them themselves. If you did not get given the task directly, as mates you helped each other out to ease the burden, the end result being constant work. Most of the guys in the Regiment did not want to go into Command troop for exactly those reasons; those who were moved into the troop normally signed off quite quickly and left the Army. It was a constant turnover of guys and no doubt why they were short once again. I had absolutely no interest in going there whatsoever. I had some brilliant friends in C Squadron, the OC and SSM were great guys, and the whole Squadron just worked really well for each other. I asked for an interview and pleaded my case to the OC. He told me he wanted to keep me but it was out his hands; this was from the top with no exceptions because they were that short of qualified personnel in Command troop.

I needed a way out and so started to ask around. Besides all the banter and piss-taking I received about going into Command troop, John S told me that there was a position vacant in the gymnasium (gym). An individual from the Army Physical Training Corps (APTC) ran the gym and each Squadron was required to supply a guy to work in there for a period of time. When exercises came up, they went with their respective Squadron and trained with everyone else, but during the phases in camp, they worked in the gym under the supervision of the Corps guy. As a group, they were responsible for the overall fitness of the men in the Regiment. HQ Squadron, which Command troop was part of, did not have anyone in the gym. I decided to do the Physical Training Instructors (PTI) course.

The course was brilliant; besides some education it was all fitness each and every day for eight weeks solid. I learnt kickboxing and qualified as a boxing, basketball and swimming coach, and became a unit lifeguard. The course was very heavy in gymnastics; God knows why they focused so much and assessed you in this discipline. I knew that as a PTI you needed to be an all-rounder and be able to play and do any sporting event, but they actually wanted you to be really good at this. Having never done gymnastics in my life, I really struggled. The ironic thing was, unlike all the other sporting events, unless I joined the APTC, I'd never ever do or teach this again. Once I passed the course, I went straight into the gym on return to the Regiment.

I met Steve, who was the guy from the APTC. He was a really chilled-out bloke compared to others of the same rank in the unit. I could see a marked difference in his man management by the fact he asked you to do something rather than tell or order you to. He then entrusted you to get on with it rather than micromanage you. He actively encouraged us not to sit on what we had learnt on the course but to get qualified in other areas and expand our knowledge; his ultimate goal was to get guys to join his Corps. Being in the gym meant my promotion took a hit; the Regimental policy was RAC soldiers were employed to be tank soldiers, and that meant being on the tank park. If you were not there, you were not being employed in your primary role and so therefore were graded down on your yearly progress report. This policy, however, for some reason did not apply to the clerks who worked in Regimental HQ. I didn't really care as my drive and goal was SAS selection not promotion.

With Steve's help and encouragement, mainly because I wasn't too keen on heights, I took up rock climbing and eventually did my instructor's course in the Alps of Bavaria and Austria. Due to my fitness, I also got roped into the Regimental cross-country skiing team, which was great because we went skiing each year for three months in Norway, Germany and France. Army recruiting saw to it that I got into several local newspapers again doing that. The write up was very well-written, there was a small piece about me personally before going onto explaining what military cross-country skiing actually involved. It included all the places and countries the Army skied in and the training soldiers had to do for it, this was then followed by all the countries I had served in up to now. Which, given my age and time served, was impressive. It was really good to be honest and no doubt inspired quite a few people to join up.

The PTI course had got me interested in medicine after studying anatomy and physiology during the classroom phase. I applied for and went on a Regimental Medical Assistant (RMA) Class three course. It was eight weeks long, divided into two parts: four weeks of theory and four weeks of clinical work. It involved, amongst other things, intubation (that's putting a tube into someone's trachea), suturing people up, putting drips into them, vaccinations and injections. I really enjoyed it; this was an area that I wanted to learn more about.

On transfer of Squadrons, I had to move out of C Squadron block and into HQ, where I started sharing a room with Gary R (Robbo). Robbo's dad had also been in the Regiment but unfortunately had died. As kids, we knew of each other, but we had never really got close, partly due to our fathers being posted to different places. In the Army, you were always getting posted all over the world; it was one of the attractions of joining up. Robbo joined years later after me and although he was an excellent guy and a very good friend, he wasn't what a lot of other people would call your ideal tank soldier. It just wasn't in his veins. One very funny and fond memory I have of Robbo was when we were on exercise. He was making us all a brew (cup of coffee/tea) using an Army camping stove. It ran out of fuel after being on for some time so he decided to fill it up. Rather than move away from the vehicle or let it cool down for a bit, he decided to do it there and then. When he started to pour the petrol into the stove's fuel tank, it ignited. The flame quickly moved up the stream of petrol to the can and set that alight. He panicked and threw the can of petrol away from himself, straight into the back of the wagon. I have no idea why I found this so hilarious given the situation, but I just couldn't stop laughing; in slow time I just kept seeing the picture playing over and over again in my head. The officer with us erupted into a furious fit; my laughing probably didn't help matters. We managed to get the fire out quite quickly and there was minimal damage caused. Afterwards, the officer decided to educate Robbo. The chat started off quiet and slow and eventually ended in yelling when he realised Robbo just wasn't getting the point he was trying to make. Might have had something to do with the fact he was talking to him like a five-year-old. All through it I just couldn't stop laughing, I had tears rolling down my face, I guess you just had to be there. So, after a short spell on the tank park, and a few exercises, Robbo decided to change his job and pursue a career as a Regimental clerk.

This proved to be a wise decision for him as he turned out to be very good at it and was promoted to full Corporal (Cpl) very quickly, thus overtaking a lot of people in the Regiment, including myself. Like I said, the rule of having to be on the tank park in order to be promoted appeared not to apply to the clerks. This was another one of those double standards that really got to people. How could a guy who proved to be a useless 'real' soldier change jobs within the Regiment and then get promoted faster than the guys on the park, who were not only doing the job we all joined up to do but were doing it well? Then to top it all off, because the Army was the Army, you had to obey orders from the person with the highest rank, not the qualifications or experience. For me it was quite understandable why a lot of soldiers took resentment and the piss (fun) out of these guys as well as the promotion system. Robbo knew this very well and would agree with me on it. To his credit, he did handle the situation very well though. He took all the piss-taking from the guys and would never use his rank to tell people how to do their jobs. Most people accepted him for who he was because of this. And like it or not, it was very unwise to upset one of the clerks, because one day you would badly require something from them, and it would be Sod's Law that the only person who could help you out would be the one person that you upset.

In my personal life, I had bumped into a German girl called Silke. She reminded me of the blonde girl in ABBA. I guess like most hot-blooded males, I had a thing for slim, pretty blondes. She was with another guy when I first met her so I saw that as her being off-limits. As time went on though, we just kept bumping into each other and it was obvious we fancied the pants off each other. Eventually, she dumped her boyfriend and we started dating. Things moved really quickly for us, and we got a flat together in a village about 25 miles away from camp so I spent most of my weekends there. I should have known better; anyone who would dump someone in that fashion and for that reason would do it again. Looking back, I think I was just blinded by sex with a beautiful blonde girl. Needless to say, we had a very turbulent relationship, splitting up and getting back together twice before I went to the Gulf.

Mid-1990 when I was in Bavaria teaching rock climbing, I met an American female soldier called Lorraine (Lori). We really clicked with each other and had such a good time together. Nothing sexual happened since she was only there for a few days and I was still going out with Silke, albeit on and off. Lori was leaving the military to take up flying back home in the States before moving to London the following year to study at university. If we were still keeping in touch by the time she got to England, she said she would like to meet up again and see if anything develops between us, assuming that's what we both wanted. I told her my unit was moving back to the UK next year, and I would love to see her again. We swapped addresses and agreed to write and see how we got on.

From here on in the book is written as if August 1990 was today. We are no longer looking back in time, we are living it now each and every day, so you the reader can experience what we went through.

Chapter 3
Pre-War Build Up

Iraq invaded Kuwait on 2nd August, 1990. I am quite sure there were other reasons why they did this but the main focus appeared to be with regards to a debt Iraq owed to Kuwait from the Iraq-Iran war in the eighties. Kuwait was refusing to wipe it clean so Iraq invaded them. The emir and most, if not all, the ruling family fled to Saudi Arabia. Ten days later Kuwait was annexed as Iraq's 19th province. The United Nations (UN) passed resolution 660 condemning the invasion and demanded the unconditional withdrawal of all Iraqi forces out of Kuwait. No doubt believing the world always just stood by and watched conflicts in the Middle East, backed up with having the fourth largest Army in the world, Iraq chose to ignore it. Therefore, an international coalition was formed under the guidance of the US to bring political and military pressure to bear on Iraq. They wanted as many nations as possible to send in military forces. Britain agreed to send in 15,000 troops. The UN issued an ultimatum in November to Iraq to withdraw its forces by Jan 15th, 1991 otherwise force would be used. This is the diary of those days out in the desert sands before and after that deadline.

At the time when Iraq invaded Kuwait the Regiment was getting ready for an Arms Plot to move back from Herford in Germany to Wimbish (Essex) in the UK. An Arms Plot is when you basically hand over your barracks and everything in it to the new unit. Not only did you want to get this correct first time around, but it was a matter of pride to stop any rumours or the Regiment getting a bad name. That meant lots and lots of work; everything from the guns to vehicles to accommodation had to be accounted for and all in immaculate condition. Inspections after inspections would be conducted until it was all up to the required standard. News soon reached us that we would be required, like all other units in Germany, to give most our kit to the units deploying to the Gulf. It was pleasing and somewhat disappointing. It meant less work for us to do on handover to the new unit, but it also meant we would not be deploying. The feelings were mixed within the Regiment, and rumours and stories soon started to spread about what it was like in the Middle East. Staying here meant we were safe; going over there to fight religious maniacs was not our cup of tea, especially since it had nothing to do with us. It was all about land, oil and a debt owed between Iraq and Kuwait. Some of the guys pointed out that there were no calls or resolutions from the UN when Iran and Iraq were having a go at each other for years, not to mention the countless other wars and invasions going on around the globe.

7th Armoured Brigade (7 Bde) was warned off that they were going to deploy to the Gulf, so the next few months saw them getting prepared and shipping out. 7 Bde were called the Desert Rats and wore the Red Rat as an emblem on their arms as well as having it painted on their vehicles. They used the fact they were the Desert Rats to take full advantage and get lots of press coverage. It almost felt like they were rubbing it in to all other units that were not deploying, and it was working, because I for one was really disappointed that I couldn't go. They got everything they asked for. All our wheeled vehicles were taken and most of the CVR (T)s were stripped of kit and equipment. They even took the new Night Viewing Systems (NVS), something we were training other units on at the time. It struck me as funny that we were only sending 15,000 guys to war and yet most of the British Army's kit seemed to be going with them; after all, each unit stationed in Germany was supposed to be fully equipped and ready for war at all times. The allies stationed in Germany regularly practised a drill called a 'Crash Out'. A Crash Out was exactly what it sounded like. From a phone call, a Regiment or unit had 24 hours in which to get its complete self, as in all its men and equipment, out of camp and deployed into dedicated battle positions and stay there until told the drill had finished. You were supposed to be able to be self-sufficient in the field for up to five days, after which you would get a resupply. The number of Regiments that would get crashed out at one time and the length of time they stayed out varied; it made no difference to be honest as the drill was the same, you crashed out and ensured you had enough supplies to sustain you for the five days. Anyone or anything that didn't make it out of the camp gates within the first six hours was swept up later on with well-rehearsed back-up plans. Monitoring teams would descend on the Regiments to check this all happened. They were not bluffing; they expected all of it to be in place by the 24-hour deadline. They would be ruthless and leave no stone unturned, even to the point of checking an individual's personnel kit to ensure they had everything they were supposed to have and that it was clean and dry. If things were amiss, you could bet your ass that the Regiment would find itself conducting another Crash Out real soon.

Sometimes when the drill ended, and especially if individuals had fucked up, the CO would roll us all straight into a Regimental exercise, and again the length of time we stayed out varied. Although a pain, it made total sense since everything you needed was out in the field ready to go. To ease the pain and ensure we got it correct every time, everyone had pre-packed Crash Out kits stored in the troop cages ready to load at a moment's notice. In other words, kit to last you out in the field for a minimum of five days. The vehicles were always fully loaded with equipment and fuelled up ready to roll. Those that were being worked on or broken down had the kit put to one side, ready to load on should we get crashed out. The kit in the cages and on the vehicles was always game on to the monitoring teams when it came to inspection time; therefore, most people had two lots. One was used for regular exercises and courses, and the other, which was never touched at all, was just left for the Crash Out.

1st The Queens Dragoon Guards (QDGs), who were also a Recce Regiment like ours, sent their A Squadron to be 7 Bde's Recce unit. The Squadron took more than the normal complement that you would find in a Recce Squadron, so it became what we termed as a Squadron plus.

It soon became very apparent that the Iraq forces had no intention of withdrawing as they were digging in and fortifying defences. They clearly were in it for the long haul. The US were amassing lots of troops and urging others to do likewise as a coalition force. Given what they were about to go up against, it made total sense. Britain agreed to send another 15,000 troops. They decided to send 4th Armoured Brigade (4 Bde) to bolster 7 Bde, the Black Rats to join the Red Rats. Together they would become 1 (UK) Armoured Division.

Towards the end of November, we in the Regiment were all told that our Arms Plot had been put on hold, and we were going to become part of those extra 15,000 men. We were being deployed as a whole Regiment to become the Division's Recce. Upon arrival in the Gulf we would be taking A Squadron QDG under our belt. This posed many questions such as: why us? Why were the QDGs not sending the rest of their Regiment, considering they already had their A Squadron out there? They also were not prepping for a move back to the UK and had not been told to hand over most of their equipment to other units so they must surely still be fully equipped? We were given a deadline of two weeks to get the whole unit prepared for war as that was when the ships were departing from the port and the vehicles needed to be on them. Given the timeframe involved and the fact most our kit had gone to other units within 7 Bde, this meant we would be working our butts off.

All personnel who were on leave and courses were immediately recalled and told the good news. Not only would we be receiving kit from other units, which would require servicing and spraying to desert colours, but we also would be increasing the manpower to get us up to our war strength. Everyone, especially all the new guys joining us, would require training to get us up to speed and prepared for war in a desert environment. The only way to achieve this within the two weeks was to work day and night in shifts. Various teams were set up including maintenance, spray and training. Enough manpower was put into each team to allow everyone to work eight hours on eight hours off, with the team continually working 24 hours non-stop. All the stuff that was left behind in Germany with other units that had not gone to 7 Bde now came to us. A lot of it was in a really poor state of repair, no doubt why it had been left in the first place. Talk about a morale boost! It was going to be bad enough just getting all the kit together and prepping it, let alone now having to repair most of it as well. If I remember correctly, we ended up with 750 men, 164 armoured vehicles and 92 soft skin ones (Land Rovers and trucks). D Squadron was our guided weapons Squadron and equipped with the Striker CVR (T). The Squadron was split down and a troop of four Strikers was attached to each of the other Squadrons.

Time seemed to fly by; you were either working, training or sleeping. There was just no time for anything else. A lot of kit that was requested or ordered just never turned up. Either units didn't have it or it had been taken by 7 Bde.

Ordering it again was going to be pointless, it would take too long to arrive. Command informed us that most of the missing kit we needed we would get out in the Gulf upon arrival. To name but a few the list included: desert combats and boots, spare water bottles, Nuclear Biological and Chemical (NBC) kit, Combination (Combo) pens (injections used in NBC conditions), ammunition, body armour, spare vehicle kits, NVS, and camouflage nets (cam nets), the list was endless. Rumour had it that all the desert kit had been sold off to the Iraqis years ago, thinking that the British Army would never need it again. Any remaining kit had all gone to 7 Bde.

For ourselves, it was very unclear on exactly what we needed to take out there, as most of the guys had never been to or trained in a desert before. Nobody was giving us any advice, and nothing was coming back from the guys already deployed out there, so guys just packed everything. We ended up packing all our normal kit and all the crash out kits, which included things like the brown and green cam nets, the logic being they might come in handy. This meant we had virtually two of everything, whether we needed it or not. Taking everything meant we at least had something, albeit we would stick out like sore thumbs in the desert with most this kit if there was no vegetation about.

B and C Squadrons getting ready

Command Troop Sultans getting ready

Guys from the Regimental training wing conducted all our Regimental training. The programme was intense and relentless. We went to Sennelarger for a few days and practised mine warfare, NBC, first aid, vehicle Recce, air defence and Recce, and zeroing of all our own personal weapons. It was all the good old military stuff that we had to learn throughout each year for fighting in Europe, crammed into just a few days. We even had a go at trying to take down a small aircraft with tripod-mounted machine guns. It was something completely different and really good fun. Until you had a go, you really didn't appreciate just how hard it was to hit a moving target that small. It was all to do with the amount of lead you had to apply, in other words, how far in front of the target you aimed and fired.

Back at camp, everyone was wheeled through the medical and dental chain like a sausage factory. Everyone had injections to ensure all the regular inoculations were up to date, before being given malaria tablets, Nerve Agent Pre-treatment Sets (NAPS tablets), Biological Agent Treatment Sets (BATS Tablets), Morphine injections, and then sent for a dental inspection. Anything that looked even slightly suspect was drilled and filled. They had 750 guys to do in a few days and had no idea if or when we would ever get to a dental centre again. I had three suspect small holes that they didn't approve of, so they were enlarged then filled there and then.

The NAPS and BATS were tablets issued for chemical warfare. They had to be started weeks in advance of you being subjected to a chemical agent, a bit like the tablets you take for malaria. We were told that they would give us some limited protection by slowing down how the chemical agent, once inside your body, reacted with your systems. This brought you enough time in which you could then administer a Combo pen. They were called this because it was an injection at one end and a tablet at the other. The tablet was similar in ingredients to the NAPS/BATS tablets but far stronger in strength. Everyone carried three Combo pens. The Combo pen was an autoject and had to be administered into a thick muscle. It needed to be a thick muscle because the needle was large (about two inches) and it automatically shot out of the pen and released the vaccine when you pressed the cap. It was designed to function like this because the chances were whoever needed to administer this to themselves would probably be in a very bad state and not functioning correctly at all. Much to the amusement of others, many a time during NBC or first aid training, when how to use a Combo pen was demonstrated, someone always managed to stab themselves by either playing around with it or using it incorrectly.

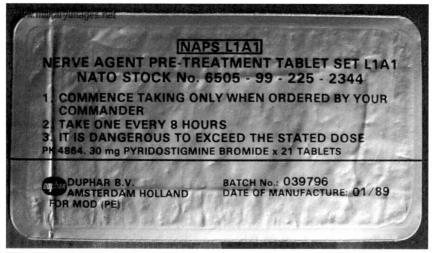

A blister pack of NAPS tablets

The Regiment was split down into advance, main and rear parties for the deployment. The parties were spaced out between each move with the advance party going first before Christmas. I volunteered to go into the advance party, mainly because I was single and believe Christmas is for children, so anyone with kids should be given the chance to stay. I also wanted to get out there straightaway; all the training I had done was about to get put into practice. There is a saying in the military of 'Never volunteer for anything', but I really wanted to get over there and get on with the job. I guess a part of me secretly wanted to show and prove to some people just how good I really was. During our short period of build-up training, I had seen guys who were not confident in their abilities at all. These same guys had always played lip service to training and found excuses to miss it whenever it came up. For some reason, nothing was ever said and they always seemed to get away with it – might have been because they had rank and talked a great deal, what quite a few people referred to as a 'bluffer'. They were always the first to slap others down if they did anything well or came up with something new, and to point out the mistakes of others to the bosses rather than helping them out. Whilst they got away with behaviour like this in peacetime, in war with your life on the line, less people would tolerate it. Personally, I had no time whatsoever for people who were bluffers or not team players and only thought about themselves and their own career. They are the kind of people that will get you killed in a firefight.

The two weeks soon went and the time came for the vehicles to depart. They were going by boat from Emden, a port in Northern Germany, and it would take about eight weeks for them to arrive in Saudi Arabia. People volunteered to go with them, and single guys were 'dicked' (volunteered) to make up the rest of the numbers that were required. I always got sea sickness on boats so decided against volunteering, I couldn't see the point of being as sick as a dog for eight weeks solid. Single guys always got the short straw in the unit, and when it was questioned, the bosses frequently joked it because single guys were deemed not to have a life. Truth was, it was a combination of laziness, ease and a quick solution to fix an immediate problem. For example, during a guard mount, if there was a man short, it was far easier to walk up to an accommodation block on camp and grab a single soldier than to send someone to drive around the married quarters knocking on all the doors. Most of which, on seeing a military person, would not be opened. Married quarters were not on the camp but split in a few patches around the local area.

Departing camp for the docks

At the beginning of December, we all had our first anthrax jab and were told to start taking the malaria tablets. We had been constantly told throughout the training that Iraq had some nasty chemical weapons and the means to deliver them. Reports had shown Iraq had used them before in conflicts and even disputes within its own borders, so logic dictated there would be no reason why Iraq would not use them against us lot. We were told the anthrax jab, which we were ordered to have from higher, was just like any other vaccination and would work in exactly the same way. Therefore, we would be requiring others later on out there for it to take full effect.

As an RMA, I was very curious since other vaccinations that were given like this followed a strict regime. There were normally three of them, and they were spaced out over a six-month period. Once the course was completed you required a blood test to see if it had taken effect, in other words produced antibodies, and if not, you had to have the whole regime again, followed by another blood test. I queried this, mainly just to enhance my own knowledge because there was no literature to read about it. A very unconvincing military doctor informed me that anthrax worked differently and that no blood test was required. Once you had the required number it worked. So, my next questions were, what was the required number, the regime and for how long does it give you protection? He said he believed it was three injections, and they had been told the protection would last for ten years. Like any other vaccination there would be side effects, that was all he knew. That implied that you would not be protected until all three were administered! Despite my reservations about having it, it was a direct order from the top, and he was a doctor so I had to trust that he had our best interests at heart and patient care came first above his career. There were lots of mumblings and quiet complaining going on from some of the guys but nobody else asked any questions and this really surprised me. Some didn't want to talk about it at all, they absolutely believed that the military would never put them in harm's way, which was ironic given where they were about to send us!

Chemical and biological agents really worried a lot of people. They had vastly changed since the days of WWII. The amount required, what they could physically do to the body, and the speed and ease in which they could do it was frightening. Even having things like the Combo pens were no guarantee that you would not suffer a horrible death. There are some, like anthrax, that once used stay around for years. The thought of having to live, work and fight in a chemical environment was scary because it would only take one wrong drill, or one hole in your suit, to allow them in. Some of the fear was down to a personal lack of knowledge and training, some of it down to a lack of trust of both equipment and what we were being told. Why? Well, different nations had different kits and all stated that theirs was the most effective. It begged the question of who exactly was telling the truth and who was only in it for commercial interests. As for training, the Soviets conducted full-scale military exercises using *real* chemical agents, our training involved going into a gas chamber once a year for a short period. Once inside, tear gas, commonly known as CS gas, was used. After completing a few drills, for example eating and drinking, you were allowed out. At times, the instructor would make you fully remove your respirator (gas mask), state your number, rank and name before being allowed out. This was done simply so you could experience the effects of CS gas. Once complete, you were then current NBC training for another year. Even this limited amount of training was sometimes avoided by certain individuals and they were still signed up as being current. Me personally, I stayed on top of the basic training we received and even read a few more manuals. I wanted to do the instructors course to further enhance my knowledge, but just like the signal instructors course, my application had been turned down several times before because I was not at the required rank.

Chapter 4
On Route to War

15th DECEMBER, 1990

At 1430 the advance party paraded outside the guardroom in our black and green combats. A few of the lads turned up to wish us luck and a safe flight, followed by the usual banter about them being able to have a beer on Christmas day, and if that wasn't enough, then one every day leading up to it, because they could. Once we were all accounted for, everyone was given a few minutes to say farewell to anyone they wanted to, mainly loved ones, before we climbed into a mini bus and left Herford to the Regimental band playing at the main gate and the CO wishing us all good luck. There were no big motivation speeches or anything like that like you see on the movies, just a simple wave. During the drive to the airport, most of the guys on the bus were very quiet, no doubt doing some self-reflection about the realisation that we were actually on our way to war and this was for real. For some strange reason, I was really looking forward to getting out there and being part of the team in a war zone. I was relieved that I was actually on my way now. I guess I always get like that when I'm going somewhere new, or maybe it was because I wasn't thinking about war at all; after all, it hadn't kicked off yet and there was still a month to go – bags of time for Iraq to get its troops out of Kuwait.

As the advance party, our main role was to pave the way for the arrival of the rest of the Regiment later on. In order to do this, the party had a representative from most of the departments within the Regiment. Their job would be to liaise with a counterpart out there and find out exactly how things were done and then start the ball rolling. Any problems encountered needed to be ironed out there and then. The idea was that when the rest of the guys arrived, they should have a seamlessly smooth transition into the new place. The Regimental Second in Command (2IC) was put in charge of us lot.

RAF Tri-Star at Hannover Airport in Germany

We departed Germany on a military plane completely full of soldiers and arrived in Saudi Arabia at 2330 local time that night. Our first scare was at the airport during the approach, when we overshot and had to go around due to nearly landing on top of another aircraft that was taking off. The aircraft captain apologised and jokingly explained this was due to all aircraft having to turn off all lights during approaches or departures in and out of Saudi. Once off the plane, we got into buses driven by Saudis and were driven to the docks area in Al Jubayl (pronounced and written on maps as Al Jubail), where we were processed. The Yanks were processing around 3,000 guys a day. The Brits, on the other hand, were struggling just to do a planeload. The clerks still had the mentality of being back home, where nobody ever rushed them, and they worked at their own pace.

Our second scare came when "GAS GAS GAS" was shouted and we all had to get into NBC kit. We sat around for ages not knowing what was going, most guys thought it was just a drill to get us into the 'swing' of things out here. We were eventually given the all clear and told that Scud missiles had been fired but they were all intercepted by US Patriot missiles.

When working overseas in the military, unlike every other UK citizen, you still paid tax. To try and help out we were given what was called a Local Overseas Allowance (LOA). Basically, it was to offset the price difference for basic food items between what you would pay in the UK and the country you were now working in. Now that we were out here and no longer in Germany, that LOA stopped, meaning you were massively out of pocket. Other nations were also giving their guys bonuses or paying them extra for being out here, but for us the UK Government would not. It had, however, agreed that we could get something small to try and offset the loss of the LOA. This would be paid daily in Saudi riyals or US dollars, depending on who collected the money for the troops at the time. In the meantime, they would look at giving a bonus or something later on that they might call 'war money' but this needed approval from Parliament. The clerks on arrival encouraged us that if we did not have one already, to take out a postal savings account rather than carry this money around with us. I signed up for one; it made total sense to me.

It took ten hours for us to get processed before being moved to Camp 4 just outside of Al Jubayl. The accommodation was basic, hard standing, mostly porta cabins with beds, showers and a cookhouse. Living in the field or this, most would elect to be here. It was no different to any other camp that I had been to in a hot country before. On the plus side, all the hospital staff was here; amongst other things it meant there were females and normal people who you could talk to.

Sitting around at Camp 4, blending into the sandy desert environment dressed in green and black combats, black boots and head dress

Over the next few days we touched base with various departments, including the Quarter Master (QM) at Camp 4. The QM was responsible for, amongst other things, accommodation and all kit issues from food to socks and boots to ammunition (ammo). We explained who we were and when the rest of the Regiment would be arriving. We also explained about what we had been told back in Germany with reference to us getting desert kit etc. issued on arrival. He informed us that there was no kit at all for us to collect. He was the QM for 7 Bde, and as such only supplied kit to 7 Bde; we had a choice: either wait for 4

47

Bde QM to get out here and get established then go through him, or we order it ourselves. He would be quite happy to send the paperwork off since we had our own Regimental QM out with us.

As new people arriving in theatre, he could issue us with some ammo though, so we got issued 20 rounds of 9mm each for personal protection on the base. It was like something out of a WWII film. What use were 20 rounds going to be if we got attacked? He informed us that the QDGs had taken all the ammo that had been ordered for the Recce Regiment, since that was what we were part of, we would have to speak to them to get it shared out until more arrived. In the meantime, he would order more but it was going to take a bit of time because it came in by ship. We told him we would also be requiring a whole stock of Swingfire missiles for our Strikers since we were bringing a Squadron worth of them out here. He said he would also put them on order but that might take even longer to acquire and arrive. He would do his best for us.

He arranged for us to have two brand new Toyota Land Cruisers and a Cressida to get around in because our Land Rovers would not be arriving for a few days yet. He then informed us that they were not expecting the Regiment at all, so no accommodation was available to receive us; units were currently being housed in camps exactly like this. A tented city was, however, in the process of being built so he would look at putting the unit in there when it arrived. The ships with the vehicles on were late and would be a few more weeks yet, so that by default helped the overall situation out. He knew that because he had kit on the same ships that he needed for other units. I wasn't too bothered about not being issued the rest of the stuff for a few weeks, but to only have 20 rounds of ammo and no body armour or Combo pens, it didn't impress me at all. Especially since we had been told that the Iraqis had Scud Missiles capable of carrying nerve agents and they could easily reach us here.

I found some old newspapers lying about. It appeared that every newspaper back home in the UK was covering what was going on out here. I decided there and then that I would start collecting clippings from now on if I could get hold of the papers.

25th DECEMBER, 1990

We had a makeshift Christmas dinner and broke with tradition by having it with no alcohol. It was a Muslim country and the British military were respecting that, so they banned it all. Anyone caught with any would get charged, no excuses whatsoever. Three people had already been charged getting beer off the Danish; the lowest fine had been £700. So, we celebrated with a small can of alcohol-free lager, which I quickly substituted for a can of Coke because I couldn't stand the stuff.

Christmas lunch, 1990

After our Christmas dinner, we all moved to the tented city, now aptly called Black Adder (BA), to check it out ready for the arrival of the main body. BA was built to house 4000 men at a time. The tents were the big 24 x 24 ones, and it was literally just tents on the sand. The idea being BA was to be used during the process period when you arrived, so you would not be staying too long. As soon as your unit was all together and your vehicles had arrived, you would be departing to make room for others.

Black Adder Camp from a distance. Lots of 24 x 24 tents

Inside Black Adder

Video link of 16/5th L Christmas OP Granby Advance party waiting for the ships:
https://www.youtube.com/watch?v=x98pW9CoXLU

That evening we were informed that the ships had arrived with our vehicles, so the rest of the evening and the night was spent unloading them. It was literally all hands to the pump to unload the ships as quickly as possible, because nobody wanted them to remain in port too long in case they were attacked. You just jumped into a vehicle that you could drive; it did not matter whom it belonged to, started it up and drove it off the ship. There was a place not too far away where we were instructed to quickly park them up and then return to get another vehicle. For speed, we simply just put them one behind each other and went and got the next one. It could all be sorted out in slow time when the boats had departed and everyone else had arrived.

Car park at the docks

The main party arrived days later and the last of the CVR (T)s arrived by the 28th. No kit had arrived for the unit so far, so we were still without what I would call 'the basics'. Most of Command troop were now out here so we had a meeting to discuss where and what everyone was going to be doing from now on. The troop leader told me that I was going on the CO's Spartan with Steve (APTC guy) as the vehicle commander because of his rank, and Cookie as the driver. To explain – In a war establishment for a Regiment, the APTC guy by default becomes the CO's bodyguard, ergo he has to be near him at all times and hence gets put in Command troop. The CO also gets a Spartan as an extra vehicle for his sole use. It made sense to put Steve on the Spartan given that he has to go somewhere but has no qualifications in Command troop roles e.g. signals. However, making him the vehicle commander based solely on his rank despite being unqualified, was questionable to say the least. That said, I was really pleased with the news; Steve and Cookie were great guys, so I thought we would make a really good crew. I expected our role was that we were just going to be used as a taxi to ferry all the CO's stuff about. The CO himself would not be joining us; after all, to command the Regiment, he needed to be in one of the Command Vehicles (CVs).

The troop leader then told me that the CO wanted me as a tactics advisor and his radio operator, given my time spent in BATUS and the courses I had done. He also wanted the wagon converting into a CV, even though we had four in the troop for precisely that role. That meant making a large map board up (and somehow securing it in the back), then getting all the stationary for keeping radio logs and marking maps, etc. The big issue was where to store it all; the vehicle was simply just not designed for this function or role. The only saving grace of all this was I could use the fact I was the CO's operator when I went to ask for kit or help. All I had to say was that the CO wanted it, and instead of getting the usual brush off or excuses, it opened doors and the kit amazingly turned up. Steve afterwards said he was none too happy about being made the vehicle commander. He pointed out that he was not in the RAC, had not done any courses and hence didn't have a clue about commanding an armoured fighting vehicle. He said he was going to go and speak to the troop leader about it. I told him Cookie and I would look after him and we would sort the vehicle out.

The OC of A Squadron QDG paid us a visit at camp 4 which we were still using as a sort of makeshift RHQ. He turned up in an open-top Land Rover in the pouring rain. They had taken a normal Land Rover and cut the roof completely off it. Both the driver and operator in the back looked cold, wet and so pissed off. The role bar had a machine gun mounted onto it with about 30 grenades strapped along it. In the back were four LAW 80s (Light Anti-tank Weapons) and loads of boxes of ammo for the machine gun. Sand traps had been attached to the front and sides of the Rover. They were obviously trying to look like the SAS from WWII out in the desert. The OC himself also looked like he was entering in for a SAS look-alike competition. Dressed in desert combats and despite the pouring rain, he wore sun glasses, a floppy hat and a very large shimag wrapped around his neck, no doubt ready to cover his face in the event of a dust storm. He had a shotgun (obviously his own and I doubted very much allowed) for a personal weapon and a pistol strapped to his leg. He never acknowledged any of us as he walked past and up the steps to greet the CO, who had just come out of the building. One of the lads called him a cowboy and commented on the fact that here we are in a vast open desert and he was goes for two weapons with a very limited effective range. The look on the CO's face when he greeted him clearly showed he was not impressed about something. They went for a chat behind closed doors for over an hour whilst we chatted to the guys in the Rover, they didn't have a single nice word to say about their OC at all. When they returned, the CO again was not looking too happy and the goodbye was somewhat lame; we never did get to find out what was discussed but we got the distinct impression that we would not be seeing the QDGs or any of the ammo for a quite a while.

Chapter 5
Desert Training

The CO expressed a wish that he wanted to get out of BA and get some training in. The sooner we got into the desert the sooner we would all start to adjust. I thought it was a very good shout given the fact most of the guys had never been in a desert environment before, just getting the basics right was going to be a challenge, let alone full-blown war tactics. The closest we had for this type of training was BATUS during the summer months, and there weren't many people in the Regiment who had been out there. We were also told we had now come under the command of the Commander Royal Artillery (CRA) and that he, or his staff, apparently had no idea what Divisional Recce actually did. No doubt like most units and personnel, they would never have exercised with a Divisional Recce Regiment before, why would they when Battlegroups have their own Recce. Even if assuming that he was ex-artillery, and that he would have gone several times to BATUS before, again he would never have seen or heard of Divisional Recce. The only guys that he would be aware of that carried out anything remotely similar to what we did were 4/73 (Sphinx) Special Observation Post Battery, who were part of the artillery. So, what exactly were we going to contribute given the fact he was in charge of A2 Echelon (rear supplies)? He apparently was unsure what to do with us.

When the Yanks found this out, coupled with the fact that we were Recce, they cried out for us to work with them. They saw Recce, or Recon as they called it, as Special Forces because that was exactly what their Recon guys were. They also had a plan of exactly how to utilise us effectively.

The training was authorised so the Regiment got organised and then deployed up north to a training area on 1st Jan, 1991. The area was a massive ten by six kilometres square, which the US Marine Corps were currently occupying together with an Artillery and Engineer unit. When we arrived, we found all the US guys had loaded weapons, so we were warned that we had to be very careful what we were doing. We still had no ammo, so there was little risk of us starting a friendly firefight. The good thing about working with the US was they attached an A10 fixed wing Squadron and an Apache helicopter Squadron to us. That would make things really easy for calling in air support now; no dick dancing around with our own guys and jets being unavailable for whatever reason. An American officer was attached to work with us as the go-between and radio guy for if we needed them.

The desert training turned out to be unbelievable, and our first glimpse of what it was like to be commanded by people who seemed to just make it up as they went along. Our Intelligence Warrant Officer (Int WO) Knocker S had spent several years in Saudi Arabia, so was pretty clued up on the desert and life out here, but no matter what he said, it got a stiff ignoring from the officers who were conducting the training. Amazingly enough, after a few of the guys started to voice their concerns about the knowledge that was being handed out, they told us about the manual they were using for guidance and expressed how this was far better than any experience someone might have. Their argument and logic being that experience was unique to an individual and would only cover certain areas, whereas a manual would cover everything. I was gobsmacked that someone in command not only said that, but actually believed it. Needless to say, we listened to what was being said because we had to, then we went and asked Knocker how it should be done.

He was the font of knowledge. As an example, basics like going to the toilet, the manual they were using mentioned digging latrines exactly as you would do for when operating in a European environment. If you were to do this, they would have attracted countless flies and you'd end up with most of your men eventually going down with disease at some point. A lesson learnt, not in any manual, was to use empty water bottles by cutting the bottoms off and sticking them together in a tube. Then you would dig a hole, put stones at the bottom, then place the tube into it, before finally filling it back in for support. All you would have now was a small opening which you used rather than a big empty hole that flies had a field day in. This was called a Desert Rose. Knocker had lots of tips like this that paid dividends for us, especially on sandstorms and what a pain in the arse very fine sand turned out to be. The stuff would somehow manage to get in every orifice going. Not only would this be a problem for equipment, but simple things like preparing, cooking, eating and storing food would get covered in the stuff unless you took steps to prevent it. He also told us about all the things that crawled along the desert floor and how to avoid them or deter them from wanting to get close to us.

Geordie L using a Desert Rose

When Command troop was out in the field with all the command elements of the Regiment, it became Regimental Headquarters (RHQ). It would comprise of well over 50 men, 10 or more of them being officers, and many vehicles. The vehicles as a minimum included: four CVs, COs and 2ICs Spartans, their Land Rovers, three Ferret scout cars, and vehicles belonging to any protecting troops given to RHQ or attached units, e.g. Artillery or Engineers. The vehicles would be grouped; one lot would become 'Main' and the other 'Step Up'. The idea of this split was to keep control of the Regiment during a moving battle. Step Up could be packed away and moved whilst Main kept control. Step Up, once firm somewhere, would then take control, thus allowing Main to pack up and move. Main, like Step Up, would move, set up and then take control back. Anyone attached to the Regiment always bolted onto Main unless they had more than one vehicle, in which case they split between Main and Step Up.

When RHQ set up, the vehicles would back up to each other to form a shape (normally a crucifix). Tents (called penthouses) extended from the backs of the CVs about three metres. These would be merged together and form a space where work could take place. Radio masts would go up and all the wires buried to prevent trip hazards. Whenever possible, we used the masts bolted to the sides of the vehicles. Once completed, all the vehicles would be camouflaged up. Crews lived and fought together so sleeping, eating and working/admin areas per vehicle would have to be made as well as trenches dug for all the men, should you need to fight. As people finished one task, you would move on to help someone else to complete their task. When this was done, you could then look at getting some food on for your crew and start the duties that needed doing, e.g. sentries. Setting this up was some mean feat, and anybody who has ever had the pleasure of working in set-ups like this would fully understand and appreciate what I was talking about. When certain individuals do not help out, it soon becomes a right royal pain and the workload massively increases.

In our RHQ, it seemed anyone wearing a rank on their shoulder (officer) always had an excuse not to help out. The best excuse I ever heard was, "It is far easier that we keep out of the way since you guys know what you are doing and where everything goes." Most of the guys just got on with it, saying it was pointless complaining, it was never going to change. Whilst I totally understood what they were talking about, it annoyed me immensely that the SNCOs were not saying anything, or as we say in the military, 'gripping' the officers. Some even made excuses up for them saying they were far too busy and had more important tasks to be getting on with. When I questioned how it was possible to not make a single brew over a two-week exercise period, I was told that it was the job of the lower ranks to do it. What was even harder for me to accept was the constant putting away of officers' kit and having to look after them on top of all your own tasks. It boiled my blood having to roll up their sleeping bags because they had not done it themselves. All soldiers were taught to square their own personal kit away and know exactly where it was at all times. If it was no longer required, then you packed it away. Not only would this reduce the time it took to pack RHQ away, but if you were unfortunate enough to get attacked and needed to bug out, you could instantly grab your kit and go because you knew exactly where it all was. In my eyes, it was totally unprofessional. They were just being lazy and expecting the lower ranks to do everything, including waiting on them hand and foot, and what was worse was the SNCOs were allowing it to happen.

RHQ starting to set up, trenches being dug

Despite not everyone pulling together as a team, normally, a well-drilled troop could get the basic set-up done in an hour or so, and the rest would take about four hours (trenches, admin areas etc.). Then it would all get titivated over the next few days as you tested and adjusted. Most of the time when we moved and set up, it was done at night. This obviously always took a lot longer with trying to keep noise and light to an absolute minimum. Because of this, it was absolutely essential to conduct a Recce before we ever moved into a new location to ensure it was suitable and that there would be no surprises in the morning that resulted in us having to move again. Taking the set-up down took just as long as setting it up most of the time because as Recce soldiers we had a golden rule of leaving no trace of our presence ever being there. This type of set-up was used for when we were going to stay for a lengthy period of time. The problem came on people's interpretation of the exact definition of 'lengthy'.

RHQ set-up minus all the cam nets

4th JANUARY, 1991

We were informed that all our deficient kit had arrived for us at last by trucks. Everyone was ecstatic until we found out that it was just one set of desert combats each. There was no ammo, body armour, desert boots, water bottles, spare NBC kit or Combo pens. In the unlikely event of an attack, we might not be able to fight, but at least we could hide a little bit, unlike the vehicles that still had no desert camouflage nets. There were also some rolls of hessian on the backs of the trucks for us to use. This was rolled out in lengths and then sewed together to cover a few of the vehicles up. If nothing else, it gave us some shade and a place to work under without being seen. For those who got it, because there was not enough to go around, it was actually quite good, and it was better than the brown and green cam nets that we had brought with us.

The desert training had given us all the opportunity to see exactly what we did and did not require out here. All the kit that we felt we did not want or need was loaded onto the empty trucks to go back into storage at the docks. Chainsaws, for example, were no good in a place without any trees. Cookie and I had a good dig out of all the kit on the Spartan and threw lots of it out in order to make room for all the other crap that we now had to take due to the CO wishing the vehicle to be converted into a CV.

We were told to stop taking the malaria tablets now because this was not a malaria country. The information had taken this long to reach us even though 7 Bde had been out here for months. There was a definite rift between the two Brigades, a lot no doubt being driven by 7's unwillingness to share information. It both amazed and annoyed me to keep hearing people ask which Bde we belonged to rather than which Regiment when we asked for something. When we explained that we were the Division's Recce Regiment, they always wanted to know what colour Rat symbol we were wearing. When we said it was a Black Scorpion, not a Rat, they didn't like that. Some even refused to serve or help us saying we were not part of their Bde; therefore, they couldn't or wouldn't help. I thought we were all on the same side out here, obviously not. I know there's always rivalry within units and especially between them. However, this was not helpful when you're all up against a common enemy. We should all be uniting to fight the other guys and prove we were better than them, not trying to compete against each other.

The vehicles had been at sea for over ten weeks doing nothing, and it was starting to show because we were now having a lot of mechanical issues with the wagons. It was a strange fact with military vehicles that if you run them all day, every day, they worked fine, but if you left them for a period of time, you ended up with nothing but problems. The Spartan's engine decided to blow up so needed replacing. The Royal Electrical and Mechanical Engineers (REME) did this as well as fix the sights, fuel and gun systems. Talk about being given a shed or what? Still, we were slowly getting there with lots of help from the REME. Like all of us back in Germany, these guys had worked their butts off repairing the vehicles that we took over. Unlike a lot of Regiments who centralised their REME, each of our Squadrons had its own REME embedded within it. Although they were badged to their Corps, they were for all intents and purposes treated and accepted as members of the Squadron rather than people who were attached.

Whilst the REME and Cookie sorted the engine out, I fitted some more radio equipment into the vehicle. Another order from the CO to make it like a CV was that he now wanted to be able to get in touch with other units when he was not in a CV. In a CV, you had the ability to monitor and talk to other units operating above you (Bde), with you (Engineers, Air, Artillery), and all your own Squadrons (A, B, C, D, HQ). These all operated on different frequencies, otherwise you'd never get a word in edgeways if everyone was on the same one. To enable you to listen to them all at the same time, each frequency needed to be on a different radio. Depending on how far away these units were operating from you depended on the type of radio, and thus antenna and mast you needed. A CV was normally fitted with a minimum of four different types of radios, large radio masts and antennas. It would always operate with another CV, so you had the ability to monitor and talk to potentially eight different units at vast distances. RHQ, having a minimum of four CVs, meant they could monitor 16 units all at the same time. The troops had AFVs that only had two radios and small antennas, one to communicate to everyone else in the Squadron and one to talk to higher (SHQ). They were simply not equipped, designed or needed to carry masts. Trying to turn an AFV into a CV would bring untold problems that anyone with a slight bit of intelligence could predict.

I had tried to explain the dangers and problems of doing it, but I was ignored. Despite others in the troop being more experienced and qualified than me, nobody was prepared to back me up. I was told, quite firmly, what the CO wanted, he got; it was not up for discussion or debate. Given my skillset and the fact it was an order from the CO, I carried it out. The vehicle now had two secure radio systems complete and two 353 radios, all running off one vehicle battery. In comparison, a CV used four batteries to do this.

I also had to make another map board; the CO did not like the last one that I made. He wanted it exactly like the ones that were used in the CVs. So, after measuring the inside of the Spartan to see if it could physically fit, I popped over to the guys in our QMs and asked if they could help out and try tracking one down from somewhere. Whilst there I grabbed a pile of sandbags and desert-coloured hessian, which Steve and I used to make the vehicle less conspicuous. First, we secured spare tank track and road wheels onto the sides and the back of the vehicle. Not only did we need to take the spares but it also added a little bit more protection. We then cut the sandbags and hessian up into strips and then shredded them; these were placed all over the vehicle to break the shape up as much as possible without restricting anything. Having no cam nets and sitting out in the open in an RHQ set-up, I felt we needed to do something. To be honest, if someone saw our set-up and was clued up on British military vehicles, they would target the CVs regardless of what mine looked like.

I received some mail today, always a welcome sight. There were three letters from Silke and eight from Lori, with a nice parcel containing some photos, a book (this diary) to write in, and of course, her homemade American cookies. Lori did not have her new address in the UK yet so was waiting to move before she would write and let me know where it was.

We moved location again because the CO did not like the last one we were in. Once set up again we had a quick troop brief. The Regiment would be conducting an exercise tomorrow night and it would include RHQ; it would no doubt be the usual 48 hours non-stop mess around. We always practised this on exercise of just continually going for a minimum of 48 hours without stopping or sleeping. They said the purpose of it was to build up your tolerance to sleep deprivation. It was always funny hearing about guys who just fell asleep driving and ended up driving into things or off roads, always good for morale so long as nobody got hurt.

Within the Regiment, one Sgt got charged for a Negligent Discharge (ND) of his weapon (that was when it fired without you intentionally meaning for it to happen). A Lance Corporal (L/Cpl) in a Squadron got demoted (bust) for calling his SSM a wanker, Cookie got promoted back to L/Cpl again and the CO sacked his Land Rover driver, again, with no explanation other than he wanted a new one. That's two now since we have been out here.

Visser had the honour, or should I say dicking, of stepping up to the plate, whether he wanted to or not. He was a good bloke, didn't really complain or make a fuss, just got on with the job in hand; no doubt that was why he was chosen. As the CO's driver, not only did you drive him everywhere he wanted to go but you also had to look after him. That included tasks such as: putting his tent up and down, laying his sleeping bag out, cooking his food, getting him hot water on for a wash, making him brews and digging his trench in case of an attack. It was a regime that rubbed off to other officers, who then also expected us lot to do likewise for them. As his driver, you basically followed him around and ensured he had everything he needed at all times. This was why most of the guys did not volunteer for it. The job did come with a few incentives. Firstly, you were left totally alone by everyone else in the Regiment, meaning nobody gave you a task or job to do without first getting permission from the CO. Secondly, if you did it really well, and you got on with the CO, you would normally get promotion out of it. Downside, if you did it badly, you got sacked and your name would be mud, and like mud, it would stick for a long time.

The CO chatting by his vehicle whilst waiting for his tent to be set up away from RHQ

Tempers were starting to heat up. Most guys felt we were no longer training but messing people about for the sake of it. This was not being helped when most tasks came with no explanation at all, and if you asked any questions you got a 'just do it' reply. The CO was constantly having chats with the top commanders in the Regiment away from RHQ. Normally, they would be conducted within the RHQ set-up for many reasons, not only did you have all the up-to-date information readily available for briefing but it was protected by sentries. To have it far away, in the open and unprotected, and then little information fed back to the troops afterwards was starting to annoy people. It was being perceived that there was no trust, with a 'need to know' policy in place. We were in a war zone, and the last thing you needed was a lack of trust starting to build up.

A report came into RHQ that a REME senior rank had been woken up last night with a gun in his face and told just how easy it was to get him if he didn't stop being an arsehole to his guys. That obviously went down like a lead balloon with the CO.

Some of the officers in our troop were not helping the situation as they were treating the whole thing like we were on an exercise back in Germany. For example, in the RHQ set-up, everyone was expected to be up and about during daylight hours and doing something. Regardless of the fact most of the guys would have done stags during the night or might have been out on a route march all night long. Driving closed down at night, with no lights for hours on end, really took it out of you. Lack of sleep was starting to show and no doubt not helping tempers. It seemed stupid to me. If you weren't required to be awake, then you should get some sleep so you are fully rested for when you are required to perform. Tired guys on stag protecting your life is the last thing I would want; your focus and judgement shifts massively when fatigued. Tactically, it also makes sense, having everyone up milling around is not good when trying to conceal where you were. Coming from Boot troop, this stood out like a sore thumb to me, and it was exactly how we found the guys most of the time when we were out looking for them on exercises back home.

'Stags' was when you did a duty for a period of time. In RHQ, we had two main stags to do. A sentry, whose job was protection, and a radio operator, who was required to listen to the radios. Being signals qualified I got the radio stags. Normally, in RHQ you always had two radio operators on and one officer, in a Squadron it was one and one. The operator's main function was to use, look after, and if required, repair any of the radio kit, including all the secret equipment. They were also taught how to mark-up military maps and read incoming signals and faxes. The officer (called a Watchkeeper) was there to make command decisions on anything that came across the radios or via signals or faxes; after all, we were in command and control of the Regiment and also representing it if someone from higher called up. During quiet periods, when we were on a Regimental exercise and had no higher authority, the officer would get his head down, assuming he trusted the operators to wake him up if required. Stags would normally be for two hours minimum before someone would take over from you. Radio stags for us were always carried out in the CV and required a handover that normally took about ten minutes. Crypto (secret kit) had to be accounted for and then signed to say you were taking control of it. Crypto is always taken very seriously in the military and comes with some very heavy penalties if it gets lost. RHQ had a lot of crypto, so to help with the handovers, we staggered the operators so you always had just one changing over at a time, this then allowed the handover to be done slowly with the guy who remained on stag. It also always meant someone had their finger on the pulse at all times with regards to the bigger picture (what was going on). Of course, this whole process was subject to change, depending on who was in charge at the time.

WEDNESDAY, 9th JANUARY, 1991

(Up to date and now writing daily in the diary).

Got up at 0630, had a wash and some breakfast. Steve wanted to take the wagon for a run, and more importantly, to pick up some important supplies; he had found the location of a garage that was open. Like I said, Steve was such a chilled-out guy. Here we were in a war zone, and he was able to find a garage which he was more than happy to drive a military vehicle to in order to get some food to cheer us up, just classic. There was a briefing after breakfast about the exercise that was on tonight. I said I would go on that, Cookie and Visser could go with Steve to the garage. The brief was as short as it was informative; the Regiment was basically going to do a route march from dusk till dawn. Once complete, we would all split up again. RHQ would break off, find a new location and set up control once more. Whilst we were doing that, the rest of the Regiment would all go into a Nuclear Biological and Chemical (NBC) state and practise working in the kit for a few hours. It would involve them wearing NBC suits, gloves and respirators (gas masks). Rather than use qualified NBC instructors, the RSM and a few officers from RHQ would be going around the Squadrons to ensure everyone was conducting the drills correctly.

Now that I had fitted the secret radios, I needed the crypto to get it all working, so I went and collected it after the brief. It involved taking a trip to the Royal Signals, who were miles away, to get what we call a fill gun. This was a piece of equipment that held the codes to encrypt radio transmissions. You fitted it to a secret radio and pulled the trigger to squirt the codes inside, hence why we nicknamed it a 'gun'. For people to be able to sign for and use this equipment, you had to be class one signals trained and what the Army call Neg Veted. This process involved the military delving into your past life, anything which they found to their, shall we say, disliking, they hauled you in for a chat. If they were still dissatisfied with what they learned, you would not be allowed to do the signals course. This was carried out because anything that had the word 'secret' attached to it attracted the stigma of you selling it to the Soviets; hence, all the background checks. In reality, we knew the Soviets just went to the manufactures to get the information; it was easier, a lot more in depth and more up-to-date. Normally, the only officer in RHQ to have done this type of course would be the Regimental Signals Officer (RSO).

I have mentioned this fact because life in RHQ was never that simple. When an officer needed to talk to the guys on the ground, they simply picked up the headgear, pressed to speak and said what they wanted to: job done. However, human nature (and soldiers being soldiers) always kicked in. There were lots of buttons, switches and lights, so to see what they did, they fiddled and pressed them. Sometimes it was a quick fix, other times it was a major problem, especially when they erased all the codes in the radios, or worse still, the guns, and we could no longer talk to anyone. That meant one of the operators had to go back to the Royal Signals and get them refilled. Obviously, because it involved crypto, they would ask how the hell it had happened. Either you had incompetent operators or you had broken the rules and allowed unqualified personnel to play with it. Either excuse was not good, and the poor operator normally incurred the wrath of the Signals unit. Going again a few days later with another problem required some serious diplomacy.

After collecting all the crypto and handing it into the CV for safekeeping, I decided to wash some clothes. I could not wash my combat trousers, as they were the only ones I had. One of the guys on radio stag informed me that my wagon had broken down again; this time it was the fan belt. The REME were tasked to go and sort it out. While waiting for them to return, I decided to push out a few letters. I wrote to Silke and one to her friend Kerstin. I was still waiting for a letter from Lori with her new address so couldn't write to her just yet.

Later on, I was sent to the Regimental Aid Post (RAP). The doctor wanted me to attend a lecture on dripping people. The RAP was made up of two doctors, a few qualified medics from the Royal Army Medical Corps (RAMC), the RMAs from the medical centre back at camp and all the members of our Regimental band who by default had the role of stretcher bearers in wartime. Like RHQ they could operate being split into two separate RAPs (Main and Step up). While one was treating casualties, the other was moving with the pace of the battle, ready to set up to receive the next lot. Hopefully, this way it would cut the time and distance down that the injured had to travel in the Squadron Samaritan. We had to be self-sufficient and treat our own wounded, given how far we would be operating in front of our own Battlegroups.

It was not the lecture I needed but the drip kits themselves. I already had the knowledge, but not the kit. When I arrived, I went and spoke to the doctor. The doc, Major W, explained that he only wanted medics who were working with him to have drips. He knew I was a qualified RMA but did not know how competent I was since I had not actually worked with him. He did not fancy the idea of giving me the kit hoping I knew what I was doing with it because if you got it wrong you could kill someone. I had to respect his train of thought, but I did not agree with him. I explained that I was the only medic in a troop of plus 50 men. If we got hit, and there was a high probability that it could happen, unlike the Squadrons who had their own armoured ambulances, we would have to call up the RAP and wait for them to turn up before we got specialist kit to save lives. Even assuming they had the vehicles and medics to send, the timeframe alone would result in needless deaths, and we were talking about the command element of the Regiment here. He said he would have a think about it but wasn't promising anything. I liked Major W, not only was he an officer that you could talk to on a professional level, but he was the kind of doc that always wanted to get in the thick of it, as in places where guys were bound to get seriously injured. No doubt he could really use and improve his skills then, and dare I say it, see injuries that you would not see being in a medical centre back in camp. To be honest, that was the kind of doc that you wanted with you in situations like this, if he'd seen it and treated it before, you would be more likely to survive.

When I got back from the RAP, my wagon had been repaired and returned; I wondered how long for this time. It had done nothing but break down since we got here. We stowed our entire gear ready for the exercise later on. Steve had brought some goodies: tea, coffee, biscuits and loads of sweets. This would probably be the last time we got hold of stuff like this.

We took the RHQ set-up completely down; once all packed and ready, we started to move out at 2100. The Operations Officer (Ops Officer) and all his kit joined us on the wagon as the CO wanted him to be part of the crew from now on. The CO elected to travel in the back of a CV for this exercise. It was the standard route march across open desert with no lights, so we all just got one behind each other and followed on, leaving a space of about 50 metres between each vehicle. This was always done so in the event of an attack, it made life difficult for the enemy to engage you all at once. The spacing distance was always increased during daylight hours. It was a clear and pretty cold night, which made for good driving conditions because the cold would keep the drivers awake. There was nothing more tiring than driving at a set speed and distance throughout the night without a single break. It also meant the night sights would be giving the drivers a good clear picture to use.

The Regiment conducting a route march

THURSDAY, 10th JANUARY, 1991

We followed each other seeing nothing at all of interest, just flat open desert for miles and miles in every direction. At 0500 the order was sent to split up and go to new locations. Once we arrived at ours, we set up again. When it was all up and running, we were all told to get into NBC kit and stay within the main set-up and look busy. Given the brief from the other day, that was a complete surprise to most of us. We realised what was going on when the radio operators were asked to leave the back of the CVs and three Captains and a Major took their places, even the CO got in the back. A Brigadier was visiting.

The visit was short and sweet since he only stayed for a quick chat with the CO. Once he had departed, we all got out of our NBC kit and into RHQ routine. A few of us sat outside the main tents listening to the BBC news on a radio that one of the guys had. It was announced that talks with Iraq had failed, looked like we would be going in on the 15th once the deadline passed. For some strange reason, I was happy about it. I guess it was a combination of factors. We were here to do a job, so now that we were here, let's get on and do it. We now had the force, and in my eyes a better force. Also, I felt I was ready for this, I had the training, the knowledge and the fitness, besides battle experience I could not be better prepared. Although you hope you may never have to put that training into practise, you must be prepared to, and you'd better get it right first time, every time, there was no second best in this game, should the time come.

Cookie received a letter from Mary back in Herford; she was a friend of ours who worked in the NAAFI. She told him to tell me that Silke was seen down Cafe Wigtig, a pub downtown where soldiers went to pick up a girl. You could always find one of these places wherever soldiers were based. This made me really mad because she knew what my views were on that pub, and there could only be one reason for her going. I was more pissed off with the fact that she did not wait that long for me to be out of her sight, and for me to be here of all places, a war zone. She obviously did not care as much about us as she made out. Somehow, I knew this would happen. It had happened before and I had let it go. She had told me at the time that she had gone to keep an eye on a friend and because I couldn't prove she had actually gone with another guy, I gave her the benefit of the doubt. Given our rocky past up to now, this was the final straw for me. I would take all of my kit out of the flat and leave her for good once I returned from here. Still in a rage I went to my vehicle, took out all the letters and photos of her, ripped the whole lot up, and then burnt everything. She was exactly what I wanted in a girl: blonde, good-looking, good figure and fun to be with. Only problem, she obviously wanted a boyfriend and the freedom to sleep around at the same time. I had made the mistake of thinking I was different and could change her.

After dinner, we were told to start packing everything away again as we were going to do another route march tonight. This time they were going to throw a replenishment (replen) into the mix. A replen is what you do to resupply your vehicle and crew with all the things you need to last you for a few days. This function was carried out by the Squadron Quarter Master Stores (SQMS) and each Squadron had one. The SQMS title was also given, and referred to, when talking about the guy who ran that troop. Normally, it was far easier for the troops to go to the SQMS rather than for them to go around all the troop locations. RHQ and sometimes SHQ would be the exception due to the size of the set-up. Taking it all up and down just to get some fuel and food was a little excessive.

We practised replens on every exercise we did, most never normally ran smoothly, mainly because people kept changing the way to do them. No sooner had everyone got it nailed, the SQMS changed over. The new SQMS, believing his method would work better, would change it and then want it tried and practised until we all got that one right. What we in the military liked to refer to as reinventing the wheel because at some point you would eventually revert to the original one. Replens were normally always done at night, the basic idea was to get in and out as a troop; getting everything you needed, as quickly and as quietly as possible. At a replen the supply vehicles would be in a long line, and each one was marked with a different coloured torchlight. Once you knew what the colours stood for, and you knew exactly what you needed, you just drove to those vehicles only, quickly collected what you required and left. That way you rolled smoothly in and out, taking up the least amount of time possible. There would be a set dedicated protected area, normally 1 kilometre away from the replen, where you would stop and stow everything correctly before moving out again as a complete troop. The only difference between a Squadron and a

Regimental replen was the number of supply lines set up. We set off at 2200, same drills as last night, it looked like another night of no sleep for everyone.

FRIDAY, 11th JANUARY, 1991

We went through the replen at 0230, this one as normal was a complete cluster. It started off with a change in the plan. Before we went through, we all had to get into NBC kit with respirators on, which added to the confusion as it made seeing more difficult. We had also never done a replen before wearing respirators at night. This would have been great practice for us, but the set-up had also changed, so when we went to what we thought was an ammunition supply vehicle from years of practice, it turned out to be the food supply vehicle. This was not the time or place to change what had been drilled into people. It was embarrassing for everyone. No doubt we will be practising that again.

Once we had gone through the replen, off we went to carry on with the route march. It ended at 0500 again, and we all split up once more to go to new locations. At 0530 it was reported that a vehicle had driven over a 20-foot drop and had landed upside down. The commander, Lt W, was killed. The gunner had head and arm injuries, and the driver was in shock. Both were very lucky to be alive and had been taken to hospital. That was one down; I wondered how many more guys we would lose before we left here.

As soon as we set up, I hit the sack for an hour before I was required on radio stag for four hours with Adam (I). Two days without sleep now, come tonight I am going to be totally knackered. Whilst on radio stag I noticed nobody was talking to us; this was not really unusual as a good radio net was a quiet one, but the troops had to send in reports at set times, and none had been sent. Adam and I checked that the radio equipment was all working correctly, and then the frequencies. Everything seemed correct as per the handover. I contacted a troop using their own Squadron frequencies and was informed that all the other Squadrons had been trying to get hold of us on another frequency. Since they were all in contact with each other, that could only mean RHQ was on the wrong ones. If we were on the wrong frequencies, it meant we had been out of contact with the whole Regiment for well over six hours. It was the job of the radio operators to make sure we were on the right frequencies at the right times, on handover between the operators you checked this, we had done that. The frequencies were changed at midnight and midday, but again, they were changed and checked. It made absolutely no sense to us, so whilst Adam started to check it all again, I went and informed the RSO. On hearing the news, he blew a fit and had a right rant at me in front of the CO, saying I didn't understand my job correctly and no doubt the fault was caused because the handover was poor between the operators. He was fuming and after blood, he went straight across to the CV and told Adam to stop what he was doing because he wanted it fully investigated.

Billy H, since he was a very experienced operator and it was his CV, was told to investigate it with me and report back to the RSO with his findings. We did a complete check of everything again. We discovered RHQ had the correct frequencies on all the radios as per the signal instructions for the day; although everyone else was on the same but different frequencies to us, they were all on the wrong ones. This meant only one thing: the RSO had given out the wrong signal instructions to the rest of the Regiment. It was his job to make sure the Regiment had the correct set of signal instructions for each day. When Billy informed him of the error, he didn't even acknowledge it or apologise to anyone, especially me, who he had ranted at earlier. He just told Billy to get it sorted out. Quite a few of the guys took exception to this.

Later on, an Orders group (O group for short) took place. With having the four CVs back to back in a crucifix with their penthouses all out and joined together, it gave quite a lot of room to work in, or as in this case, a nice, warm dry place to hold an O group. If you were the enemy, this would without a doubt make a beautiful target: one bomb and you didn't just take out the CVs, you got all the top men of the Regiment at the same time since it was them who must attend the O group. There was never any extra protection put around RHQ when O groups happened, there was just the one sentry as usual. I really do believe they thought they were invincible and would never be attacked. That belief, or bad practice as I saw it, might have stemmed from all the exercises we had done in the past, where RHQ never ever got attacked. Even when we practised artillery coming down on our heads and you had to get under cover, the penthouses, despite being made of fabric, were always classed as hard cover. Besides the inconvenience to the top lot, taking out the control with all the top players would undoubtedly grind the exercise to a halt, and we always played to win, so no doubt the reason why it never ever happened.

It was always wise to listen in on these O groups if you ever got the chance, because a lot of what was said and discussed was never passed onto the blokes (lower ranks). Most of it was normally not relevant as it turned into a bit of a social gathering for the officers, but if you were lucky enough not to lose interest in it, you could pick up the important things that were said. Of interest from this one was that Regimental training was now over, and we were going to have three days of grace for everyone to sort out any last-minute issues. It was going to be our last chance before things started to happen. A truck would be turning up tomorrow to take any kit back, including any personal items, that we no longer required. Replen might become an issue when the Regiment moves forward; therefore, everyone was to be made aware we would be taking plenty of food, water and ammo onto the vehicles. Room needed to be made available for when this tipped up. Another General will be visiting tomorrow, so no doubt some more messing about will come with it as normal. Rumour has it we are going back under the command of 1 (UK) Division but will be keeping the US attachments (A10s and Apache helicopters). Seems someone up top has questioned what the hell we are doing working with 1 (US) Corps and not our own guys. Given what has transpired up to now with trying to get help etc., I know whom I'd rather be working with. We are also getting four Multi Launch Rocket Systems (MLRS) and a command wagon from Sphinx Battery attached to us. They will tag onto RHQ for ease of control. Having all this firepower attached now, I really wished I was back in one of the troops again. There would be zero chance of using it being in RHQ, that was for sure.

In four days' time, the deadline will be up and we could be going in, *yet here we were in a war zone still without any ammunition, body armour or desert cam nets for the vehicles.* We were the British military, and we prided ourselves on organisation and getting things done. Besides not having other important things, no ammo or body armour at this point in time was just unacceptable in my mind, yet nobody at the top appeared to share my opinion, that or they just didn't want to make waves and upset people. It was a good job the Iraqis had not decided to attack us.

A CV trying to hide itself using cam nets designed for Europe

Members of RHQ blending in with the sandy desert...or maybe not

Mail arrived and I got one from Silke's sister. She was wishing me all the best and telling me to look after myself. That cheered me up a bit. Mail was such a morale boost for everyone; if anyone ever denied it, all you had to do was watch them when they didn't get any, you really did see a change in behaviour from them. It was one of the reasons why most of the guys, especially the young lads, took to writing to pen pals, that and the fact there really wasn't much else to do stuck in a desert in the middle of nowhere.

After stag, I helped Steve, who was busy cooking our dinner over a stove. As a crew, we tried to take it in turns to cook whenever possible, but it normally ended up with Steve doing it because Cookie and I were always on stag. When Steve cooked, we would do the washing and clearing up afterwards; the Ops Officer, who was now part of our crew, like most officers in the troop, was far too busy to help out. Always ensuring that the officers were fed and watered was one of the reasons why we believed everyone had to be awake during daylight hours. God forbid that we would make shift patterns up, or that an officer actually took a turn in cooking or making a brew. Once we had eaten and everything was washed up and put away again, I got straight into my sleeping bag. I was feeling so knackered; sleep deprivation was starting to build up and so was my frustration.

SATURDAY, 12th JANUARY, 1991

Everyone was woken up as normal by the sentry at 0630. This time we didn't have to prepare breakfast as the cooks had turned up. Whilst centralised cooking seemed totally unprofessional for a Recce Regiment, it was such a Godsend not to have the hassle of cooking as well as the hundred and one other jobs you had to do in RHQ. The cooks we had were a good bunch of blokes, and they looked after us really well. They were always left alone just to do their job of cooking, but boy did they work some hours. I always remember a funny story about a cook on exercise. After having his head ripped off for not having his weapon and webbing during a mock attack, he was asked what the hell he would do if the Russians came over the ridge. He replied, "Give them the menu and ask what they wanted for dinner."

After grub, we were all told about the need to make room on the vehicles to carry extra water, food and ammo. We moved our vehicle out of the set-up and once more took all the kit off it. We still had far too much kit on board. It meant being ruthless and only keeping the essentials. It was a good job back in Germany that the REME had welded a cage on top of the wagon to carry any extra kit. It made it larger and less inconspicuous but without it, there was no way in hell's chance we would have been able to carry the kit.

I asked the Ops Officer to sort his kit out and explained that he needed to be ruthless with it. Officers always seemed to bring ten times what they actually needed when they went somewhere; normally this was not a drama because you had the room available. We managed to persuade him to get rid of over half of what he had. All personal kit in the troop which was not needed was placed in a pile to be collected later on and taken back to Al Jubail, where it would get put in a container and sealed up. Because only a single truck was turning up to collect the kit, all the kit off the vehicles that we did not need was disposed of in deep trenches that were dug. It was amazing the amount of actual kit on a vehicle, all taking up space, which you really did not need or for that matter ever use. Most of the kit was designed for a vehicle to operate in a European environment, and as we were now in the desert, it was pretty useless. The first things that went into the pit was all the floatation gear required for crossing rivers and that was quickly followed by a lot of other needless crap.

The truck that turned up to take our kit back had some desert cam nets on the back of it. However, the driver told us that only some had arrived for the Regiment and there wasn't enough to give out for every vehicle so the QM had decided the priority was the CVs. The Squadrons had received two each for their CVs, he had brought four for RHQ. He also told us there was still no news on the arrival of any ammo or body armour.

At 1200 it started raining, it was that annoying drizzle rain, the one that just went on and on for hours instead of just giving you a quick downpour and then stopping. Most of the guys did not have waterproofs with them, but they did have a poncho (a sort of waterproof mac) which we all carried as part of our webbing. In the Regiment, it was always frowned upon to wear waterproofs. The belief being that in a heavy downpour you could hear the rain falling on them and that they also rustled when moving about, thus giving your position away to the enemy. You were always told: your skin is waterproof and you were a man if you could take the cold and the rain. No amount of reasoning was going to make someone see the flaws in the belief or those statements. We all started to build makeshift shelters; anything would do just to keep the rain and wind off us. Steve, Cookie and I actually managed to build quite a nice little home. It is amazing what you can do when you put your mind to it.

Another filling fell out; that was now two since we had arrived out here. I will have to go to the dentist and get these sorted before they start to become a problem. This was all because of the rush jobs the dentists did back in Herford. When there were 750 odd guys to do in such a short time, it was no wonder the work was of poor standard. I went and saw the 2IC. He told me the CO was writing a letter back to the dentist in Herford as they had seven other people so far with exactly the same problem. He then radioed the Dressing Station (DS) to get their location and to let them know he was going to send a guy down to them in the morning for dental treatment. The DS was like a mini hospital. It deployed in the field and sat behind the front line of your own troops, awaiting casualties that were brought to it by ambulance from the RAPs. Amongst other things, it was the first place in the medical chain that you would find a dentist and a minor trauma surgical team.

No mail got delivered today, which cast a cloud over most people. It was still raining when I went on stag at 1830. During the handover, it became apparent that three of the fill guns, loaded with codes, were missing. We were talking a court martial offence here. After a quick flap, we grabbed a few of the lads, explained the situation and then started a major search. After hours spent searching, we found out the Regimental Signal Warrant Officer (RSWO) had taken them without telling anyone or checking them out using the crypto register. He just laughed it off, had one of us done that, he would have ripped our nuts off, and rightly so since both were offences when dealing with crypto. After stag I hit the sack, everyone else was already in bed, mainly because it was still raining.

SUNDAY, 13th JANUARY, 1991

I was woken up at 0415 by the sentry for my stag at 0430. Deep joy, it was still raining. Rain was one of the many joys endured being in the Army. I didn't know why it was, but every time you went on exercise, or were ever deployed anywhere, it always rained. The briefs we had back in Herford about the weather out here informed us it was not going to be a problem, and it only ever rained about eight inches a year. I think we just had those eight inches last night. The main weather problems we were to focus on were the sun and heat type illnesses. Since we had been out here, the weather appeared to be operating in a four-day cycle; we got two days of sunshine followed by a sandstorm and then a day of rain. I wondered what other information they had given on the briefs was not as accurate.

When I got on stag, I found out that for some reason, we were only doing one-hour stags today, so I decided to do the next one as well and give the other guy a lie in. It was pointless going to bed as everyone was being woken up at 0600. Once everyone was up we were told to move the CVs. The news really impressed the guys as it was still raining, but the CO was absolutely right, the sabkha they were in was flooding and becoming boggy. Sabkhas were where water collected in a desert. Given the information on the yearly rainfall, it made perfect sense to use these areas. They were nearly always flat and in low ground, thus it afforded you a little bit of protection by hiding you and made the formation of the crucifix a lot easier. Putting stakes and pegs into hard mud was easier and held things down far better than in loose sand. Luckily, we had positioned our vehicle on higher ground, slightly away from the CVs.

After giving the guys a hand moving, I returned to my vehicle only to find our makeshift home was leaking. We rearranged all the covers to try and stop the water from getting in. It really made no difference now as I was already soaking wet through from helping the guys out earlier, it just meant I could now sit in a dry place in soaking wet clothes. Steve made me a brew to cheer me up, he was really good at looking after Cookie and I. Mail arrived and I got three letters and another CD off Britannia music, really useful that, especially since I do not have anything to play it on. I had already written to them twice before deploying and explained where I was going and not to send me any CDs. They obviously thought it was just an excuse to try and get out of the monthly subscription, that or they simply didn't give a shit and just wanted the money off me.

The mail driver was on his way back to his location and would be passing by the DS, so I caught a ride with him. I was really worried about going because I had a phobia of military dentists. I'd yet to meet one who hadn't inflicted pain on me. Why was it you could go to the medical centre in pain and you left afterwards in no pain, yet you went to the dentist with no pain, and after they had finished with you, you left in pain? This visit, however, turned out to be pleasantly different; I had temporary fillings put in due to them not having the correct kit to do proper ones. Not that I was complaining as it involved no injections at all. They told me they would require changing to proper ones at some point as they were only meant to be in for six months.

While I was waiting for transport to come and pick me up, I got chatting to some of the guys there. They told me the vehicle that had gone upside down happened right by them. They pointed out the drop that it had gone over; it was over 50 feet. They said the kit and doctors were on the scene within minutes but there was absolutely nothing they could do for the commander.

My lift arrived and off we went. When I got back, I had to go straight into a brief. It was to let us know what the plans were for the coming days. We were supposed to be moving up north but this has now been delayed until around the 22nd January; I guess the war was not starting on the 15th then. We would, however, still be moving in two days' time to a new location. The CO would be conducting a few Recces of those areas before we moved. That was good news of sorts since we still did not have any ammunition, amongst other things. I wondered if maybe we were not the only troops without ammo, and if that had anything to do with the decision to delay. There was a plan to hold a church service today for Lt W, but because of the weather it had now been cancelled until tomorrow, hopefully the weather would improve by then. Nothing much else came off the brief. We all had dinner then we retired to our 'home' to play cards and tried to make the best of the poor weather. Another early night was in store; there wasn't much else to do.

MONDAY, 14th JANUARY, 1991

Everyone was woken up again at 0600. This did not impress certain people such as the CO, who voiced his displeasure at breakfast. Yesterday we did it because the CVs needed moving, today should have been back to 0630. It all arose from a bit of confusion, the RSM had asked to be woken up at 0600, this was interpreted by the sentry that he wanted everyone waking up at 0600. It was still raining. The sabkha was now starting to show just how much rain had fallen; massive puddles were now forming on it. This meant it would start to rise soon and were it not for the fact we were moving location tomorrow, it might have required RHQ to move yet again, so much for the eight inches.

Podge G in front of a puddle forming in a sabkha

Since it was raining and there wasn't a lot else to do, I got all the weapons off the vehicle to clean them. The mounted machine gun badly needed it. It was starting to rust on the outside of the barrel again. This was a direct result of what happens when you scrubbed the protective coat off them and then exposed them to the elements. This was borne out from the insistence of having clean, shiny weapons in the armoury. Back at camp, the weapons were cleaned and inspected weekly, any marks or rust found on them and you were charged. Guys, therefore, ended up using wire brushes to remove any stubborn marks or rust; doing this also removed some of the protective black coating. You now ended up in a vicious circle, first bit of moisture and they instantly rusted, so out came the wire brush again and so it went on. I was a great believer of if guns were supposed to be shiny they would have been made like that. I just used to ensure that the inside of the weapon was clean and lightly oiled and that it was working correctly. The outside would just be dry-cleaned because out here you had the added problem of fine sand, if you oiled the outside of the weapon to prevent it from rusting, it would get coated in sand. It was a dilemma but either way, if a boss saw the state of the weapon and it wasn't shiny, or had rust on it, standby. At lunch time, it eventually stopped raining, so I replaced the cleaned weapons and went for grub.

After grub, we all formed up and had a church service for Lt W. I was not into religion at all, but for one of the guys I would always pay my respects.

Afterwards, we had a quick brief from the RSO and were informed the press were coming to visit our location today. Everything had to be put away, all trenches were to be dug deeper, and the set-up of RHQ generally smartened up. For security reasons, they were not to be allowed anywhere near the CVs, and under no circumstances were they allowed to see or get inside them. The CO, 2IC and Ops Officer would keep them busy whilst all the NCOs were to be in and around the CVs to ensure this happened. A few guys commented that although the security card was played, we all knew damned well that the reason they wanted the NCOs to be together and well away from the press was because the CO did not want any of us talking to them; someone might say something that was the truth. We were, after all, more than happy to be here, we had everything we needed, we all knew why we were here, what we were fighting for and we all totally agreed with it. The party line as we called it.

If someone did say something other than the party line, the fact it was the truth would be neither here nor there. It would not look good for politicians, or the military top brass, if the people back home read in the papers something that contradicted what they had said. A world of hurt would descend on you if you spoke to the press without permission (and presence) from above. In truth, most of us had not got a clue why we were here; there were no briefs on it before we left Germany or even when we arrived out here. Sure, we could make an educated guess; after all, we do read the papers and listen to the news. Guys had all sorts of reasons from it being all about oil, to companies just wanting contracts so the rich could get richer. But the simple fact was, every time we asked our bosses or tried to engage in an educational conversation, we just got brushed off with remarks like, "you're a soldier and paid to go where you're told", or, "it's to back the UN up because nobody in Iraq was listening". All those answers did was provoke more questions amongst the guys such as, if that was truly the reason, then why have the UN stood and watched countless other wars go on around the globe and done absolutely nothing about them? As for fighting in a foreign country, if I'm putting my life on the line, I wanted a better reason to understand and believe in, than "you're a soldier, do what you're told". Our superiors should have been boosting our belief of exactly why we were here and what we were doing was the right, honest and just thing to do. They should not be sowing seeds of doubt by just spouting a party line and then brushing guys off when it was challenged. Could it be that they simply just didn't know themselves, or didn't want to know and were blindly following the people above more worried about their own careers, rather than 'rocking the boat' as we called it? Either way, not being honest and truthful with the guys eroded respect and trust.

When the press did tip up, we were still on the 'digging trenches deeper' phase. At the continual rate we were digging, soon nobody would be able to see out over the tops of them unless they were seven feet tall. On sighting the press, a few of the guys left to ensure the CVs were secured but it made no difference anyway. The CO intercepted the press and whisked them off in another direction away from us. Cookie decided he was not going to be unnoticed, so placed a black NBC glove on his head and ran from vehicle to vehicle. This had most of us in fits of laughter, all except a few of the bosses, who saw this going on and obviously did not find it funny in the slightest.

Once the press departed we were told we could stop digging and the RSO had a word with Cookie about his behaviour. I went back to our makeshift home, stripped off and washed my combats and sweaty body. This might sound like an easy task, until you find yourself in a desert with a lack of water. In this scenario, a shower becomes more of a strip wash. This involves standing naked in a bowl and using a flannel or a bit of cloth and a cup. You first use a couple of cups of water to wet yourself, then you wash your body with soap from the top down. You then rinse off using the same water out of the bowl first, followed at the end by a couple of cups of clean water. Getting someone to give you a hand with the cups of water makes it so much easier; there's no time for modesty in our world. We all had a 'shower' then hung all the wet combats on a line outside; it wouldn't take long for them to dry in this heat and wind. Whilst they were drying it was time for some more card action in our underpants.

When we were not writing letters, playing cards was the next best option to keep you occupied. It was also our default for stress and something to do whilst we listened to the BBC. I had brought with me a normal pack of cards and a card game called Uno. In Uno, there were four coloured suits (blue, red, yellow and green), numbered zero to nine. Then there were some other cards that indicated either change direction or suit, pick up some more cards (two or four) or miss a turn. The game was very simple; you each got dealt seven cards, the last to get rid of them lost, or you could play that when the first person got rid of theirs, the game stopped and the cards would be scored (each one having a different value). Another card game we liked to play was 'hunt the queen', also referred to as 'hunt the c**t'. This involved more skill and cunningness. All the cards in a pack would be dealt out and you played trying to avoid collecting any of the hearts or the black queen (worth 50 points). Sometimes players would gang up on someone just to get them to 'bite'. This was when they lost their patience or temper. It was what soldiers did, there was no malice in it and everyone got a turn somewhere along the line; the idea was to try and see it going on and not to bite if it was directed at you. The thing about cards is, not everyone is good at playing them; sometimes we had such a good laugh when someone was taking a game very seriously and someone else was not. It got even more hilarious when they eventually realised that the other person didn't even have a clue how to play the game in the first place.

After dinner, I sorted out more kit and the boards in the back of the Spartan. I decided to hit the sack at 2200, which proved to be a waste of time as we were all woken back up at 2350. The ammunition had finally arrived for our troop, and the 2IC wanted it issued there and then, ironic given how long we had been here without it. 200 rounds were issued per person for our submachine guns. The rest was broken down and split between the vehicles. We got three grenades, one Law 80 (An anti-tank weapon) and 15 boxes of General Purpose Machine Gun (GPMG). I was not entirely sure what to do with three grenades given the fact there were four of us on the crew, so I just stowed it all on top of the vehicle. Someone asked about body armour and the other kit and was told there was no news on it at all; we would get issued it when it arrived.

Chapter 6
UN Deadline Now Up

TUESDAY, 15th JANUARY, 1991

I had been here exactly a month now.

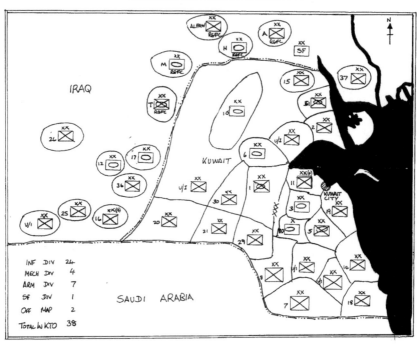

A trace showing what they thought we were up against. A cross inside the box meant it was infantry, a racetrack was armoured and together it was armoured infantry. Sizes/Strengths were placed on top of the box, XX was the sign for a Division

Everyone was woken up at 0630 by the sentry informing us all that we had just two hours in which to get everything away and ready to move. That meant no breakfast and rushing around literally just chucking kit into the vehicles rather than stowing it away properly. As we started to leave the location, the CO called a halt and had a right rant at the crew of OB for not filling in two trenches. Steve looked at me with a puzzled face and commented that it was not like someone was ever going to fall into one of them out here in the middle of nowhere, besides which, the next sandstorm would fill them in within minutes. I told him that whilst he was absolutely correct, drills were drills and it was a poor one not to do it as Recce soldiers, the rule being we never leave a trace of our presence ever.

The CVs were called OB, OC, OD, OE in order of importance, pronounced Zero Bravo, Zero Charlie, Zero Delta and Zero Echo. The CO would always operate from OB (Main) and the 2IC from OC (Step Up). The other two could be used how you liked, normally OD was the Intelligence (Int) wagon with the Int Officer and Int WO on it. OE was a spare CV that could be used for rebroadcasting (rebro). (I will explain more about these roles later on.) When a CV had control of the Regiment, it automatically changed its call sign to ZERO, regardless of which CV it was or who was actually operating from it.

We moved just three kilometres away and set up again. At least the sun was now out and shining. This was one massive bit of flat open land, and you could see out to the horizon in any direction. The Regiment spread right out because of this; everyone trying to ensure that the nearest other vehicle was no closer than one hundred and fifty metres away.

Some bright spark decided that because there was another report of an ND in the Regiment, nobody in RHQ was to have any ammo on them. All ammo was to remain inside the vehicles. This sparked a massive debate in the troop between those just wanting to do as they were told and those who thought it was an absurd idea given where we were and the potential to get attacked at any time. It was a classic case of those more worried about their careers and blindly following orders, to those who were thinking about the implications of what they had just been told to do. No way was I walking around out here unprotected, knowing the ammo was stored somewhere in the vehicle. I could not believe someone had actually thought that idea up in a war zone and implemented it.

Once set-up was complete, I decided to get all the kit back out of the vehicle and re-stow it properly, putting the ammo where we could easily get to it should we urgently need it. The GPMG, which was mounted on top of the vehicle, now had four boxes opened up and ready to use, with two belts clipped together for immediate use. I placed the LAW 80 just behind the turret hatches so if required, Steve or I could easily grab it. The grenades I put into an empty ammo tin next to the LAW 80 and secured it. Whilst I was busy doing this, Cookie was digging some shell scrapes and Steve was sorting out all the new maps for the whole of RHQ ready for the next area we would be going to. Once Cookie had finished he gave me a hand to clean all the weapons again. After a quick sweep out of the back of the wagon to remove most of the sand, we put everything back in its rightful place and then got our new set of maps off Steve to stick together. On looking at the maps I thought Steve had given me the wrong ones: there was nothing on them at all. It was just plain desert: no houses, roads, trees, wires or water holes, not even any contour lines. We might as well have been given brown-coloured sheets of paper. I had never seen maps like this before in my life, I thought they had to be misprints.

Mail arrived and I got one from Michelle. At least I now knew mail was getting through. I was busy reading my letter when the RSM came over and asked me if I had any medical kit on the vehicle. I always kept an ammo box full of medical kit for emergencies. He asked me if I could have a look at a bloke with a cut head from one of the troops. They'd brought him to RHQ because nobody could find the RAP due to it being on the move, and they were not answering up on the radio. So much for the one foot on the ground principle. I went into my vehicle to fetch my box while the RSM went and fetched the guy. When he arrived, I cleaned and examined the wound. It was a straightforward cut about three inches long that did not require stitching, which was a good job, because I didn't have the kit to do it. After I patched him up and he left, the RSM returned and told us all to get our berets off and our tin hats on. He said we were no longer on Regimental training now and officially at war. I asked him if that was the case could we load our magazines up then and got told no way: magazines stay unloaded as per the CO's instructions. I was surprised that the RSM was going along with it as he always struck me as a very level-headed bloke and someone who I looked up to. Most RSMs actively go around their own units and 'let' you know they are the RSM, almost like a power trip, but this one didn't. He treated and spoke to you like you was a human being, and all the guys I knew respected him for it. Hence why I dared ask the question in the first place.

The RSM (Dave I) in wartime had the role of being in charge of Provost troop. Those were the guys, who when back in camp, ran our guardroom and looked after any prisoners. In wartime their role was to look after any Prisoners Of War (POWs) and they were bolstered up with extra guys to help them do it. Until we got some POWs, they were bolted onto RHQ to help with the guarding of it. The RSM got a Ferret scout car as his own vehicle so he could get out and about, because he would sometimes be asked to act as a Liaison Officer even though RHQ had two dedicated officers for that role. His driver, Ade R, was a good bloke. Ade was training to be a PTI, so I knew him through that side of life.

On the BBC radio, it said all talks with Iraqi diplomats had failed but they would carry on trying until the deadline was up, that being 0001 UK time, 0301 out here. I don't know why they were bothering, they'd been trying since August last year, hadn't they got the message yet? Saddam Hussein was not going to move his troops out of Kuwait full stop, the longer the talking went on the more his forces dug themselves in and prepared their defences.

Once everything was sorted, I got into my sleeping bag as I was on stag at 0300 in the morning.

WEDNESDAY, 16th JANUARY, 1991

Woken up at 0245 for my stag. Old newspapers had started turning up so I cut a few more clippings out whilst on stag. The media appeared to be trying to cover everything that was going on out here for the public to read. There was also a lot of speculation in the papers about other countries joining in, especially Israel. The US wanted them to try and stay out of it, no doubt because of all the Arab nations involved so far. The firing of Scud missiles into Israel by Iraq was clearly an attempt to provoke them into joining in. One paper stated that if they did join in, Jordan and Iran would join in on Iraq's side. If this was all true, we were looking at World War III starting. There was already a hell of a lot of countries involved and enough military out here as it was; it would not take too much to tip it into a world war. Rather than allay all our fears and keep us current of the situation with briefs from above, we were being told nothing and had to rely on newspapers and the BBC radio from back home for any information. Maybe there was something to be said about the saying, 'ignorance is bliss'.

I sat in the CV and listened patiently to the radio, **War was officially declared across the military radio net at 0305**. I wrote it in the radio log in bold capital letters and stuck my name next to it. **That meant I could say I did the first stag of the war**; let's hope it wouldn't be my last. As before, I asked the sentry not to bother waking the next guy up for stag. Had I have been tired I would have swapped, but I was wide awake now so it was pointless me going back to bed to try and get some sleep for an hour and a half. Even when absolutely shattered, I'd always find it very hard to get to sleep; it normally took me a few hours of tossing and turning before I eventually nodded off. It was either stress or insomnia.

The sentry woke everyone up at 0630 as usual. After breakfast, we had a brief and were told that the CO had decided that most of the troop would be moving out and joining in with a Squadron exercise that was taking place today. He said it would save everyone sitting around getting bored. Our wagon was going to be left behind so Cookie could be used for sentry, and I had two tasks to do. One was to mark all the maps up with the new traces RHQ had received last night from higher, the other was to fit some more signals equipment into the wagon. A trace was normally a thin film of plastic which was marked up using military symbols (As shown at the beginning of the chapter). It was the quickest and easiest way to pass on information from one map to another, especially if there were several maps that needed the information transposing onto.

Signal operators were taught what all the symbols stood for and exactly how to mark a map up military style. That way, when you were on stag, you could instantly look on a map and see exactly where everyone was, including their size, unit, equipment and strengths. Operators also listened to the radios and read the faxes and signals that came in, including the secret ones. On takeover of a stag, in order to catch up on all events and be abreast of the current situation, a good operator would read back through the log books to the last entry that they had previously read, since everything had to recorded by writing it down. You then had a pretty good idea of what had happened and what was about to happen. When an officer then asked what was going on and where everyone was, you could give them an accurate picture of the whole situation instead of, "I don't know, sir," which was not very professional at all. In reality, depending on the visitor, the Watchkeeper would jump in and do the brief. You'd then be placed in a very awkward situation if they gave an incorrect brief.

Part of the handover/takeover process between operators was to conduct this brief and pass all this information on; the rest could be read in slow time whilst you were on stag. This process was why we always found it strange and very frustrating when certain officers would not pass information on. As operators, we either already knew it or we would find out about it when we next did a stag. It was the main reason why I chose to write the diary during my stags, the information was right in front of me recorded in all the log books.

AJ – One of the signal operators marking enemy positions on a map in OD with his 200 rounds of 9mm ammo all ready for use in the event of an attack

We also got told on the brief that we were still not moving before the 22nd, this was to give the coalition air forces a chance to do some bombing. When we eventually move, we are going up north to a place near the Egyptians and Syrians, it will be very interesting and a bit nerve-wracking as they are both equipped with Soviet equipment, exactly like the Iraqi Army. After the brief, I was given some more radio kit to install in the vehicle, instructions from the CO, so I nipped over to see the REME for some cables in order to make the leads up that I required. I spoke to the electrician and explained that although I was being ordered to do this, I was concerned that the batteries would not be able to handle it and I wasn't exactly sure what the result would be. I didn't think the CO quite got electrical load sharing; either that or simply just being told something by a L/Cpl. It was not being helped by the fact none of the senior operators, or even the RSO or RSWO, who were actually passing the tasks onto me, were saying anything. After explaining to me about military batteries buckling up and exploding, he said he would have a word with his boss, if nothing else just to cover my arse for being ordered to do it.

On getting back to the vehicle, the RSO came around and wanted to inspect all the weapons. He found some rust on the barrel of the GPMG and wanted to know when I had last cleaned it. I told him we'd cleaned all the guns only yesterday and the fact they were left out last night in the elements was why the barrel now had some rust on it. I tried to explain to him what over cleaning the guns with wire brushes was doing, but he wouldn't have it. He said it took days of neglect for rust to form, so he was going to charge me for not cleaning the weapons, he told me to get it cleaned with the brush and then stormed off. Besides the fact there were four of us on the crew, it always amazed me that the default approach to any problem in this Regiment was to always charge someone first, rather than listen, understand or educate.

I was absolutely furious. I got the gun off the vehicle and removed the rust with a wire brush. This was going to be a never-ending problem, so I nipped back across to the REME to have a chat with the armourer for some advice. He was not impressed by the fact that I had used a wire brush on the gun, but there was no way rust was going to come off with a bit of cloth. He told me to slightly oil the barrel then place a condom over the whole barrel. It may look unprofessional, but it would help keep the sand and rain off it and if we were required to use the weapon, it wouldn't cause any problems at all when firing it. He said to pass it around the guys and do it for all the weapons, not just the GPMG. He also said not to worry about the RSO. He would have a chat with his boss and get him to go and speak directly to him. We shouldn't be scrubbing the outside of the barrels out here; it would just result in more rust forming quicker each time. I felt relief after that; at least someone had my back for once.

I walked back across the desert to my vehicle, which was about 800 metres away. Going back and forth across lose sand with all your kit on in the blazing heat was quite tiring so I decided to chill for a bit and write a letter to Michelle. After I finished the letter, since nobody was about, I got all my 9mm ammo out from the vehicle and loaded my magazines up. I know the RSM had told us not to do it, orders from the CO and all that, but we were now at war and anything could happen. It would be no good moaning after the fact and saying things like, "I wish I had…" or, "It was his fault we had no ammo". In my eyes, having ammo in its boxes in the vehicles instead of on you in a war zone was fucking ridiculous, especially if the enemy attacked you. It reminded me of that Zulu film where 1,800 British soldiers died because the QM would not allow them to open the ammo without his permission. True or not true, here we were years later in a similar situation. I would rather not find out the hard way, I would just do it and keep very quiet about it. What everyone else chose to do was their business.

It was now getting very late and the troop had still not returned, either they were still moving about the place or they had decided to stop somewhere for the night and would return in the morning. There really wasn't anything else I could do so I hit the sack, knowing that when they returned in the morning there would be plenty to do with setting RHQ up again.

THURSDAY, 17th JANUARY, 1991

Up at normal time. To my surprise, the troop had arrived back in the early hours of the morning. I must have been dead tired, as I didn't hear a thing, which was a little concerning. The air forces of the coalition had started their bombing raids on Iraqi positions in the early hours. So, it really had kicked off; I guess there was no turning back now. It felt weird though, war was kicking off and when you looked around, everyone was in a cheery mood as if it was not affecting them. Guys had no ammo on them or body armour and the officers were still wearing berets despite what the RSM had said. They couldn't decide whether we should wear or carry the helmets. I was still going to wear my helmet, no matter what they decided.

At 0920 we all had our first panic attack. The CO dived out of OB and screamed at everyone to get under armour. Like most people, I instantly grabbed my gun, webbing and helmet but then just stood there for a few seconds with my brain playing catch up. It was trying to work out if it would be better to get into a trench rather than inside a vehicle sitting in the open. If it was an air or ground attack, I would stand a far better chance of survival in a trench, if chemical then the vehicle was the better option. The CO shouting his head off interrupted my thoughts. He was like a madman in total panic, so needless to say this got most of us flapping, including me. If he was that worried, it must be really serious and scary as hell. I guess it was the unknowing coupled with a bizarre unfamiliar call of "Get under armour". Normally, a call would be something like, "Incoming", indicating something from the air like rounds falling onto you. "Gas, Gas, Gas," indicting a chemical attack, or "Stand To," indicating you were under attack from ground forces. That way your training kicked in and you instantly reacted rather than do what most of us did and just stand there which potentially could get you killed.

I headed at full sprint for our vehicle, still thinking to myself that if we were under attack by tanks we could kiss our arses goodbye. I was scared as hell not knowing what was going on. As soon as we got in the vehicle and the door was shut, the CO shouted at Cookie to get the vehicle running and pressurised. He then put his respirator on and told us all to do likewise. We instantly did it. Now I really wanted to know what was going on. If we were under a gas attack, putting our respirators on should have been the first thing we did before sprinting hundreds of yards to get under cover, that was the basics of NBC warfare that was drilled into every soldier. A shout of "Gas, Gas, Gas!" would instinctively have made everyone do this. I asked him what the hell was going on. The five of us who had managed to get inside the vehicle were dying to know.

He said it had come over the radio that Scud missiles had been launched, no other information as to numbers, direction or potential targets. On hearing this my heart stopped racing now. I took my respirator off and politely reminded the CO of the brief we had been given during Regimental training. We were told not to worry about Scud missiles this far south for two reasons. The first being, when a Scud was launched and headed this way, a Patriot missile would intercept it on the border. Since I had been here, there had been three attacks. During one attack, six Scud missiles had been fired and not one of them managed to leave Iraq; Patriot missiles had intercepted them all. The second reason was because, if one had been fired and not been intercepted by a Patriot missile, it would have already hit its target long before it was reported over the radio nets. In all the other attacks in places where they had no Patriot batteries, the attack had been reported three hours after they had landed. Whilst the brief was very informative, it had been really annoying to find that information out so late in the game, it should have been disseminated a lot sooner because on each of the attacks, we had all gone into NBC kit and then sat around for ages waiting to find out exactly what was going on.

We had also been briefed not to take our NAPS tablets, because although the Scud missiles had the capability to carry chemical and biological weapons, given the heat and vastness of the desert, unless a whole lot was fired in one go, and actually hit their targets, the spread of any chemical weapons out here would be minimal. The heat alone would kill it all off quite quickly and the sand would absorb most, if not all, the liquid agents. They would let us know, if and when, it was necessary for us to start taking them.

The CO didn't hear, or didn't want to hear, what I had to say. He told me to put my respirator back on until we were given the all clear. I complied and we all just sat there in silence with the vehicle running. The clearance came about 30 minutes later, when someone came over from the CV, opened the door and told us it was an old report. The missiles had been fired five hours ago; only one had actually managed to evade the Patriots and it had landed in the desert 200 miles away from us.

That little episode completely eroded my confidence with the CO. His intention was there but the lack of NBC training/knowledge clearly showed. If that was the example of how he reacted to something like that, what was he going to be like when we closed with the enemy? Next time he tells me to get into a vehicle, I will go into a trench and take my chances. I was not getting killed because of his lack of training. Most of the vehicles in RHQ besides having limited protection, had no fighting capability whatsoever. Sitting inside a vehicle trying to figure out what was going on because information was not being passed could be the difference between life and death. In most situations, you needed to be outside in all-around defence with the knowledge of what was going on and what you're up against, and then be prepared to react to a changing situation.

Later on, a Land Rover was going to A2 Echelon (A2) to pick the mail up, so grabbing my gun and webbing I jumped on-board for a lift. A2 was what we called the base rats. They were the people in the Regiment who were the furthest away from the front line, people who would normally stay back in camp when we deployed on exercises back in Germany. Amongst other things they would be comprised of the QMs department, REME base workshops, the postal guys, all the Regimental clerks and all the cooks. They held all the stocks for resupply and had the ability to carry out major long-term repairs of the vehicles. That was ultimately why they had to be that far away from the front line and all the fighting. The set-up of A2 was massive because of the sheer number of vehicles they had, most of which were soft-skinned and totally unprotected.

When I was there, I met Robbo and Si (another clerk), and we had a chat. They told me that when we move up north they would all be coming with us. I told Robbo about the diary, and he said he would start to collect newspaper clippings of the war for me since they were getting papers from back home in A2. They were a couple of days old but it was better than nothing and gave you something to read. I asked him if he could put some into our mailbags for the lads, even if we had to wait for the guys at A2 to read them first. He said he would. We all knew the guys at A2 received papers; the troops only got them if someone could be bothered to send them on. Mail was picked up, but I never got any. I said my farewells to the guys and hoped to see them again soon, up on the front line.

When we got back, we decided to play cards again. Visser was our humour point today. He didn't have what you would call a good understanding of card games, which I found highly amusing. Quite a few of us found him to be such a nice guy that you really couldn't get mad at him at all, he just made you laugh.

The CO with the RSM decided to carry out an unannounced mock attack on the troop to test our drills, since nobody had loaded weapons, they were fairly safe doing this. Afterwards, we all had to parade for a chat. They were not overly impressed with the reactions of the guys, including me, who just couldn't be bothered to play their stupid game. After our bollocking (telling off) and all being told, we would be dead if we acted like that during a real attack; I pointed out that most of us would be dead no matter how good we were. The 200-metre dash across open ground to get to the vehicles where our magazines and ammo were, assuming they and ourselves were not hit, then having to ask the Iraqis to hang on for a few moments whilst we loaded up, might prove somewhat a bit problematic. The RSM agreed and suggested to the CO that we should be allowed to load our magazines up but only carry them on us. Nobody would be allowed to put a magazine on a weapon unless told to do so. The CO agreed.

A sentry wearing an NBC suit doing protection for RHQ

Chapter 7
And So It Begins

FRIDAY, 18th JANUARY, 1991

Woken up at 0600 to be told Scud missiles had been launched everywhere in the night, and we would be getting an Intelligence (Int) brief later on about it; in the meantime we were to start taking our NAPS tablets. That was one tablet to be taken every eight hours starting from now.

After breakfast, all the radio operators had to go and see the RSWO. We all had to form up before he gave us a bollocking, because someone had not changed the frequencies on time. The guys told me afterwards that most people never took any notice of him whatsoever, mainly because of his frequent bollockings, which always seemed to be when someone with rank was within earshot. Almost like it was staged for their benefit. It just so happened to be the CO on this occasion. I didn't really know the RSWO that well and had hardly worked with him, but he personally struck me as a guy to be very wary of. Only the other day, he had given the wrong codes out to over half the Regiment and then tried to cover it up by taking the crypto guns without signing for them, nothing was said about it, which really pissed the guys off. I wondered if that was why he was so quick to point out other people's mistakes, that way it would shift the heat from his own. The direct result from his approach to any mistake that was made was that when anybody made one, nobody told him anything about it. He was kept out of the loop whilst we just got the situation rectified, learned from the mistakes and then moved on.

After he had finished, we had an Int update from the Int Officer.

Int Update:

Enemy – Nine Iraqi planes had been shot down, seven Migs (that's a Russian fighter plane) and two Mirages. All of their airfields had been bombed, but only one was reported destroyed. All static Scud sites had been targeted and hit, only two remained operational. 30 mobile Scud launchers were still to be found. Last night 17 Scud missiles were launched, five were at Turkey, three at Saudi Arabia, five at Israel, and one at Syria, the other three had misfired. Patriot missiles that had been deployed destroyed the ones that were launched against Turkey and Saudi Arabia.

Friendly: Eight coalition planes had been hit; four of them were shot down. 18 soldiers were reported wounded so far. It was believed we had an air advantage, so the bombing would continue until they were sick to death of it.

OD was the Int vehicle whose job it was to collect all Int from various sources and keep RHQ constantly updated, both of enemy and friendly forces. The crew of the Int vehicle was made up of people from within the Regiment. It comprised the Int Officer (Capt T), the Int WO (Knocker S) and training wing personnel (Podge G and Dave C), who had done various courses to enable them to carry out this role. AJ was their signals operator. I always looked up to these guys as they seemed very clued up and knew their stuff, especially on Soviet tactics and equipment. The training wing was on my radar to serve some time in to get clued up to their standard.

The Intelligence wagon (OD) and its crew

Orders came in from higher: the Regiment was to move up north on the 21st to an area in front of allied troops, it was just 70 kilometres from the border. We were to wait there for further orders to move up even closer. That seemed to be a change of plan as we were originally told that the Arab nations would go in first not the British. That was a political decision to further show we were out here helping the Arab nations, not the other way around. Even the Americans were staying 120 kilometres away from the border.

After the Int brief, we were all told that due to the Scud firings last night and the potential threat of chemical weapons, the priority was now to get on and repair the NBC seals on all the vehicles. The function of the NBC seals was not to stop air getting in (although ultimately that was a by-product), but rather to stop air escaping, so you could pressurise the inside of the vehicle. This was done by the NBC pack that would draw air in from the outside, filter it of any potential chemicals and then force it into the vehicle. The problem was, most of the NBC packs on the vehicles were not working correctly, if at all. They had not been serviced or repaired since a new ruling came out a few years ago after an accident stating that only qualified personnel could do it. Before then, all RAC soldiers were allowed to do it. Someone had incorrectly fitted the filters and poisoned a crew on an exercise. Because we didn't have many qualified personnel in the Regiment, quite a few NBC packs got neglected and were never even checked on vehicle inspections. Hence, most of the NBC seals were neglected as well. As an urgency, all NBC packs now needed to be correctly checked, serviced, tested, and if required, replaced. Doing the seals would be a complete waste of time if the packs were not working correctly, how would you guarantee the air you were about to breath inside the vehicle was free of chemicals?

Guys, and especially the NBC instructors in the troop, tried to explain this to the bosses to pass it up the chain of command but they were not having it. The CO had given his direction and it was not up for debate. It seemed certain officers were getting far too paranoid about NBC. No doubt driven by a lack of training/understanding. A few days ago, it was pointed out to the Ops Officer that he didn't have the right water bottle top on his water bottle. They had been changed well over a year ago so that you could fit it directly to a tube on your respirator, negating the need to remove the respirator from your face to have a drink. Had he of been to any of the NBC lectures or been in the gas chamber, which was a yearly compulsory training directive for all soldiers, he would have found this out.

Some of the guys went back to A2 to get the glue and seals whilst the rest of us started on the vehicles. Before we could start, we had to take a vehicle one at a time out of the set-up and remove all the kit from the outside of it.

To do the seals on a vehicle correctly, you needed to strip it right down. This involved removing all the engine decking, disconnecting all the driving controls and then removing the bulkhead, that was the part that separated the driver from the engine. All the viewing sights, (these allowed the crew to see outside the vehicle from inside it), had to be removed and all the mounted guns that protruded out of the vehicle needed to come out. The belly plates under the vehicle for draining water out of the engine and gearbox compartments also needed to come off. You then needed to remove all the old seals from around the edges and the rims of the remaining holes, ensuring they were dirt and dust free before gluing the new seals down. Once completed, the glue needed time to set before you could replace any of the parts and put the vehicle back together again. Every hole where a bolt went was a potential air leak, so they had to be plugged, preferably with the correct bolt. Once done and the vehicle was back together, the REME then tested it with specialist equipment. If it was not pressurising correctly, you started all over again, because there was no way of knowing where the leak was. Doing this in a sandy environment, rather than in a vehicle hangar over a pit back in Germany, was not ideal.

The guys returned from A2 to inform us that there were not enough sealing kits to do all the vehicles. We had to be seen to be doing something, so after a chat with our NBC instructors, it was decided to concentrate on just doing the main areas, those being all around the drivers' cab and the turret. You always found holes everywhere on the vehicle, normally where bolts used to be but were no longer there. Some of the missing bolts were because the thread had gone and so a bolt simply couldn't be fitted. The holes needed to be rethreaded. Plugging them up could be overcome out here, not, I must say, to the standards laid down by the Army or the NBC cell. But when needs must, they must. REME, strangely enough, were not available for testing afterwards.

No mail arrived again. Silke was getting further out of my mind now, probably because I'd had no mail from her in ages. It wasn't the mail system either because her sister had written seven letters in ten days to Eddie, her boyfriend, who was also in the Regiment. Robbo sent me a few clippings from the papers. One was from *The Sun* newspaper. The unit was front cover with the headline 'SAS on tracks' and a picture of two CVR (T)s on a patrol. That was no doubt from the press visit the other day. The article then proceeded to say exactly what our role was and where we were operating. Guys commented, "Why don't they just hand our arses on a plate to the enemy?" Good job we would be moving again soon.

After my stag, I started thinking about my time left in the Army. I only had shy of 20 months to go now. I might just can the idea of the SAS, sign off and ask for a posting back to Canada to complete my last year. I didn't think this Army was for me any longer, not given what I have seen so far out here. It was the sheer willingness to please the highest rank and blindly follow orders without thinking or questioning that worried me the most. All the training I had seemed to count for very little and would certainly not protect me from getting killed based on someone else's poor decisions or training. Whilst on radio stag, I had sat and watched the officers working out battle plans; they were using books to do it from and I'm not talking about enemy capabilities either. I was horrified because I bet the Iraqi officers had those exact same books; after all, most had been trained at Sandhurst.

If there's one thing my two years in Canada taught me, it was never to religiously stick to the books. Books gave you the basics, a template so to speak, for training. Once you know the basic templates, stop using the books and start being flexible and adaptable, because no plan survives first contact and there wasn't a template for every situation. The enemy always has a vote and they won't play your game, they are there to kill you. You stick to templates and the enemy knows them, you will be out-manoeuvred every single time. Look at history, there are countless examples of it. This was why they taught us all to understand and know your enemy if you want to defeat him, you get him to dance to your tune, not the other way around.

SATURDAY, 19th JANUARY, 1991

Up at 0400 to do a stag. We were back to doing two-hour stags again, which was good as it gave the guys more time to get some kip. On the operators' board was a reminder to tell the sentry to get everyone to take their NAPs tablets. The times were to be 0700, 1500 and 2300. It was the sentry's job to make sure everyone took them at the correct time; if guys were asleep, they were to be woken up.

I was on stag with Sean L (Geordie). Obviously, he was from the North East with a name like that. I got on really well with Sean, helped no doubt by us both being Newcastle football supporters. There was a comic magazine called *Viz*, which focused on life in the North East. A few of the lads used to get it sent out to them from people back home. One of the characters in it was called Biffa Bacon. I managed to get Sean to read out aloud, this and other stories, since he had a very strong accent. It made it more authentic and used to have the guys in fits of laughter. It was a trade-off; he would do it if I would allow him to read what I was writing in the diary. I totally trusted him not to mention it to any of the officers.

We were getting ready to go to the ranges after breakfast when "Gas, Gas, Gas!" came over the radio nets. The reason it was sent across the radio nets was to ensure others nearby got the message and everyone was safe. They may not have been the intended target of the attack, but if it involved chemical weapons and the wind was blowing, it could shift the chemicals downwind onto someone else. Therefore, you got the call out to one and all and then quickly followed it up with more detailed information once everyone was safe. In that information was the exact time and location of the attack, the chemical weapon used and the direction and strength of the wind. Knowing this and where your own position was, you could then work out if it was going to affect you and what to do about it.

The call put most people into a panic and of course, straight into the NBC drills. The first and most important part of the drill was, when you heard the alarm you had nine seconds in which to get your gas mask on, otherwise you ran the risk of inhaling whatever it was. This was followed up with getting under cover or your NBC kit on if it was available. It turned out, one of the troops in B Squadron was testing out its NAIAD (a piece of kit that detects nerve agent gas) when they accidently set the alarm off. Before anyone had chance to explain what had happened, it cascaded all the way up the chain, with everyone reacting accordingly. This, of course, did not impress most people at all. A little bit of pre-warning from B Squadron about conducting NBC training, and the plans for if any of the alarms accidently went off, would not have gone amiss.

When the panic was over, and everyone was content that it was just a false alarm, half the troop left to go and fire their weapons on the range, the range being some sand dunes somewhere in the open desert. I was part of the troop that stayed behind again, so I went and hung around the CV to see if they needed a hand and to find out what was going on. Whenever half the troop went anywhere, either to carry out the role of step-up, or as in this case, off to the ranges, the workload increased, and stags came thick and fast.

Israel was attacked again last night with Scud missiles, numbers unknown as of yet, but they think Iraq was now running low on them. US Marines attacked an Iraqi artillery position, killing 40 Iraqi soldiers. Other than that, it was really quiet. A Squadron QDGs had now joined us and were under the control of our Regiment. Most of us had no idea what they had been doing up to this point in time. Speaking to the guy who dropped the post off today, it seemed the guys in the Squadrons were getting messed around something rotten. The OCs were conducting their own training as well as all the stuff RHQ kept getting them to do. The guys didn't appear to be getting a minute's rest. I wondered if that had come from the top, like us, to keep the guys busy at all times.

SUNDAY, 20th JANUARY, 1991

Up at 0315 for another wonderful two-hour stag. Considering war had just broken out, all was quiet on the radio nets. The guys were still on the ranges, having decided at the last minute to also conduct a night shoot; it made total sense as they were already there, so why not take the opportunity. Adam, with his dry sense of humour, commented that given the length of time it took to get ammo to us; we best put a request in for some more right now. After stag, I went and lay on my sleeping bag until it was time to get up for grub.

The rest of the troop returned just in time for grub. After breakfast, we all had to assemble in front of the CVs. We expected another bollocking; after all, it had been a few days since we had our last one. The CO addressed us this time. He told us that the RSO was being replaced for reasons that were of no concern to us. He said it was not because he was useless or anything like that, they had simply decided he'd be better off in another troop. Of course, nobody believed that speech. We all knew damned well why he was getting replaced, and so did the RSWO as he had had a lot to do with it. After my episode with the RSO over the GPMG, I was not too bothered to see him go. On the bright side, we all knew the Captain who was taking his place. He was another one of those rare cavalry officers who was very well-liked and respected. So, in the grand scheme of things, it worked out better for us as a troop. As one of the guys said, "All we need to do now is get rid of the RSWO and Command troop will be brilliant."

I was cleaning the inside of my vehicle when "Gas, Gas, Gas!" was shouted. Into the kit again and waited inside the vehicle until someone found out why it was called this time. There had been no explosions, aircraft or any shootings, there was no wind blowing and no alarms had gone off from any of the detectors placed around the RHQ set-up. It was no doubt another false alarm again. After sitting around in the kit for what seemed like a lifetime, the all clear was given. It turned out to be B Squadron yet again. This time they were firing on the range and one of the gunners had fainted inside the turret. "Gas, Gas, Gas!" was instantly shouted. The fact that none of the rest of the crew was affected, nor nobody in the immediate vicinity of the vehicle, or even on the range itself, coupled with no alarms going off, might have got them to pause for just a moment. Had it been any other time or place, machine gun fumes would have been the first and only logical thought, the paranoia of chemical weapons simply just took over.

During a briefing afterwards, they tried to justify it by saying, "It's better to be safe than sorry." Whilst you couldn't argue with that statement, to me it once more highlighted certain individuals' lack of understanding and/or knowledge of NBC.

Another ND was reported. This time the bullet had ended up in the hip of one of the guys, and it was his mate who had shot him. Guys joked that with mates like that you didn't need an enemy to fight. I just thought about how awful it would be to go back home and then have to tell everyone that you were shot by one of your own guys. Besides all the jokes and banter (and believe me when I say there would be loads from the lads), it would be pretty embarrassing and very hard to live down. On a serious note, it was really bad. People's own professional skills and drills were woefully poor; someone sooner or later was going to end up dead. There was no excuse for it in my eyes, especially when you ended up with results like this.

Some unknown people visited us later on, bringing with them laptop computers. All the operators were informed that we would be getting a few in RHQ so we needed to know how to use them. We spent a few hours with the guys going through some training and were shown a few of the programs that were installed before they left. I don't know why we bothered, because no sooner had they left than the Ops Officer muttered he thought he should personally have one to work on, this was quickly followed by the 2IC. I never touched the laptops again.

Good news, our second set of desert combats arrived, meaning we could now regularly wash a set without the fear of getting into trouble for wearing shorts whilst the only set we had dried. I always wondered how the officers managed this, did they have two sets, did they hide them, or did they just not bother? The only reason I had such questions was whilst I mentioned previously that all crews lived and fought together, this did not apply to the officers who came into Command troop from HQ. They had their own admin and sleeping area away from the rest of us. No way was the CO, 2IC or Ops Officer for example, ever going to mix with us lot and to be fair, it worked both ways because we would feel uncomfortable if they did. Still no body armour or cam nets for the rest of the vehicles and we were moving up north tomorrow to within 70 kilometres of the border, easily within enemy artillery range. We know they do not have aerial Recce, but they do have Special Forces (SF) and ground Recce. Let's just hope they are not close by or as good as us, because out in the open with no desert cam nets, you'd be able to spot our vehicles from miles away and call in artillery to destroy them.

MONDAY, 21st JANUARY, 1991

Up at 0630, had grub then started to pack everything away. Before lunch, we had a brief on what was going to happen with regards to the move. Basically, we were all going to move out and meet up at a given grid later on. Only the commanders of the vehicles would be told the full details and given the exact grid. Once there we would await the arrival of the rest of the Regiment. When everyone was all together, the commanders would then have another brief to be told what was happening next. The information was deliberately being withheld for security reasons. On hearing that last bit, a lot of the guys immediately flashed and interpreted it as they simply did not trust people in the Regiment; given the time frame involved and where we were, it made no sense not to inform everyone. We had lunch, and then set about filling in all the trenches and packing the rest of the kit away before leaving the location at 1400. It was a very short drive, lasting just over an hour to the 'secret' grid. We arrived at the meeting point to find most of the Regiment was already there parked up in long lines. We just joined on the back of one of them and parked up.

The Regiment all lining up waiting for orders to move up north

This was the first time the Regiment had all met up again since we had deployed on the 1st of this month. We parked up, and like everyone else, sat around waiting to be told what was going on. Steve B and Nigel Z (Zeb) found me, so we sat and had a brew and a chat. Zeb, also being an RMA, was now part of the RAP. Steve was now in 1st troop C Squadron. Both told me they hadn't a clue what was going on, and it had been like that since they had arrived out here, like most of the guys in their troops they were getting really pissed off with not being told things and constantly being fucked about. They asked if I knew anything being in Command troop, and I told them to join the queue with the rest of all us pissed-off guys. After putting the world to rights and getting things off our chests, we had a laugh about the good old days and having beers downtown in Herford. It cheered us all up.

O groups were eventually called, and afterwards we were all told that we would be moving out at midnight, details to follow later. This later got changed to *we* would all be staying the night and leaving first thing in the morning at 0800. That meant we would all be getting up at 0500, because everyone would have to be washed and fed before leaving. Everyone was instructed to just sleep where they could; no tents or cover was to be put up at all. The only good point was the cooks set up a cookhouse in preparation for the morning.

Mail went around. I got eight letters. Lori had written me a really nice letter, but it was dated from November. Thinking about things, I decided to write to my German bank and stop Silke from using my cashpoint card, just in case. I had left it with her for safekeeping, that and a few other things. I guess I wanted to show her I was willing to trust her, a big mistake me thinks now.

The call went around for everyone to take their NAPS tablet. Since I've started taking these I'm getting a lot of stomach-aches now, and I am not talking about food poisoning type pain. This was a completely different pain and really hurt like hell. It's that bad it instantly doubles me up when it comes on. Other guys were also experiencing the same problems; some were really bad and had the instant need to go to the toilet during the pains. As soon as they straightened up to go, they just shat themselves. They seemed to have no control over it whatsoever, it just flowed out like water, albeit the dark, smelly type. We were putting so much shit into our bodies all in one go I was surprised that we didn't drop down with something, that or we started to grow a second head. To top it all off and cheer us right up, it started to rain again, so we all got soaked.

Civilian low loaders turned up during the night, waking most people up. Those not awake were soon woken up, and everyone was told to get up for a brief. We were told they were going to be used to take all the vehicles up north, and we were to start loading them up straightaway, all kit and the drivers were to stay with their own vehicles. It took ages but once they were all loaded and, on their way, the rest of us tried to find a bit of dry ground where the vehicles use to be to get some sleep again; it was still raining.

TUESDAY, 22nd JANUARY, 1991

Everyone was woken up at 0500 as predicted. Breakfast was on but when we got there we found there was a problem. They had no plates, diggers (knife, folk and spoon) or cups and all of ours were on the vehicles. This coupled with the fact that the queue was massive resulted in most people not getting fed, those that did were equally disappointed; the food was stone cold by the time they actually got to it. Four tonners (military trucks) turned up later to collect us all. There weren't enough trucks for everyone to get on, so the rule of only 18 people maximum per vehicle went straight out of the window. Nobody wanted to hang around in the middle of nowhere in a desert without protection or water. Most trucks had between 30 to 40 men in the back: it was ridiculous.

Instead of going up north, we were driven back down south for a few hours to an airport. Someone joked we were actually on our way back home. We got dumped off and told to wait there until called forward to board our plane. While waiting around, a planeload of American soldiers arrived. As they were marching past us, a horn was sounded on a vehicle and a gas attack was shouted. This was obviously something the Americans did to all new arrivals, no doubt to get them focused and into the swing of things. It was soon noted that none of us Brits had reacted, we had just sat there and watched them put their respirators on; this did not go down very well with a high-ranking American officer, who happened to be with them. He was straight over and demanded we go through the correct drills. Just to show our American colleagues our NBC drills, "Gas, Gas, Gas!" was shouted. I think it really impressed them, the fact we didn't just sling a respirator on. We had a very lengthy drill that we went through, which included decontamination. After that little demonstration, we got out of our NBC kit. We sat for ages in the rain before being called forward to board our plane. The RAF was then very unimpressed when asked to wait because someone had forgotten his respirator. We were flown to an airfield up north, where we boarded some more trucks.

These drove us for hours across the desert to a place where we met back up with the drivers and the vehicles; well over 30 hours had passed from when we had first set off. What a complete waste of time that was! We could have driven up here, or at the very least, all gone with the vehicles and not just the drivers. It would have been far quicker, not to mention the fact none of us got any food all day long. Being away from your kit was never a good thing; you always wondered if you would ever see it again, that was why we always carried so much crap in our webbing and rucksacks. Even the drivers were pissed off; they'd been there for over 16 hours waiting for us lot to turn up. When we asked what was the point of that exercise, we were just told, "Ours is not to reason why, it's just to do as we are told." I fucking hated that saying with a passion for so many reasons. I replied that I bet it would go down in the history books as a masterpiece of military planning despite the fact that the only thing that seemed to go to plan was that we all eventually got here.

Once everyone had found their vehicles again, it was time to depart and go to pre-arranged positions. Our new location was in the middle of nowhere, and the land was as flat as a pancake again. We were told this was going to be our new location for a few days and the Engineers would be turning up tomorrow to dig the vehicles in. It was the only way of getting some protection and trying not to be seen out here; it was pretty dark now but you could see for miles in any direction. RHQ was set up and then stag lists were drawn up; it was now well past midnight.

So, this is to be our last location before the big push, once we get that order, it will be no stopping until Kuwait is taken back. It was frightening to know that artillery could come down on our heads at any time, and we were all sitting out in the open, just classic, you couldn't make this shit up if you tried. It was a case of just don't think about it, then it won't bother you until it does happen. When that time comes, I guess it is a case of pure luck if you are hit or not. A nice thought as we all drifted off to sleep.

WEDNESDAY, 23rd JANUARY, 1991

Up at good old 0630 again. Most of the guys were starting to look so tired now; fatigue was building up, especially after that move yesterday. Most of us were only getting around four to six hours uninterrupted sleep a night if we were lucky. If we keep going with this regime, we will have serious problems when the fighting starts because us Brits like to conduct most of our fighting at night, which means nobody will get any sleep at all.

Another guy was brought to the troop for me to give first aid to. He had cut his finger right through to the bone on an open tin can. I cleaned it up, put some sterile (butterfly) strips on, dressed it, and told him to go to the RAP the first chance he got as it required stitches. Failing that, he could come back and see me in the morning, because the dressing would require changing.

Whilst on stag in OB I had a look at the new trace that was on the map board. It appears we were now in a Divisional concentration area called 'Area Keyes', and it's full of Americans, namely 7 (US) Corps, who amongst other things have three armoured Divisions in it. That was good news because that meant there was more firepower about for a bit of support should we require it. We were sitting just to the south of where the three borders met between Iraq, Kuwait and Saudi Arabia.

The Engineers did not turn up to dig our tanks in. We were told that when they do eventually get here they will be doing the Squadron troops first; after all, they were even closer than us to the border.

Int Update:

Iraqi Special Forces posed a real threat to us here; six were shot dead last night to the south of us by American troops. News had it that 2,500 Iraqi soldiers had defected. Morale was reported as being low. 75% of their chemical stocks had been destroyed, so from the top we were to revert to NBC state 'low', which meant we could stop taking NAPS and carrying our NBC suits around. The CO, however, still wanted us to carry on taking them due to where we were, but he was happy for us not to carry our suits. An NBC instructor had pointed out that if the threat was deemed high enough to warrant taking NAPS tablets, then you should be carrying all your NBC kit with you at all times, as per the NBC policy. His advice was ignored.

I was stopping mine because the stomach-aches were killing me, and it was getting worse. I experienced first-hand what a few of the guys had been telling me about already. I actually shat myself today, no warning whatsoever, just the normal severe pain followed by an increase for a few seconds, and then out it flowed like water. Not a damn thing I could do to stop it. I had no control whatsoever, which was a little bit concerning having never experienced anything like that before in my life. If that was not your body telling you these NAPS were bad for you, I don't know what was. It was a good job I had that second set of combats now.

No mail arrived. I guess it was because we were now up here, so the postal system would be delayed until they caught up and got things back into place. I wished Lori would hurry up and get in touch. She must be settled in London by now, and it would be nice to write to her. If nothing else, it would cheer me up.

THURSDAY, 24th JANUARY, 1991

Woken up at 0745 to find everyone was as happy as punch, it was almost like a small victory had been won. We had actually managed to have a lie in. Nobody was entirely sure how it had happened, because it certainly wasn't planned. We wondered if the sentries had fallen asleep, but it was not the case, they simply hadn't woken people up. Given the fact everyone slept in, it clearly showed the guys needed a good night's sleep. The CO at breakfast made sure everyone knew he didn't approve of it though, so we were all quite positive that it would be back to 0630 tomorrow morning without fail.

After grub, we had yet another shout of "Gas, Gas, Gas!" not bad considering yesterday's Int brief. Turned out to be another false alarm. We were briefed/bollocked afterwards that the CO was now starting to get really annoyed with all the false alarms and us lot clowning about conducting NBC drills. That only happened because the guys took the piss, having been told yesterday to stow all the NBC kit inside the vehicles.

When I was on stag later, we sat and listened to all the bosses in RHQ discussing building a training program for the Regiment. It was to be conducted over six days, during which there would be some more visits by certain individuals, exact details would follow later. If you didn't know any better, you would think you were on an exercise and not at war. Here we are sat out in the open desert, well within enemy artillery range, no body armour, half of us with no cam nets, there were reports of enemy Special Forces about, and we were doing Regimental training and having visits arranged.

Int Update:

The French Air Force has just bombed the Iraqi Republican Guard Force (RGF). These are meant to be Iraq's best fighting troops. They are regular soldiers equipped with all the best Soviet equipment and as such they will be kept in reserve to reinforce forward positions when needed, good old-fashioned armoured warfare tactics. To do this quickly they are equipped with T72 MBTs and APCs (called BMPs and MT-LBs). Let's just hope that the air attack was a success and they have managed to kill a lot of them. It had now been a week of bombing from the coalition air forces, and we have not even used any artillery yet. It was looking better every day, but I could still see us having to go in sooner or later as nothing had changed: it was still stalemate.

No mail again today. The Engineers managed to get out to the troops to dig holes for their vehicles to go into, but they didn't show up at our place, so another day was spent sitting out in the open.

FRIDAY, 25th JANUARY, 1991

We were all woken up at 0630 by the sentry, who apologised and said it was direct from the CO. The apology did not stop the guys giving him shit about it though, all good banter. After breakfast, the Engineers turned up with diggers. Whilst they got started we took everything down and stowed it all away. We were expecting them to dig holes exactly like they had done for the rest of the troops, so we could simply drive the vehicles into them and no longer be sky lined. Instead, after they had been briefed by one of our officers, they started to pile the sand up into large sandbanks and formed a huge square berm with just one entrance into it.

Engineers constructing the berm for RHQ

Before we moved any vehicle back into the berm, we had a brief and along came the next surprise of the day. From somewhere the QM had managed to get hold of an 18 x 24 tent and a pile of six-foot tables and chairs for the CO. We were told that the CO wanted the tent put up in the middle of the square and then all the vehicles backed up onto it. That would allow the whole of RHQ to be co-located together in one place, plus it would give a much larger space to work in and conduct O groups. We set about getting the tent put up and into place. Because pegs were useless in the sand, to secure the tent and hold it down, we had to physically bury the bottom flaps under piles of sand.

The 18 x 24 up, now to get the vehicles in one at a time

Once the tent was up and secured, we drove the vehicles in one at a time and parked them up with their backs and penthouses facing into the tent. The tent then had to be adjusted so you could physically get in and out of the vehicles with the tent still remaining in situ. Once the bosses were content with the set-up, we then set about getting all the radio masts up and the vehicles covered as best we could whilst they arranged the tables and chairs inside the tent. Because the CVs were now side by side either end of the tent, it freed two cam nets up to be used elsewhere. When we had finished that task, as a crew we then made our admin and sleeping area up next to our wagon. We built a small makeshift house, where the four of us (Visser included) could kip and play cards out of the way. We then used one of the spare cam nets to cover it all up. When we were happy it was all done, we set about making a urinal area and a bog (toilet) for everyone to use now that we were all inside the berm. Whilst we constructed that, some of the other guys started building fighting pits at each of the corners of the berm; these could be used if we got attacked. Just when we all thought we had completed everything and was about to get grub on, we got told to dig trenches inside the square in case we got hit with artillery, this most of us found highly amusing, but it wasn't so funny when we found out they actually meant it.

Our admin area at the side of our vehicle

The sentry on return from his stag told us to take a walk just outside the berm and have a look back at RHQ. He said if we weren't a target before, we certainly were now. A few of us left to see what he was talking about, I decided to take my camera with me for a photo. We didn't have to walk very far to get the point he was trying to make. The whole set-up now looked like a Divisional HQ, except without any of the protection afforded to one. It may be nice and cosy, but tactically it stank; it was huge and attracted attention from miles away, especially in the flat open desert. It would only take one bomb to explode in the middle of it all and it was goodbye to the whole of RHQ. All the years of Recce training that we had done, that spread out you become harder to take out, especially if you were in open terrain, appeared to have gone out the window.

The enemy may not have the freedom to conduct air strikes whenever they like, but they still have the capability to do it, and they certainly can reach out and hit us with artillery whenever they feel like it. Tactics now seemed to be taking a backward step to be replaced by comfort and ease. Some of us chatted about it and kind of all agreed; it was difficult to say what drove this type of behaviour, the pure arrogance of thinking you're invincible, the need to be different or as they say eccentric, or just plain stupidity with no thought of the consequences. Mind you, considering we deployed with no ammo, body armour or desert combats, why should this come as a surprise to any of us? All we needed now to complete the comfort was the cooks with a cookhouse.

RHQ inside the berm

Int Update:

Today American and British forces recaptured an island just off Kuwait; a Kuwaiti flag now flies on it again. More bombing of Iraqi forces had taken place, this time they went for all command and control type places and major installations. The HQ of their Armoured Corps was bombed to bits, accompanied with a few RHQs and SHQs. If they were anything like ours, as in co-located altogether and out in the open with no cam nets, the air forces must have had a field day.

No mail again today, I would say I wasn't too bothered, but I was running out of people to write to as nobody seemed to be replying, so I had nothing to write to them about. I will no doubt probably get a massive amount all in one go, if the post ever got going again that is. Some old newspapers arrived from A2 for the troop, so once everyone had finished reading them, I cut out some of the articles to save. All the articles written about every country wanting to join in was a little bit disconcerting. We were all just hoping it was the press blowing it out of proportion to sell newspapers and not what was actually going to happen. The Regiment appeared to have made the front page of *The Mail on Sunday*, albeit nobody actually recalled the picture ever being taken in the first place and most of us were not convinced it was us lot at all. I cut the article out as a keepsake.

The Regiment made the front pages

I was on stag at 2130 for two hours, after that I needed some sleep. I was not sure what was fatiguing me the most, shitting through the eye of a needle all the time or the lack of sleep. I could try and do something about the lack of sleep, but as for my bottom, it looked like it was simply going to have to be a case of dry your eyes and get on with it. Other than stop taking the NAPS and hope my system would eventually flush it all out, there really wasn't much else I could do about it.

SATURDAY, 26th JANUARY, 1991

Up again at 0630. The early rising and everyone having to be awake during daylight hours was clearly beginning to get on people's nerves now, because the guys were all starting to make comments and complain about it. You know things are getting really bad when that starts to happen. Amazingly, and for some reason that I couldn't quite fathom, the officers were just not getting it. Besides the fact we were doing most, if not all the manual labour, they seemed to be failing to grasp that while they slept all night long, we were staging on, it was no wonder they were not tired. Simply shouting at the guys when they made mistakes would not make them any less tired. No doubt they just put it down to us being weak and requiring more training at sleep deprivation to get our bodies used to it. After all, that was the logic of why we had those 48-hour nonstop exercises, to try and condition you too little to no sleep at all.

After grub, we started on the training program that they had worked out the other day. You could almost be fooled to thinking you were somewhere else in place and time. The sun was shining, it was peaceful and quiet, and here we were sitting in the sand having some chilled-out lectures. I had to teach the guys first aid. Everyone seemed to enjoy it, which cheered me up as that was what I always tried to do when I taught any subject. I even had two officers turn up, which selfishly made me feel good. They actually admitted they needed the training as they were totally unsure of what to do. Fair play and I respected that, so when they were making a total pig's ear of it, I just gave them more help and advice. I jokingly said to one of them, if I'm ever in need of any help, please fetch someone else; he just laughed. A valid question was raised by one of the guys to the RSM: where were all the other officers, and why were they not doing any of the training? He never got a reply.

After the training, we had a game of football and again no officers joined in that, even though I was absolutely sure some wanted to. We all had a great time, and it eased a lot of tension in people, allowing them to blow off some steam. It also gave everyone a run about; something we had not had in a while. The guys in the sabre troops would never get a chance to do something like this, because they were in their three-man crews spaced out on their own. Even on an exercise back home we would at least all get together at some point for a Squadron BBQ, but out here, that was just never going to happen. So, I did feel for them, at least we in RHQ were co-located together and had more than just two people to talk to. I guess like everything in life, there were pros and cons. I am quite sure most of the guys had no idea what life was really like in RHQ for the lower ranks, and probably for the same reasons, exactly like me, they would absolutely hate it.

When we got back after the game, the CO blew a fit on us all about nothing in particular. We were not sure if it was because we had been playing football and enjoying ourselves, or because he was simply just in a bad mood and wanted to vent. No mail again today, but there was a rumour that six large bags of the stuff was waiting for collection, so hopefully someone will get hold of that tomorrow.

Later on, Steve and Visser went out and about on the scrounge in the Rover. They came back with a 9 x 9 tent and a heater for us. Nights were starting to get really cold now, so they would be very useful. We set it up as our new sleeping place, the other makeshift tent could now be used by the guys as a place to meet and play cards out of the way. It didn't take too long before our new tent was spotted and the Ops Officer came over to have a chat. He suggested to us that the 2IC and he have it so they could work in it. As a crew, we protested; Steve pointed out that we had all been told the whole reason the 18 x 24 was put up was for that exact purpose. He just left, none too happy that we had not agreed with his idea.

After we finished everything, I stripped off and had a wash before washing all the kit I had been wearing. I hung it up and then we all sat in our old tent and played cards to pass the time away. It was the safest place to be, venturing into the big tent would undoubtedly incur being given a task to do. One of the guys decided we should start playing for money, so we had a few games later on without being stupid about it.

Int Update:

Reports came through that Iraqi troops were moving south. It was unclear where or why, either a need to know basis again or the Int wasn't that accurate. Either way we'd soon find out when the firing started. It wouldn't take too long for them to spot us lot sitting out in the open.

SUNDAY, 27th JANUARY, 1991

Woke up to that glorious sound of really heavy rain. We got out of the tent to find water was flooding everywhere inside the berm because it had nowhere to drain other than the trenches that we had dug, which were now half full and filling up by the minute. Outside the berm was just as bad, there simply wasn't anywhere for it to run this time; there was no low ground or valleys for miles around. The holes that had been dug for the troops to hide their vehicles in soon started to fill up. Those that attempted to move positions soon encountered another problem, they quickly got bogged in. It was such a deceptive terrain because on top it looked quite solid, but the ground underneath was being turned into a bog by all the rain. As others moved in to try and attempt to help out, they too soon got stuck. The REME spent all day going from one vehicle to the next to pull them out.

Ken G and his Scimitar stuck in the mud awaiting the REME

Our wagon started leaking. The CO, clearly not pleased about the situation, soon pointed it out and started shouting at me to get it rectified. CVR (T)s were notorious for leaking, as were most of the British Army's vehicles that were older than ten years. The waterproof sheet that came with the vehicle was barely large enough to cover it in the first place. Now we had the added problem of all the extra gear and the cage on top. It was an art to use the sheet to cover the vehicle up and yet still be able to use the vehicle at the same time. Example being, the vehicle needed to be started and run up every now and again to charge the batteries. This meant all the engine intakes and the exhaust area, which ran the entire length of the top of the vehicle, needed to be free of any coverings to prevent any fires. Removing the waterproof sheet then allowed pooling of water on top of the vehicle, which eventually found its way inside. Normally, you just accepted you would get a few drops of water inside; we were after all, soldiers. Cookie and I got totally soaked removing all the kit from off the top of the wagon so we could take the waterproof sheet off. We replaced it as best we could and then put all the kit back on top. Good job we had a tent and a heater so we could get changed into some dry clothes and hang the wet ones up.

The rain stopped at 1300 just as mail arrived. I got three letters, from my sister, mum and a pen pal. I also got yet another CD. They were all dated 15th Jan. Reports kept coming in of vehicles getting bogged in and requiring REME assistance, even though the sun was out shining and most of the puddles had disappeared.

Later on, we had an hour of wearing just our respirators for NBC training. It seemed totally pointless to a few of us given that most of the guys were doing jobs or tasks with their skin exposed to the elements. Some were even sunbathing with the thing on whilst allowing their wet clothing to dry. The bosses all seemed content though so nobody got shouted at.

Int Update:

Seven Iraqi planes had landed in Iran; the Iranians had detained them and the pilots. Scud missiles were fired at Saudi and Israel again, some had hit, most were intercepted by Patriot missiles. The Iraqis have started to pour oil into the Gulf Sea from a major oil pipeline; it is believed that this is possibly an attempt by them to stop a Kuwait invasion by sea. It really infuriated me hearing about them doing that. How many poor animals were now going to die because of that action? I really want us to go in now and get this ended once and for all.

Artillery was now being used and has started to rain down on Iraqi positions. American Infantry troops have moved up alongside us and are digging in by the border. Their armour is starting to amass just to the south of our positions. Seems there is a lot going on but we are still being kept in the dark by our bosses.

MONDAY, 28th JANUARY, 1991

On stag 0500–0700. The sun was up first thing, so after my stag I decided to get the rest of my kit washed. Once done I hung it up on a line with the wet kit from yesterday to dry. Quite a few others followed suit to utilise the blazing sun, but it didn't take too long before we all got told to remove it because the CO was not impressed; he said didn't want the place looking like a laundry shop when the Brigadier was visiting. People decided to press their luck for a bit until their kit was dry, which didn't take too long given the heat.

Cpl Keith E tipped up from the RAP with all the kit necessary for me to stick cannulas and drips into people. He told me the doc was impressed with my medical work that he had seen of people coming to them, not to mention quite a few good words put in from other medics who knew me. Coupled with the situation of RHQ, he had decided to cut me a bit of slack and trust me to get on with it. We had a brew and a chat, and I told him about how it was getting me down being in RHQ. I explained that the blokes in the troop were brilliant and we always had a really good laugh; it was the endless running around after officers all day and night doing tasks and constantly being on call to make them brews every two minutes that I hated. What really boiled my blood was having to roll someone else's sleeping bag out when they just stood and watched you do it and then afterwards wanted to know when you were making them their food. I didn't join the Army to do this shit, it's so degrading and has nothing whatsoever to do with being a professional soldier. He said he would have a word with the doc and see if I could be moved to the RAP given my qualifications. I thanked him for trying.

No mail today. After lunch, we got down to some more troop training. It was lessons on how to use and clean your own personal weapons. I clearly was not in a good mood today, because I had a right moan to the RSM who was overseeing it all. I said after eight years in the Army, including the time we knew back at camp that we were coming out here, and the time we had actually been out here, if I couldn't use and clean my own personal weapon by now, I needed beating or shooting to death with it. A couple of guys burst out laughing even though it was not meant as a joke. The RSM said it was from the top; and it wouldn't hurt if everyone just brushed up with training. "Fair point," I said, "so why isn't there one single officer present?" A few of the lads then chipped in and commented on their lack of presence throughout all of the training we had conducted as a troop, both before deploying and now, and this time they were not letting the subject drop. He said he'd have a word with them all to encourage them to join in from now on.

Int Update:

The NBC state has gone back up to 'high' and everyone is to start taking the NAPS tablets and carrying full gear again. Int suggested they'd carry out a chemical attack against us tonight or tomorrow morning using Scud missiles. The 'us' part didn't clarify who that actually was; did it mean the Regiment or everybody? If they manage to successfully conduct an attack, it would show just how unreliable the Int was that we kept getting because the missiles shouldn't even be getting off the ground anymore, let alone across the border. There were more confirmed reports of Iraqi troops having moved south, and artillery was now being fired across both sides of the border. Why they couldn't take the enemy artillery out was beyond me; we had been told that we had air power and control of the skies; therefore, as soon as they fire and give their positions away, we should be following it up with airstrikes or counter battery artillery. Another major artillery dump in Iraq had been hit and was confirmed destroyed.

Over 50 enemy planes had now landed in Iran. It was still unclear as to why they were going, and being allowed to land there. These countries had had countless years of war between them, and yet Iran now appeared to be helping them. We were hoping it was just pilots deserting and not some sort of cover-up whilst preparing for a future attack. Four Fencers (Bomber aircraft) had been shot down; seven others managed to escape to Iran and land safely.

Electricity has been cut in Baghdad, and food and water is scarce for all Iraqi troops. We hoped this Int was correct and it was not just morale boasting propaganda for us lot. It was bad enough being out here as it was without being deprived of food and water as well. If it was true, they would not put up much resistance when we steamroll through.

On stag, I read back through the orders logbook; it seems Iraq is our destination once we go in and not Kuwait as previously briefed. We are going straight for Baghdad. The place on the map where we are going to enter has eight Iraqi Infantry Divisions and currently no armour in support. They are being left alone by the coalition for the time being. Other positions, mainly in Kuwait, are getting the shit kicked out of them. No doubt to try and give the impression that is where all our main effort is being focused, and ultimately, where we will invade.

Although from all the reports it appears that we are winning, the Iraqis somehow are managing to build up a force for some sort of attack against us. The Int reports of them moving south could not be vaguer if they tried. The basics of position, equipment, size and direction were missing, and nobody seemed to be asking the question: why? Was it complacency, or was it under control and they were just not informing us like everything else that seemed to be going on around here?

TUESDAY, 29th JANUARY, 1991

Woke up to another sunny day, which appeared to cheer most people up, given all the banter going on at grub; it was that or the fact no chemical attack happened last night. We wondered if it would happen this morning. Just in case, I had all my NBC gear to hand. We were all hoping it was just false information or poor Int and that there wouldn't be one at all.

I received over 20 letters today. Importantly, there was one off Lori. She had now settled and was studying in London. I was really chuffed as I'd now got her new address so I could write to her.

One of the lads, Richo, for some reason, decided to tell me that he'd slept with Michelle when he was in Canada. He had been posted over there after me to do the same sort of job. Knowing Michelle, I could not see her sleeping with him at all, but why would he lie? More to the point why did he feel the need to tell me something like that given where we were? I was trying to gauge if he just wanted to clear the air and get it off his chest, but his manner was that of someone who wanted to wind me up and get me biting, more to the point someone who had been pushed into trying to wind me up. No doubt by the lads that were joining in. What was he hoping to prove, and what did he think my reaction would be out here, or had he not even contemplated it? He clearly did not know me very well. Lucky for him he wasn't the kind of guy I would fill in because there was just no threat there at all; he just wasn't what I would call a fighter. I just let it go and told him there was not a hope in hell Michelle would sleep with him and to keep dreaming on.

Later on, all the lower ranks got booted completely out the berm so the Squadron leaders (OCs) and certain other officers could have a chat about some secret mission. One of the guys commented that we best hope our officers don't get killed, because as each one gets taken out, that's a troop, Squadron or indeed the Regiment that would grind to a halt not knowing what the hell was happening or what was expected of us from higher.

Whilst we were all sitting out in the open sand, the Ops Officer came over and asked me to come back inside to start making piles of maps up just for the officers in the meeting; he said nobody else was to help me, I was to do it on my own and say nothing about it. That task took me until 0230 in the morning to complete. Judging by the maps and the traces, it seemed the Regiment would be heading into Iraq, then straight up north towards Baghdad. Was this what they had been talking about earlier on? If it was, we already had wind of it from the radio logs and secret faxes.

By now, not only had quite a few of the guys seen me writing in the diary when on stag but word had also got around. At first it seriously worried me because some of the officers found out, but it had actually worked out in my favour as people were now starting to tell me everything they knew that had gone on. Even to the point of being told what an individual had done. The individual would sometimes furiously deny it, which then prompted others to join in confirming it was actually true. Sometimes the individual would then try to make excuses as to exactly why they had done it, or worse still stick to their original story and deny it. Most of the guys just laughed it off when I said I was putting what they had done into the diary; a few of the officers, on the other hand, were less than impressed, which just spurred the guys on to dishing more dirt out. I was not sure which annoyed them the most: the fact I was actually going to record it, or the fact the guys were insisting on me to do it because it was true and nobody would believe someone could do what they had done. A bit of self-embarrassment creeping in, I thought. It was clearly short-lived given that within a few days they were mentioned again in the diary for something else. It was funny because my diary was now becoming part of the handover at stag times. I was allowing anyone to read it so long as they were on stag with me, that way I knew it would not disappear. A few comments/threats had already been mentioned from certain individuals, but once the guys had started on them they quickly dropped the subject saying they were just joking or that they had my best interests at heart knowing how the CO would view it. To be fair, most of the individual stories that were told, I never actually recorded them, but they were always good for banter for everyone to hear them.

Int Update:

Not a lot had happened today. The concerns from higher were it seemed more and more likely that Iran was going to enter the war on Iraq's side. They believed this could be due to religion and the fact they both had a mutual dislike for Israel. If they did, it would start a world war off without a doubt, because there would be no way Israel would sit back and take strikes from both Iraq and Iran no matter what the USA said. With Israel involved, other Arab nations were bound to join in, and then there was the problem of the ones already involved as part of the coalition, would they switch sides? Not only would we be totally surrounded from all sides, but the balance of military power would massively shift against us. The longer we dithered about not getting on with this, the more potential for the situation to escalate out of control there was.

WEDNESDAY, 30th JANUARY, 1991

Up at 0710, amazed. Steve must have told the sentry to let me sleep in a bit longer, that or he forgot all about me. When I was up and about, the 2IC came into the tent, and we had a coffee and a chat. He was another officer that most of us had a lot of respect for. So much so that a lot of the guys said they would rather it was him running the Regiment out here. He was very down to earth and in touch with reality, he also talked to you like another human being rather than someone who was beneath him and only there to serve. He told me today was going to be a 'quiet one' for me. It was a reward for working my ass off last night. I asked him what's the catch, because nobody got a 'quiet one', regardless of what they had previously done. He just smiled and left. That was Major F for you. I had absolutely no idea what that was all about, but I took it that a 'quiet one' would mean I would not getting any tasks given to me today.

I cleaned all the guns again and tidied the inside of the wagon up. Washed more kit, hung it up to dry, and since the sun was out and very hot again, I decided to hide out the way and get some sunbathing in while writing a few replies back to the mail I received yesterday. It was going to take me ages to reply to all these. So long as I could push one out a day to Lori, I'd be happy.

Later on, we got together for our normal troop brief before the Int one. We were warned that people were now being watched with regards to NAPS. It had been rumoured some of the guys were refusing to take them. Anyone caught not complying was now going to be charged. The boss then stood there whilst everyone had to take one. I took mine as ordered, first sign of stomach-ache and I will be quitting, charge or no charge.

Int Update:

An Iraqi convoy was destroyed last night, 24 vehicles in all. The Navy sank five gunboats yesterday. More planes had flown to Iran; the air forces were trying to shoot them down before they got there. It was estimated to be 90 planes there now. An Iraqi ship was hit, but it managed to sail into Iranian waters; the crew was rescued. Iran has said it will remain neutral for the time being even though Iraq has asked them for 100 Scud missiles. Iraq launched three attacks across the border last night, all were repelled but both sides took casualties, numbers were not known as yet.

There was still talk of this enemy force massing near the border, but exactly where it was, still remained unclear. Given all the assets we have available they must know, so why the information was not being passed was beyond us.

Talk was that we might attack sometime between 15th–18th of next month. Not only was it high tide but also the night will be one of the darkest. It would be perfect conditions for a land and sea assault into Kuwait. They didn't believe the Iraqis had much night-viewing equipment or the capability to fight at night. In comparison, we not only had lots of equipment but we had also been trained to fight at night.

The oil being pumped into the Gulf sea has been stopped by sheer bombing. The oil that was already pumped into it should hopefully be naturally dispersed by around 10th February.

Chapter 8
The Iraqi Army Attacks

THURSDAY, 31ˢᵗ JANUARY, 1991

Before breakfast, we all assembled and were given an Int brief.

Int Update:

The Iraqis invaded Saudi this morning with around 4,000 troops and armour in support. They took a village and reports said 12 American and 8 Saudi troops were killed. A counter-attack was launched and the village was retaken, killing hundreds of Iraqis and destroying most of their armour, numbers were not yet known. Someone asked if we were being filmed because it sounded more like a report you heard on a Hollywood Vietnam film to keep the troops happy rather than an Int report sticking to facts.

60,000 Iraqi troops were said to be massing on the border just north of our positions, preparing for an attack. We'd either actually found those forces that have been massing for days, or this was another lot and the 4,000 troops from this morning were the ones they were on about. Questions sprung to mind such as: how was it possible for that sheer size of force to get together and so close to the border without us bombing the shit out of them? Or was our bombing not as effective as we were making it out to be?

After grub, Maj W, with a few of the bandsmen, tipped up. They had brought with them the second of the anthrax injections. As a doctor, he was supervising whilst letting them carry out the vaccinations. A lot of guys stated that they wanted to refuse it, especially after seeing people get sick from the first lot back in Germany. After my little chat with the doc back at camp, and the fact they were not prepared to write it in our medical documents, I wasn't too keen on it myself. To get everyone on board, or should I say, 'in line', we were all told that we had to have it; the order came directly from higher and anyone refusing it would be charged. The Army was giving you something that would protect you, by refusing it you were trying to commit self-harm, which was against Army policy, therefore you couldn't refuse it.

Major W overseeing the anthrax injections being given to RHQ personnel

I really did believe that in times of war, industries and governments utilised the period to test new and experimental technologies, equipment and drugs out. Sometimes war actually drives the production of it. You only need to look at everything that was developed during the Second World War as a prime example. If these items worked, as in combat proven, then selling the products to other countries afterwards becomes so much easier. All good news for the economy and industry. Unfortunately, the soldier is the poor soul that is the 'lab rat', and I have absolutely no doubt that if you asked questions you would be told anything to get you to take part. This would include being ordered to by your bosses, who just go along with it rather than give you the information and option/choice. I strongly doubted very much that the company that had made the anthrax vaccination had tested it on people over a ten-year trial period and during those trials had included giving it with cocktails of other vaccinations/tablets at the same time to see what the side effects were. I remembered watching a documentary about the atomic bomb tests, where they swore blind to 150,000 troops that there was no such thing as radiation; therefore, no danger whatsoever. They had all the top scientists on the project; they knew what they were on about.

I asked the medics that turned up when our next supply of NAPS would be arriving since most of us only had seven days left. They said resupply had been requested but there was no news on it. Command had not factored in that we would be taking them for this length of time. Like everything else, it was a case of wait out and hopefully, they would turn up at some point.

Given that news and the limited knowledge we knew about NAPS, a few others and I decided to stop taking the tablets. It would be at least two weeks before we go in if not longer, (the longer the better). We were going to try to keep some just in case that supply, as normal, failed to turn up. Once we got wind of a resupply we would start taking them again, or failing that, wait until 24 hours before we knew we were going in and then start. It was a bit of a double-edged sword really. We were told that NAPS gave you some limited protection after two hours of taking a tablet and that this protection increased with further prolonged doses. What we were not told were answers to questions such as: how much this protection increased to, could it be increased to 100%, how long could you actually take the tablets for, could they be taken with other medications and if so what the drug interactions and contraindications were, and how fast and at what rate did the protection decrease when you stopped taking them. These were questions that as a medic I wanted to know the answers to and hence why I wanted to do the NBC instructors course.

Afterwards, we had another game of football again using our guns and NBC kit as goal posts. Although another great time was had, I badly twisted my ankle and it hurts like hell now. To add to that my hands were starting to crack with the cold and the wind. They were bleeding this morning; I need to see if I can get some cream from somewhere.

Later on, a few of us managed to hide at the side of our wagon and get some more sunbathing in, my top half was now starting to look slightly brown. Wrote some more letters. I was still waiting for a reply off the bank to confirm Silke would not be allowed to use my account. What a mess, and I still had the problem of getting all my kit back from her flat on return from here. After that, I just laid on my sleeping bag thinking of things back in Germany until I drifted off to sleep.

FRIDAY, 1st FEBRUARY, 1991

We were woken up by the sentry to be told that all hell had broken lose; we needed to grab our kit and get ready for a fight. We were getting an Int brief straight away. Excited as hell, I grabbed my kit and headed for the CV.

Int Update:

Iraqi forces have started an advance towards the border just to the north of us. Reports coming in said the advance column consisted of over 1,000 vehicles and 15,000 troops. B52 bombers were now carpet-bombing them. If these got stopped before they reached the border, it would really bring home the truth to the Iraqi Army of the capability and exactly how well-prepared the coalition forces were.

A-10s just flew over our heads, good old tank busters, no doubt on their way to spoil some Iraqi's day. Apache gunships and Kiowa helicopters were also on route, we could see them in the distance just off to our left flank.

Apache gunships and Kiowa helicopters on route to engage

We waited by the CV listening to the reports coming across the radio net. It was confirmed that during the fighting to take back the village yesterday, 11 American and 12 Saudi troops were killed, 200 Iraqis were killed and loads taken prisoner. Only a few enemy vehicles had actually been destroyed, and these were mainly wheeled ones. No T72s (MBTs) at all were hit.

1400: Reports came in that it appears the bombing was mainly ineffective; mind you, carpet-bombing from the height the B52s fly at would be stuff of WWII accuracy. There was now a wait out on the exact location of the column and where it was heading. An American jeep and 14 men were missing; it was bound to be Special Forces because they wouldn't say anything else about it, not even a location. We couldn't really help them out if we knew little information.

British Main Battle Tanks (Challenger 1) had been called up to join us and were now starting to get into positions just in case that column made it over the border. The Regiment was already in the Recce screen positions so they would get loads of warning of exactly what was coming. The MLRS that was with us had now set up ready for use. No doubt the rest of the Division's artillery located miles behind us would have done exactly the same. Hopefully, the Iraqi tanks would be stopped before getting here, something that large would stick out like a sore thumb in the desert so shouldn't be too difficult to find and hit. The Yanks also have a few armoured Divisions up here with us as part of 7 (US) Corps if required. I was quite sure they were getting ready just in case; they wouldn't want to miss out on the action, that was for sure.

Challenger 1 MBT

1605: The Iraqi forces had been relocated and tracked. They were now starting to cross the border. Dug in troops opened fire on the first three tanks across with anti-tank missiles, instantly destroying them. Our guys started to call in air and artillery strikes, and it was not long before the MRLS behind us opened up. It was awesome watching them firing right over our heads; normally, you were quite a way behind these things due to safety constraints. When they had finished firing and started to reload, we could hear the sound of friendly artillery firing from the rear. Whilst we had been listening to all the reports coming in, most of us loaded up our weapons ready for a fight. The anti-tank weapons and machine guns had been taken off the wagons and placed on top of the berm wall that was facing north ready for use. We now got into positions and just laid there waiting to see if anything appeared. We could see smoke just to the north, so had a rough idea of exactly which direction we needed to concentrate the firepower in. It was now a case of sit and wait.

The column didn't get very far over the border before it was stopped in its tracks. Over 100 tanks were reported ablaze, mainly the old variant T55s. The rest turned and headed back to where they had come from, being harassed the whole way by air and artillery fire. Fuck being in one of those old tanks, one on one against our CVR (T)s you would have the upper hand, but you really didn't stand a chance against modern tanks like the Challenger I and the M1A1 Abrams. Not only could they outgun you in range and accuracy but also even if you managed to get within range to fire your own weapon, the chances were your shell would just simply bounce off the modern armour that was used. Still, that was a few less enemy tanks and soldiers to worry about now and a major kick in the teeth for them, not to mention a morale booster for us lot. First major battle and we won it; hopefully, none of our lads up front have been injured or killed in the process.

Burning BRDM2

Destroyed Iraqi T55 tank

UK Challenger 1 compared to an Iraqi T55

The RSM came around and told us all to remove our magazines off our weapons again, not because the attack had been stopped, but because another person had had a ND in the back of a truck full of guys. He said it was damned lucky it went through the roof and not through somebody instead. So far two Sergeants (Sgt) and a full Corporal (Cpl) had fired off their weapons. Given their rank, they should have known better. He then said a senior rank would inform us when, and if, we could load up again.

This made me mad as hell after what had just taken place and the fact we had had no senior ranks or officers with us on the berm. I asked the RSM if a senior rank would be around when we next get attacked. Just in case we needed help with any stoppages or problems with the weapons that we might get, since it appeared we couldn't be trusted with our own personal weapon drills. This, to say the least, did not go down too well.

Later on, after everything had calmed down, the doc turned up and told me he had been to see the RSO and it had been cleared for me to do training with the RAP for the next three days. He said I needed to turn up wearing an NBC suit and carrying the rest of the kit. He then left. It sounded interesting, and at least I would be away from RHQ for a while and doing something constructive. It was so bizarre, we had just been attacked and here we were, a few hours later, back doing Regimental training again as if nothing had ever happened!

Mail arrived and I got another six letters and a parcel to cheer me up. Three were off Lori, in one of them she actually admitted that she loves me and will do anything to be with me. A bit of a bolt out the blue but really fantastic news, so now all I needed was for this to finish so I could get my ass back over to see her.

I was on stag later with an officer from Sphinx battery, he had just been on selection for 22 SAS, so we had a good old chat about that. He gave me some tips on how to train and what to try and prepare for. He advised me to do pre-selection to get a flavour for what was going to come my way. He also told me a very funny, but very serious, story about a guy that we both knew.

On a major NATO exercise in Germany a few years ago, this guy was in charge of a troop as a Cpl. They had gone outside the exercise area with the intent of getting around the back of the enemy. They decided to stay in a local barn for the night, something we always did if for no other reason than to foster good relationships with the locals. However, they did not ask permission from the owner. On seeing them, he reported to the police that he had seen suspicious people in his barn. They had no vehicles but were dressed in combats, wearing balaclavas and carrying weapons. This was in the days when the IRA were targeting British soldiers in Germany and killing them. The police, who had previously been informed and briefed about the exercise, phoned up to make some enquires. They were categorically told on several occasions that there were NO British soldiers outside the exercise area. Checks had been conducted and everyone was accounted for. The actual troop had received several such calls and thinking it was exercise play to try and find them, they gave another location as to their whereabouts.

The police informed GSG-9 (A German Counter Terrorist unit). GSG-9 turned up to the barn and started to take up positions. The troop, obviously being well-trained, spotted them doing this, and still thinking it was all part of some sort of training for their unit and what they do, opened fire (with blank ammunition). GSG-9 returned fire with real rounds and tear gas. Being completely surrounded, the guys quickly surrendered. Amazingly, nobody was injured at all. They were all taken blindfolded and rather roughly to the local police station, where they underwent interrogation. Like us when we go on exercise, they carried nothing on them that would give a clue as to who or what they were. Every question they got asked, they answered, "Sorry sir, I cannot answer that question." They just kept repeating the big five (number, rank, name, date of birth and religion) as per our training. GSG-9 and the police insisted someone high up from the Army got their ass to the police station as they were convinced they were British soldiers. The Army still insisted they were not because everyone had been accounted for but they agreed to send someone. Needless to say, the whole story unravelled, much to the embarrassment and displeasure of the high command. All the NCOs in the troop were busted and posted out the unit over that incident.

More bombing continued on Iraqi forces as B52s kept flying over our heads. From our positions, you could actually see the explosions where their bombs were landing. Night time the whole area to our front was continually being lit up, followed by the sound of explosions shortly after. Sod being under that lot.

Iran has now said officially that if Israel joined in the war then they would join in on Iraq's side. From the information we were receiving in the troop, it appeared they wanted to; they were just looking for an excuse to do it. Most of the guys in the troop thought they seemed to be hiding something, but nobody knew what. Everyone was convinced that they would be joining in sooner or later, and it was all going to get very ugly, very quickly.

Chapter 9
US Cavalry Fly In

SATURDAY, 2nd FEBRUARY, 1991

Got up at 0630 as normal, had some breakfast then got into my NBC kit and walked over to the RAP, which was now co-located 500 metres from us. Everyone was hanging around waiting for one of the Samaritans to return, it had been called out to pick up a guy who had been shot. The doc did not want to start any training until this was out of the way.

Operating well ahead of the Battlegroups in enemy territory did have some major drawbacks, the medical evacuation chain being one of them. During peacetime exercises, we practised the evacuation chain. From the point of wounding, your own troop guys treated you since they were right there with you on the spot. Each Squadron had its own RMA, who was co-located in SHQ with the Squadron Samaritan. Upon request from a troop they would be dispatched, assuming you were the only troop that required them. On arrival, the RMA was capable of administering advanced medical treatment, either at the scene directly and/or whilst being transported rearwards to the RAP. At the RAP, you got to see a doctor, before being moved by one of their Samaritans rearwards to a DS. Treatment, and surgery if required, took place before being moved rearwards once more to a hospital. The whole transportation from the point of wounding to the DS was done across country in a tracked vehicle that rattled and shook like hell and took a very long time. Something, that depending on your injuries, you didn't have on your side. What was not made clear to people was the fact that whilst we practiced this evacuation chain, it was designed and set up from the Battlegroup rearwards. You would not find a DS set-up in front of a Battlegroup. So, in the 'real world' you would be travelling a lot further for a lot longer to reach a DS. For us, as far as using helicopters went, we were told our own Army Air Corps (AAC) and RAF would not send helicopters that far forward into enemy territory to pick up casualties. It was far too valuable an asset to lose, not to mention they were not trained to do it, as in they were not a dedicated Search and Rescue or Casualty Evacuation (CASEVAC) platform. Another factor was if they did send one, it would require protection, be it extra helicopters or fast jets above them. There just wasn't the appetite to send that many aircraft that far forward into enemy territory just to pick up a wounded guy.

Luckily for us out here, since we had done lots of work with the Americans now, they and our own Royal Navy had offered to come and get our seriously injured in helicopters once we go in, regardless of where we were operating. That was a big relief, not to mention a massive morale booster, knowing that in the unfortunate case of you getting injured, someone would come and get you should you need it. It also meant you would be going very quickly and smoothly straight to a dedicated hospital rather than spending hours getting thrown around in the back of an armoured vehicle on route to a DS.

The ambulance returned with an injured trooper. He had shot himself in the foot when coming off stag. He claimed his webbing had somehow managed to cock his weapon while he was climbing out of the trench, as it released, the gun went off, resulting in the injury. In other words, an ND. Putting aside that he should have had the safety catch applied, therefore preventing the working parts from physically being able to go backwards in the first place, I was finding it pretty difficult to see how the hell he could have done it; the angle alone that the bullet had entered his foot made it almost impossible. Still, that was what he was claiming, and his SSM was backing him up, saying it was an accident.

He was given some more morphine before his boot was removed. The doc then insisted we all had a good look at the effects of a bullet on the human body. In this case, he was very lucky. The bullet had gone straight through his boot and foot and somehow managed to miss all the bones. Because the boot was tight fitting, the damage from the bullet wound was minimal. It was not what I was expecting at all. He was treated before being sent back to Al Jubail, never to return to us again out here.

I did four hours of training at the RAP, I didn't learn anything new but it was really good practice. It was all stuff I already knew: straightforward dressings of wounds, to gunshot injuries to blast injuries. We also had a few practices of putting drips into each other and spoke about what to do in the event of collapsed veins. The doc reckoned we were going to be doing something different tomorrow, and we would be sweating just a little bit, full NBC kit was required again. Afterwards, I went for a quick chat and a brew with Zeb on his wagon just to catch up on gossip and things.

Two Apache helicopters and a Kiowa came to visit us later from the Squadron that was attached to us. The pilots wanted to see what kind of vehicles we had so they would not shoot at us by mistake. Not very reassuring at all, considering they had already shot some of their own vehicles up and they should have known what the hell they looked like. We lined up a display of the vehicles we were using, much to their surprise due to the variants of the CVR (T). They couldn't understand why we had so many variants, and more importantly, why the ones that were supposed to look the same looked totally different. This, of course, was because of all the add-ons we had attached in order to carry all the extra kit we had been told to take. We assured them that since we had air power as soon as we crossed over the border, we would all be displaying a big fuck off luminous orange marker panel on the top of the vehicles. We also, like everyone else, had the inverted black Vs painted on the front, back and sides. Whilst they had a look around our vehicles, I had a look around the helicopters and took some photos.

A CV with all the add-ons and extra kit. A stark change from those that left Germany

Video link of AH visiting and us getting ready. 16/5L getting ready to cross into Iraq: https://www.youtube.com/watch?v=CryIQMqqMzU

Two Apaches and a Kiowa helicopter visiting RHQ

Billy H by an Apache helicopter

I had a very good chat with one of the pilots before they left. The Apache, like the Scimitar CVR (T), had a 30mm gun. The Scimitars 30mm was loaded by hand. The rounds came in clips, three rounds per clip. They were then individually fired one at a time. The 30mm on the Apache was belt fed and it fired in bursts. The minimum burst being ten rounds, which took just one second to fire. The max being all in one go, and it could carry 1200 rounds. It also carried two pods of Hydra 70 rockets, 19 in each pod, and 8 Hellfire missiles that he claimed could destroy any known tank armour in the world today. What a beast, one Apache had nearly as much firepower as a complete Squadron of our CVR (T)s, and they had quite a few of them out here. I was glad it was on our side.

We watched more B52s fly overhead, saw the flashes, heard the explosions and then saw the planes return. The more they bombed the better; hopefully, they were actually hitting something. A guy came around with a box, and we all got issued one NBC first field dressing to carry with our normal field dressing. One of the guys asked me what exactly was the point of the dressing, because he was struggling to see its benefit over a normal field dressing. He said the only scenario that you could possibly benefit from the need of having to use one of these was if you got wounded and then were under a chemical attack afterwards with a liquid agent. However, the more likely scenario would be a chemical attack first, followed by an assault, and you then having to fight and being wounded in the process. If that was the case, the chemical agent would already be inside your body. To stop any bleeding then, any dressing would do. I agreed with him and said, "At least we all now have two field dressings."

Received some mail and a parcel off Lori with some games, grub and a *Penthouse* magazine. No doubt I would be fighting the blokes off later for that.

Still not heard from Silke, it's really proved to me that she doesn't care about me at all and that what I am doing is the right thing to do.

SUNDAY, 3rd FEBRUARY, 1991

Up at the normal time and off to the RAP again in my NBC suit for some training. We had lectures on burns, chemical and casualty treatments, and then we practised it all. An ambulance crew at a time would be sent off to a make-believe incident about 15 minutes' drive away. When they arrived, they would have to treat the causalities they found. Once they were happy the casualties were stabilised, they would get them into the vehicle and then they would drive to a vehicle decontamination point, where the vehicle was decontaminated, removing any potential chemical agents on board. Once given the all clear by the chemical decontamination team, they would then come back to the RAP, where we would all treat the casualties. The whole exercise was done in full NBC kit, including wearing respirators, and boy did we sweat like pigs! It was really educational, as we had never done anything like this before, not at this pace and in an environment like this under these conditions. Each crew went through it, so we all got stacks of practice. It was amazing just how difficult it became to use basic equipment once wearing NBC gloves, not to mention your respirator eye pieces kept steaming up, preventing you from seeing what the hell you or others were trying to do. Putting a needle or cannula into someone's vein can be tricky at the best of times, NBC conditions thrown in added a whole new set of a challenges.

When I got back to RHQ, the pay people had tipped up to give us our water money and some more mail. I now had over 400 dollars on me.

Another O group took place, and once again all the lower ranks (non-officers) were asked to completely leave the berm area and go and sit out in the open desert. Two hours later when it was finished, we were called back in and informed that there was a Divisional exercise planned for tomorrow. The basic idea was for everyone to practise going through the berm and the Iraq defences when we crossed the border. The plan was for the whole Division to move to a staging area and wait there until the Americans had notionally cleared a minefield and breached a berm; this was all going to be pretend at a set secret location. On call the MBTs (Abrams and Challengers) would go through first and secure the area to the front of the breach in case of a counter attack. Once secured, we would be called through to break out of the breach. We would simply drive through the lot of them and continue on route to carry out the Division's orders. The rest of the Division would then follow on behind.

One of the guys questioned why we kept being asked to leave the berm, he was told that things were discussed that were not for our ears. There was a lot starting to happen now, but the people in the know were keeping it to themselves, and this was causing a big rift between the lower ranks and the officers. Why they had this secrecy was beyond us. Soldiers do not like being kept in the dark; they like to know what the hell is going on and what is happening around them. More so if they are a specialist in that area or subject, because they might just have an idea of a better or more efficient way of doing something. They especially like to know details such as why they are doing something, what the bigger picture is and how vital is the task they are being asked to conduct. This was not 'insubordination', as most of the dinosaur people in charge called it. Soldiers were now being trained by the Army to get the task done the best way possible to achieve the end goal. It was exactly why there were courses for soldiers to attend and become qualified instructors and specialists in certain areas. We rate ourselves amongst the best in the world because we say we are very flexible; the truth is, most people in this unit are very inflexible when it comes to change and rank always overrides qualifications.

We had another Int brief later on but there wasn't much detail in it. The news on the radio wasn't much better either. They reckoned the bombing was not having much effect on the ground forces at all due to dropping most of the bombs into desert sand. The force that came across the border was part of that 60,000 which had been moving south for days. It has now been stopped and had dispersed, but for how long was anybody's guess.

When we go forward for real to cross the breach, B Squadron, as the OC keeps hounding the CO to allow him, will go through the breach first. Once through they will then form a line and advance north until they contact the enemy, or until the enemy contact them. The CO estimates we will lose about 150 men straight off during the crossing, or put another way, nearly all of B Squadron. If that does happen, then what's left of B Squadron will hold the line and A or C Squadron will come through them and carry on with the advance. Whatever remains of B Squadron will join A2 and await further orders to join another Squadron.

MONDAY, 4th FEBRUARY, 1991

Up at the normal time, had grub, then we were all called for another briefing. We were informed that since we had a few hours to spare before we were required to practise going through the berm with the Division, we were going to conduct a Regimental practice beforehand. We obviously could not practise a Divisional exercise at Regimental level, or a crossing of a minefield or a berm since we did not have any Engineers with us. Therefore, we were just going to practise all leaving our current locations and meeting up at a new one before forming up into Squadrons. To make it more realistic for RHQ, we would be leaving in two hours' time; we were then dismissed to get on with it. That now meant we had to run around like headless chickens and get everything packed and squared away into the vehicles.

The 2IC, for some reason, had been working in our vehicle and had left all his kit everywhere inside. Because he was not part of the crew and there was literally nowhere for his kit to go, I had no option but gather it all together and take it across to his wagon. He was nowhere to be seen and the guys were too busy packing the kit away. I had no idea where it was supposed to go on their wagon, and I also needed to get back to my wagon to carry on packing everything away. I just put it all in a pile outside his vehicle, told the crew and then left.

Once we were all ready, off we drove into the desert. After an hour of driving around, the Regiment all met up and formed up into Squadrons. The whole thing only took two hours in total. We still had time to spare before being required at the berm with the Division, so it was decided that the Regiment should conduct another route march rather than just sit in the open desert. Once everyone had managed to take a suck of gas, off we all went again. After 11 kilometres, a halt was called, and everyone was told to return to their old locations from this morning.

Back at the old location, we were told that the Divisional exercise had now been pushed back until tomorrow, so we had to set everything back up again. Whilst setting up the CO, for some reason, blew a fit on everyone because of the state of the place. Nobody had a clue what his point was because the set-up was always untidy until complete. The crew from OC told me that the 2IC had found his kit where I had left it when we were packing up; he was fuming and after my blood now for not packing it away correctly on his vehicle.

Once we had finished setting RHQ up again, I went and saw the RSO and asked for a troop transfer to the RAP, or any other troop if that was out of the question. He didn't ask what my reasons were, he simply told me to "fuck off", adding that I was too good an operator to lose. I would have taken that as a compliment, but it was more like there was nobody to take my place because they certainly wouldn't get any volunteers to do this.

Int Update:

They reckoned that their own guys had shot the Marines that were killed in the last battle. Ten of them were in an APC when it was taken out. 25 US planes had now been shot down, there were no details of where or the fate of the pilots, so we took that as they were killed in action (KIA). The ships had now started to engage targets in Kuwait to soften it up. Looks like the build-up was getting bigger, 15th to 18th was looking good for the go.

TUESDAY, 5th FEBRUARY, 1991

Everyone was sharply woken up at 0600 and told everything had to be packed away ready to move by 0700. After frantically rushing about again, and literally just throwing kit into or onto the wagons, we were ready to move out; we then got told we wouldn't be moving before 0830. Since it was only an hour and a bit, there was no point in trying to hide or set anything back up, so we all just sat around in the open like spare parts.

Mick T (one of the clerks) came over and asked if I could dress his foot as the RAP had already packed up and moved out. The doc had removed one of his big toenails because it was in-grown. I got my medical kit out and changed his dressing. I gave him some extra dressings and cleaning solution and told him to try and get it cleaned and changed daily; otherwise, he would have fun with it trying to heal out here.

We started moving out just after 0900 and were all in the staging area by 1200. It was unbelievable, the sheer number of vehicles here. I had never seen so many wagons anywhere before, even BATUS paled into insignificance compared to this. I wondered how many would make it back home after this was all over. There was a defence review currently going on, and there had been rumours going around ever since we deployed, that nearly all the Regiments out here were earmarked for amalgamation or disbandment. Guys had already discussed the impact of this on several occasions, and the main focus always seemed to come back to the vehicles followed by the men. If the rumours were true, then the wagons would end up in storage once they got back home. It would be far cheaper and easier if they simply just did not return. Profit-wise it would be better to sell them on, failing that, leaving them out here if they were not already destroyed. This then always got the debate going of did this logic equally apply to the men as well; if we all got killed, wouldn't that make life so much easier for the people doing the cut-backs? Again, even with these debates going on, nobody up top wanted to discuss it or reassure the guys.

The CO decided he wanted to control the Regiment from his Spartan rather than a CV, so the Ops Officer and he got in the back and kicked Steve and me out. We went to take some photos and for a chat with the guys at the back of OB.

I (UK) Division formed up. Warrior APCs of the Royal Scots on our left, Staffords on our right

The Division formed up

The whole Division waited in the staging area until 2200, simulating the time it would take for the berm to be breached. A staging area was a tactic that the British Army always used when conducting a crossing of an obstacle. A few of the guys commented that they hoped it didn't take this long for real, because sitting out here in the open made a target that was just too good an opportunity to pass up on, especially when you were in range of enemy artillery.

On returning to our vehicle, Cookie told us the batteries in the back were now flat and no longer able to hold a charge. Due to our sitting around for so long with the CO using the vehicle to control the Regiment rather than a CV, they had been drained to the point of damage. They would now require changing at some point, but until then we would just have to constantly have the vehicle running to provide electricity.

At 2200 the Division started to move out, doing about ten miles an hour. Orders came from higher that each row of vehicles was to simply tag onto the one in front and follow it. We were all going to conduct a route march of around 100 kilometres; the aim was to confuse the Iraqis by letting them know we were here. Someone commented that judging by the fact they attacked us the other day, you could pretty much bet they already knew we were here. He didn't know about confusing *them*, we were all confused. Looked like a very long night ahead.

The Divisional route march just before last light

WEDNESDAY, 6th FEBRUARY, 1991

Early hours of the morning, the light is just starting to cut through the darkness in the distance, it's very cold outside and we are still on the route march. The CO and Ops Officer were now starting to get right on my nerves. They wanted me to make them coffee every hour and said nobody was to sleep at all. Apparently, it was 'good training' for everyone. On top of that, every time the CO could not contact someone on the radio, he had a go at me for it. He kept complaining about the limited range of the radios compared to when he is in the CV. I explained the basics of antenna theory and power output to him. We only had a small 2-metre whip antenna bolted onto the roof of the vehicle, whilst the CV had an 8-foot mast with a 3-metre whip antenna on top of it that could be put up to reach 30 feet. It also carried enough batteries to supply the power that was required to boost the signal. He told me, no arguments, he didn't care how I did it but he wanted me to fit two radio masts to the wagon when we finished the exercise. I pointed out that there was absolutely nowhere for the extra batteries to go, and they would be required for the extra power, but he just ignored me.

I really wished I wasn't here right now; I felt I was slowly being worn down with each passing day and new bonehead ideas that kept coming from the top. I really wanted to come out here, and when I found out the Regiment was deploying I was so pleased. Yes, I wanted to be back in a fighting troop alongside my mates doing what I did best and had been trained to do, but I was stuck in command troop. That said, there was no way I would not have wanted to deploy knowing all my mates did. Since we had been here though, I felt I had slowly gone from being a trained combat soldier specialised in quite a few areas to just being a slave and told exactly what to do. The very real and scary thing that had dawned on me was the high probability of getting killed by someone else's poor decision-making and bad ideas. What made it even scarier was there was absolutely nothing you could do about it; you had to follow orders as a soldier. What made it worse was nobody up top would care if you did get killed, you'd just be a casualty of war and another statistic. The more casualties there are, the less you will be remembered and the sooner you will be forgotten, the world would move on.

If I was going to die in a war, I wanted it to be on my terms, doing something I believed in for the right reasons, not just following an order for the sake of it.

Route march into the distance

Endex was called across the radios at lunchtime. The Regiment broke off, and everyone was instructed to return to their last locations. We returned to our berm to once more set RHQ back up. Once complete, I went and had a wash before washing all my clothes and putting some clean ones on. Afterwards, I geared myself up (weapon, webbing, helmet etc.) and took a trip across to the REME and QMs to see if I could get hold of some masts and cables. The guys at the QMs told me they had no masts at all but not to worry, they would find some for me by the end of the day and said to return tomorrow to collect them. It always amazed me the effort that was put in when you said it was for the CO and not for yourself. Sometimes for a laugh, I would not mention the CO until they said NO, then I would tell them I would pass their message onto the CO; amazingly, it soon became a YES. Whilst I had been doing that, Steve had managed to get away for a bit with Visser again in the Land Rover. They had found the location of the American PX (A shop similar to the NAAFI, but a whole lot bigger and cheaper). He bought me a cheap camera, which I thought was really nice of him. Now I could take loads of photos for the album I was going to make on return. Visser said he would go in the Land Rover tomorrow morning and collect the masts, save me walking all that way again, besides which, how was I going to carry both masts and all the cables back on my own? It was now 2200, I was on stag at midnight and needed some sleep; I went and tried to get my head down for a few hours.

THURSDAY, 7th FEBRUARY, 1991

Did my stag at midnight. Everything was quite on the radio nets, not a lot happening at all. I handed over to Tim E-L at 0200 and hit the sack again for a few hours. I woke up freezing. I couldn't believe how cold it was. The temperature during the night had plummeted down to well below zero. I felt it on stag but it must have continued to drop.

I decided to approach life with a new head on today and try something different. Instead of trying to explain, or get more information because what I had been told made no sense to me, I would just do what they asked, no questions or comebacks whatsoever and see if that worked. Hopefully, that would stop me feeling so down in the dumps and looking miserable all the time, which was not in my character. It might even prevent upsetting certain people ranked above me by being a 'yes man' for a while.

Visser brought me two masts first thing. He ended up having to collect them from the guys in A2, so it was a good job that he had gone in the Land Rover given how far away they were. I managed to secure them onto the wagon, one either side at the rear, and connect them all up. The only problem I encountered was where I had managed to fit the leads on the roof so they went straight into the wagon itself, since the vehicle was not designed to carry masts at all. I needed something to stop the leads from being damaged when people were on top of the wagon erecting the masts or getting kit off or onto it. This I overcame by dismantling two spare antenna base units designed for other wagons and using the protective metal base part of them, which I then fitted to the wagon. The RSWO saw what I was doing and came to have a look. He blew a fit at me for wrecking the kit, said he was sick and tired of me 'bodging' things for the wagon, who the hell did I think I was? The next time I did something like this he would charge me for it. I was to reassemble the bases and return them to him, because he needed to keep them as spares in case someone else needed them in the future. I bit my tongue and said nothing. After he left, I went and explained the situation to the RSO to get his advice. He told me to leave it all in place and he would speak to the RSWO; great, situation resolved but at the cost of now having the RSWO pissed off with me.

Once that was sorted, I had lunch then went over to see the REME about the vehicle batteries. I explained the situation, and they told me to try and fully charge them first without any load bearing at all and see if that worked. It meant taking them out of the wagon and putting them on charge for at least ten hours before putting them back in to test them. I headed back to the CVs and found

Geordie on stag. I told him what I was going to do and asked if I could use his wagon to charge the batteries. CVs have an external socket box at the rear of the wagon that you can run power leads from; one of them was designed solely for battery charging. While I got the batteries out of my wagon, he looked for the battery charging lead on his wagon. The batteries on the vehicles were about three times the size and weight of a car battery, so very awkward and heavy. After getting them out and carried across to the CV, Geordie told me that he couldn't find the lead on his wagon; he had searched all over it. His stag was now up so we both went and had a look to try and find one.

After searching all four CVs, we went to the RSWO to see if he could shed some light onto the situation since CVs should be carrying a battery charging lead. He said he'd never brought them out in the first place as he did not see the requirement or the need for them. He told me to try to make something that would do the job. Whilst trying to figure out how to bodge a lead up, one of other guys asked what Geordie and I were doing. Geordie explained it all before he told us that all the leads had been brought out to the Gulf. The reason we couldn't find one now was because the RSWO had told someone to throw them all away when we were ditching the kit we didn't need. Unbelievable! Logic would have dictated that at least one out of the four was kept in case it was required.

Given the power involved and the potential for this to go horribly wrong, I went and spoke to the REME for advice. Gary, one of the REME electricians, told me not to try and make a lead and that he would help out; if I brought the batteries over to them in the morning, I could use their wagon and lead.

Int Update:

It was fairly quiet on the Int picture again. They reckoned up to 134 planes have now flown to Iran, and everyone is still unclear as to why Iran is allowing this to happen. Jordan was now starting to voice opinion and threatening to join in as well. Two ships were pounding targets in Kuwait, and the RGF were getting bombed every chance possible. Baghdad had been the target of 33 air raids, 12 hours in all just to show that not only could we reach into Kuwait, but we could now reach that far inland straight into Iraq unopposed and untouched.

Mail arrived and I got five letters plus a parcel off my mum.

FRIDAY, 8th FEBRUARY, 1991

Up at 0630 again to another freezing cold morning, now I know what they meant when they said deserts get very cold at night. I knew it got cold and you would really feel it because the temperature drop was large, but nobody said anything about it dipping into the minus figures. It was going from plus 25 during the day to minus 5 at night now.

Once I had managed to get the batteries back out of the vehicle again, I had to carry them across to the REME. I wasn't cold any longer after doing two trips. They told me they needed to be left with them for at least 24 hours on charge before they could test them. They would send word when they were ready to be collected. Steve tipped up with Visser and a few others from the troop in the

Land Rover. He asked if I wanted to come and visit the Yanks 'across' the road, and of course go to the PX, so I jumped in the back and off we all went. Took about 40 minutes to get there. On getting out at the other end, the first thing I really noticed was all the women, and I mean real women. You'd be surprised how much you take for granted until it was no longer there anymore.

Had a chat with a few US guys and we swapped kit, it was what soldiers did when given the chance. There was always kit out there used by other nations that was far more practical and would do a job better for you than your own kit, or as in some cases, you didn't even have kit to do it in the first place. The main items they wanted were our food and our NBC kit, mainly the respirators, as they believed ours to be far better than theirs. We wanted their food and camping cots. Their grub was perfectly suited for the role we did. Our food (Compo, short for 'composite rations') came in large tins and was designed for four men to eat at once. Afterwards, you then had to cart the empty tins around with you until you met back up with the SQMS again to off-load them. It was not very ideal when you were in three man crews and normally always on the move; hence, a lot of the time guys went without or simply ate it cold. Theirs came in individual small bags called Meals Ready to Eat (MREs). They just required heating up, or you could eat them cold if you were hiding. We mainly traded grub for grub. Unfortunately, we only get issued one respirator, so that was completely out of the question for trade, as was their personnel weapons, which one of the guys tried to trade for. A few of the guys did manage to get some camping cots. We said we would return again to do some more trading. All in all, it was just great to get out and chat to someone else, especially since they were brothers in arms.

Driving back to RHQ, Steve, who was sitting in the front, told us all to take a look ahead. From miles away we could see RHQ because there was now a massive Regimental flag and three Union Jacks flying above the position. Visser commented, "Fuck me, talk about highlighting your position or what?" When we arrived back, the sentry told us the press was visiting and we were all getting a brief on it; they were just waiting for us lot to return. We had a parade inside the berm and the CO addressed us. He told everyone that when the press arrived, only the officers were allowed to speak to them in case we said something that was of military importance. He wanted all lower ranks out of sight when they arrived. The officers would do all the radio stags until they left. Once they had departed and were clear away, RHQ would resume normal operations.

Flags flying above RHQ

A lot of the guys took real offence to the CO's address. Me, I just took the opportunity and went and wrote some letters in our admin area.

Int Update:

Two 15,000lb fuel air bombs (Daisy Cutters) were dropped just north of us by the US today. What a sight that was! They just burst into one gigantic ball of fire which then sucked up all the oxygen for around 4 x 4 square kilometres. They were designed so that if the fire didn't get you, the lack of oxygen would. They had a few more of them, which they plan on delivering later on both day and night. The day one was very impressive, so I cannot wait to see one go off at night.

US troops went across the border today. Once they encountered Iraqi positions, they opened fire on them and then retreated. As the Iraqis chased them to hit back, they were taken out by waiting Apache gunships. Talk about a come on or what! At this rate, their military machine was going to be crippled, which could only be seen as good news, since that was less for us to face when we go in.

SATURDAY, 9th FEBRUARY, 1991

Up at 0630 as normal. After grub, we were told to prep the wagon as we might be doing a signals exercise tonight, there were no other details. I explained about the batteries and was told not to worry, we wouldn't be using them. I did not press the issue, there was clearly no point, but I found it really frustrating because I wanted to. It was not so I could look like a smart ass or a know-it-all; I just thought people sometimes had a lot on their minds and missed things. What was then obvious to one person might not be obvious to someone else. A signals exercise required radios, they in turn required power that came directly off batteries, no batteries equalled no radios. Not to mention that driving around at night out here with no radios surely wasn't such a good idea.

We got the wagon all packed and ready to go then I nipped across to the REME to find out what was happening, because we had not heard from them. They told me the batteries had not charged correctly but they thought it was another problem that had caused it, so they needed another 24 hours. On return I tried to get some sunbathing in with the other guys, but this was cut short by a sandstorm that just appeared out of nowhere. It was blazing sun one minute then we were eating dust the next. Within minutes, we couldn't see a thing, so we retired to the admin tent and decided to play cards instead. We seemed to quickly end up playing for money now; I won 80 riyals and 20 dollars.

Got some more mail. I was now actually finding it difficult to find time to reply to them all. Guess I needed some more early morning stags to catch up.

Later on, we had a visit from the Egyptians, who turned up in T72 tanks. They wanted to have a look at our wagons and see what kit we had. It also gave us an opportunity to have a look at Soviet kit in the desert environment rather than the European one we were all used to.

Egyptian T72s came for a visit

During the visit, I chatted to one of the Egyptians, whose English was really good. He was both surprised and impressed that I had been to Egypt. I told him I intended on going again at some point because I only got to see Cairo and the pyramids. I hadn't realised that most of the other things were miles away down south. I especially wanted to see Abu Simbel, the place really fascinated me.

After the visit, Steve told me that he had just been informed that the wagon was now not going tonight. It would be first thing in the morning instead, after I have fitted the batteries. Later on that night, it changed again to it was not going at all now. There would be another signals exercise on the 12th or 13th, and we would be going on that one instead.

Int Update:

The US has said that it is stopping the aid it gives to Jordan this year for siding with Iraq. It is believed to be about 53 million dollars. Jordan's reply was that they were Arabs and they wanted to stick together and show support. Nobody challenged them back, which seemed odd to me given this was a perfect opportunity for some politician to point out that they didn't hear them say that when Iraq invaded Kuwait, or the fact we had Arab nations fighting alongside us now. That's politics for you, I guess.

Chapter 10
The Green Carpet

SUNDAY, 10th FEBRUARY, 1991

Up at the normal time before getting on with the daily rituals of wash, breakfast, tidy admin area up, burn rubbish, hang sleeping bags up to air, wash kit, and then sit around waiting for some officer to come and fuck you around with another task to keep you busy.

Today's fucking about was just epic. The QM had managed to acquire a very large green carpet, which turned up in the back of a truck. It was about half a centimetre think, very synthetic and very tough, no doubt made to simulate grass out here. Our first task today was to lay it in the big tent, anything left over could be used for the floors on the inside of the vehicles to make them look nice. Firstly, we had to clear everything out of the tent. Then the sandy floor inside the tent needed to be levelled off to remove any lumps or bumps. We were told to try and compress it as much as possible to prevent dips when we laid the carpet down. We tried various methods but it proved impossible in the end because we were on very fine sand. We then laid the carpet down, ensuring it was as flat as we could possibly get it, which was quite a feat because walking on it just kept making dips underneath as the sand gave way. Once done, wooden pallets were dug into the sand at both entrances to the tent for people to knock the sand off their boots before standing on it. All the tables and chairs were then put back in, before brushes turned up for us to sweep any sand off the carpet that had managed to find its way on there. We were told sweeping it would now become a regular task for a couple of guys each morning to keep it clean. Who would ever have believed that we had put a massive tent up with flags flying above it, and then carpeted the inside of it in the middle of the desert in a war zone? The set-up was now starting to look like some sort of bizarre hotel.

A piece of the 'green carpet' at an entrance

Afterwards, we were told to paint inverted black V's on the wagons. Some had already been done but we had run out of paint and were awaiting more, it had now arrived with the carpet. They were to be at least one-foot-high by six inches wide and visible on the front, back and sides of all the vehicles. All the Black Scorpion symbols that hadn't already been removed were to be painted out and replaced with a Black Rat.

Tim E-L asked why we were doing that when we were supposed to be the 1 (UK) Divisional Recce force working for both 4 and 7 Bdes. The Black Scorpion was for Divisional Recce troops. If we were painting Black Rats on the vehicles, that meant we were part of 4 Bde; therefore, were we just going to be working for 4 Bde? The answer given was, we were still going to be working for both Bdes as Divisional Recce, but the Red Rat was unique to 7 Bde only; we were attached to 7 Bde, not part of them so were not allowed to have it. The looks on everyone's faces showed it had cleared that question up. This was followed up by other guys arguing the point that we were all well aware that the Red Rat was unique to 7 Bde, as was the Black Rat unique to 4 Bde, and the Black Scorpion unique to us. It did not explain why we were putting the Black Rat over the Scorpion. They would not be told to paint their Rats out if they were attached to someone else; therefore, why were we being made to do it? What about the QDGs attached to us, are they changing their Red Rat to a Black one now they are with us? With an almost red face, we were all told rather sternly it had already been discussed and decided upon higher up and was no longer up for debate. The only symbol allowed on a British vehicle out here was a Rat. We were not part of 7 Bde, so we could not have the Red Rat. That just left the Black one, so just get on with it and get it done. Someone piped up that it was nice to know that the real important things were being addressed at higher whilst we were out here awaiting orders to attack.

Steve and Cookie did the painting on our vehicle whilst I went back across to the REME with Visser. The batteries were good to go, so we collected them and fitted them back into the wagon. I quickly tested them, they were all fine. We were now ready for the signal exercise on the 12th.

1900 and the sentry came and got me; I thought he had come early to get me for stag, but it turned out the CO wanted me in the tent. When I got there, the CO asked me to fold his map up and put it into his map case (a see-through plastic sheet with a zip). Once completed I stood there waiting to see what he had summoned me for whilst he chatted to the other officers; after a while I realised that the map folding was all that he had called me for! The 2IC saw me standing there, no doubt looking like an idiot, and told me to get my hair cut, even though his was three times the length of mine. He was not joking either. I guess I would have to try and get one of the guys to do it somehow. I took that as my cue to leave.

Later on when I was on stag, the guys were all venting what had pissed them off the most today and wanted me to enter it all into the diary. It had been without a doubt the worst day since we had been out here of getting bone tasks. Cookie said he was going to drop (punch) the Ops Officer if he carried on picking faults up with things he knew nothing about. He had had a go at him about the hubcap oil levels being too low on our wagon. Cookie, being a driver mechanic, tried to explain to him about oil levels and heat. Out here, you didn't fill them to the same level as you did in the UK/Germany, because oil expanded slightly more in the heat of the desert and would blow the seals. To prevent that from happening, you slightly under-filled them. The Ops Officer obviously thought he was trying to pull a fast one for not doing his job correctly and was having none of it. He told him to fill them exactly how he had been shown to do it in Germany before going off to inspect and inform the other drivers of their errors. Once more demonstrating to everyone that rank won over qualifications.

Standing around the CV and venting was probably not the best place to do it as anybody could have heard us. Whilst most of the guys in RHQ would not have minded, after all it was what soldiers did from time to time, other members would not be impressed. I told the guys I was not going to put everything into the diary, simply because it would end up focusing on all the negative side of things, something we are very good at being British. Someone mentioned about starting a 'piss-me-off book'. It would allow everyone to get things off their chest and vent a bit, with our weird sense of humour it would also allow others to have a laugh at your expense. Every time someone pissed someone off, it gets put into the book. The guys all thought it was a great idea, so one was started. It was to be left in the main CV (OB) for all to read when on stag.

There was no Int brief today and the only thing on the news was some statesman from the USA had arrived today to check on the current situation and decide if, or when, we needed to go in. Went to bed at 2200 as I was on stag again at 0400.

MONDAY, 11ᵗʰ FEBRUARY, 1991

On stag 0400 until 0600, all was quiet. Had an Int update come in. From the 13ᵗʰ we are going on immediate Notice to Move (NTM), that meant no more tents or cam nets up. Only 19% of Iraq's kit had been destroyed so far because they were dug in, we needed to get them into the open. If it meant committing troops to ensure that happened, then so be it.

An artillery gun blew up yesterday; it did not say which nation it belonged to but I guessed it was either British or American, because it did say that it was the second one that had exploded and so an investigation was being conducted. No information on cause or casualties yet. I logged it all down in the Int log book.

After breakfast, a few of the officers went on a Recce again in the Land Cruisers. Once more they never told anyone where they were going, why, or when they would be back and hence had no protection with them yet again. Cookie found the Ops Officer's NBC stuff and asked what he should do with it. In a flippant remark, I told him he should bury it as that would be about as much use as it was going to be to the Ops Officer out on the Recce, he obviously thought he was immune to chemical warfare. So, Cookie did. Unbeknown to us, this hadn't gone unnoticed by another officer, who rather than have a word with Cookie decided that the best course of action was to report it to the Ops Officer upon his return. Later on, when I was asked about it, I obviously denied it all. You just don't grass mates up, especially when you were about to go into battle; after all, I knew who would be fighting alongside me, and it certainly would not be the Ops Officer. The kit was dug back up and placed back in the vehicle.

After dinner, the RSM came and had a word with us both. We tried to deny it, but he informed us that Visser was not as loyal as us two and the beans were spilt. For the time being, AJ was now going to be driving the CO instead of Cookie, who would be going to A2. We were both to await our fate tomorrow, as we would be getting charged. The RSO also wanted a word with me. I went and found him.

The RSO didn't really say much, not after he started off by asking me how I was feeling. I told him how pissed off I and most of the troop were with certain individuals within RHQ. I reiterated the fact I desperately wanted a troop transfer and would accept anywhere rather than staying in RHQ, I had simply had enough of it. I joined to be a soldier not a slave. He did the duty officer part of trying to calm me down, explained that he knew exactly how I felt and told me not make a rash decision or say something stupid that I would regret later on, especially tomorrow, when we were to go in front of the CO. It would work out for me in the end; I just needed to stick with it for a bit longer. He then briefed me about the signals exercise tomorrow and said my stag had been brought forward to 2200 until midnight because I was going on it.

TUESDAY, 12ᵗʰ FEBRUARY, 1991

Up at 0400 and off on the signals exercise. The weather was really bad and the visibility less than 20 metres in dust and rain; it made driving horrendous.

Sketchy reports came in of two CVR (T)s going into ditches, one was believed to have overturned. Not sure which Squadron or if anyone was hurt as we could not get all the information. The communications seemed to be very poor as well; weather no doubt was affecting everything.

On return from the exercise feeling very tired and with the visibility still poor, we accidentally clipped one of the makeshift tents and ran over the Ops Officer's bed. It really was a total accident; he however told the 2IC and the CO that it was deliberate sabotage given the respirator incident. Steve suggested, to keep him happy for a while, that I should give him the one I was using that I had borrowed off Visser, otherwise things might just get out of hand given the fact we were getting charged later on. I took his advice. Steve kindly lent me his little Army one, which was better than sleeping on the cold sand. Visser, when I told him, was not impressed that I had lent the Ops Officer the bed. I can't say I blamed him but we were trying to keep the peace here. Without saying anything, he took it back. It sent the Ops Officer into a rage. He came straight into our admin area and demanded to know where his bed was. I pointed out that it was not his or my bed and I had wrongly lent it to him without the owner's permission. He had obviously decided to take it back, and he would need to speak directly to him about that. He decided instead to have a rant at me, adding that I should have stopped him. He then spotted the bed Steve had lent me and asked whose it was and could he borrow it? Thinking about getting charged later on, I just gave in and said he could have it; I would sleep on the wagon tonight and try finding another bed later on. He didn't appear interested in my problems at all, only that he got a bed, which he took and left.

We were told that before anyone was allowed to get any kip, we had to clean all the kit and weapons, sort the wagon out, get a faults list into the REME, and then sort the Ops Officer's bed space out that we had run over as well as get some hot water on for him to have a wash. It was a peace offering, because he was still sulking about his bed.

Cookie and I both got charged later on; they set it all up in the tent like it was a court martial back home. The CO was at the top of the table with the 2IC on one side and the Ops Officer on his other. We were marched in and out by the RSM, which if you had ever tried it on a cloth covering fine sand, was strange to say the least. Cookie was transferred troops, just as he was expecting, he also got demoted and given a £350 fine. He was totally fine with it and relieved to be leaving RHQ. I got given a disciplinary hearing. That meant it would affect my promotion, or put another way, stop it now, for a minimum of two years. The CO said because I was so good at my job, I was staying on the crew and the incident would be overlooked this time. Great, I'm still in RHQ but now I was on the wagon on my own looking after the CO and the Ops Officer until they found a replacement for Cookie. That was punishment enough.

The RSM grabbed me on the way out and said he fully understood why I'd done what I did, but he was not forgetting that I lied to him. Fair shout, I couldn't argue about that one and I did feel really guilty about having done it, but grassing on mates didn't sit well with me. How were you supposed to be trusted if you did that?

Received another seven letters today; that cheered me up a bit.

Int Update:

The bombings by coalition forces had increased. More Iraqis soldiers had surrendered, even though there were rumours of execution squads going around shooting people who, as they put it, were deserting. Morale was low and nearly all food supplies had been cut off; poor bastards. I actually felt sorry for them. I guess I was putting myself into their shoes and how I would have felt if it happened to us lot. Thing is, would they have felt the same if it was the other way around? I bet they wouldn't have.

WEDNESDAY, 13th FEBRUARY, 1991

I was woken up late for once, 0830. Were people giving me breathing space because of yesterday and my chat with the RSO, or was it that they had forgotten about me? We had a briefing first thing, well more of another talking to. We were all told not to spread rumours about things we might overhear in the tent or see in the CV when on stags. Nobody in command had a clue when we were likely to go in or any other Int of value that was worth passing on to anybody, so we were to cease doing it. The guys in the troops were being told everything that they needed to be told; if they asked questions, we were to refer them to an officer.

I finished the film in my camera so sent it to my sister. Hope it turns out OK given all the fine sand that keeps getting into every gap possible.

Visited the Yanks again to exchange some more kit. Had a brew and a chat. They said they were going in tonight and would be getting a few briefs later on explaining exactly what they would be doing. They were not sure if it meant for good or just doing another incursion again to shoot some more people up. We would soon find out as it was to our front once more. It would be funny waking up in the morning to find all the US troops gone and us lot left twiddling our thumbs in the desert because we had missed a trick.

Int Update:

We were all now on immediate NTM, but the tents and cam nets were staying up. In other words, nothing about the RHQ set-up had changed, and it would still take us at least two hours, if not longer given we now had the big tent with us, to pack it all away. This went totally against everything we had been taught. On 'immediate notice' meant exactly that. Everything was packed away, trenches filled in and the crews were in the vehicles ready to go. As soon as you got the call, you immediately left.

The standard NTM times used were set at immediate, five, ten, fifteen and thirty minutes, one and two hours, you could have others if you wished. The manuals also stated generically what to have out, and what you should be doing depending on the NTM time given. These NTM times were constantly used and practised on exercises so everyone got the feel of exactly what they could and couldn't have out in order to meet the timings since troops had different roles and thus carried different equipment.

On the BBC news, it said Saddam had agreed with the Soviet's peace plans, but nobody seemed to know what they were. Iraq was claiming a bomb shelter got hit with over 500 people in it; it was all over the TV back home.

Tomorrow we are moving further west and even closer to the Iraqi border. That should be fun; we will get to see all the bombings at really close range. More Daisy Cutters had been dropped, lovely weapon. If nothing else, it would not do your morale any good having that thing dropped either onto yours or someone else's position. The two vehicles that went into ditches yesterday, neither had overturned and the crews were all fine, just bruised a bit.

A CVR (T) in a ditch

THURSDAY, 14th FEBRUARY, 1991

Up at the normal time. We were all told to get everything packed away ready to move by 1400. Besides having to help out getting the big tent sorted before then getting our own vehicle squared away, I was told to pack all the kit away belonging to three officers, who all decided to sit in the CV and have a chat. I cannot put into words how it felt to constantly be clearing up after people who in my eyes were just being lazy. At camp, they paid people to clean their rooms and make their beds. That was fine because they were paying them and thus it was a professional job. But we were not being paid; we were just expected to do it. I could not for the life of me understand why the SNCOs thought this behaviour was acceptable and actually told you to do it rather than grip the officers to square their own kit away.

During the packing away of all the kit, the 2IC came over and took the 9 x 9 tent off us; he said he needed somewhere for the Ops Officer and himself to work, we would just have to find somewhere else to sleep.

Once everything was packed away, we had a short brief before setting off. We were moving 80 kilometres to the west and deploying on the Iraqi border, RHQ would be set up 12 kilometres from it. Rather than it just be a straight route march there, the bosses have decided to play a little exercise on route, RHQ would be playing the enemy, exact details to follow later on.

One of the guys spoke and mentioned that yesterday during the visit to the Yanks, some of the guys had been told that as of yesterday, we were now all going onto G DAYS, and it was a countdown of eight days until we went in on the ground. They believed in sharing information if it directly affected you. Given the fact everything they have told us so far has turned out to be correct or true, he wanted to know if the G stood for ground and if it was true or not. He was told straight it wasn't true, end of story.

1400 we started to move out. The CO and Ops Officer decided they wanted to travel in the CVs to control the exercise that was going to happen. So, Steve, AJ and I were left on our own to follow on behind OB. We never had a clue what was going on, we just followed the wagon in front, which was simply following the one in front of it. Whatever the exercise was, nothing came across the radio nets, and we stayed as a packet throughout the move.

Int Update:

A Scud missile was fired at a place not far from us; it was the first one that had been fired at troops on the ground instead of going for the towns and cities miles away to the rear of us. They think the intended target was the airfield we had landed at.

FRIDAY, 15ᵗʰ FEBRUARY, 1991

Been here 2 months now. We were now up very close to the border and were still driving around. Reports started to come in of vehicles being spotted coming towards the troops from the west. We found out it was 1 US Cavalry Division who went through the Squadrons as they were repositioning onto our right flank. That caused concern to a lot of the guys in the Squadrons, who no doubt wondered if it was the Iraqis again, because no one had been told this was going to happen. We were sure the bosses knew since they were not concerned at all when it was questioned why other vehicles were driving through the Squadrons. Good job the guys were well trained in vehicle recognition and nobody opened up on them. That would have been very embarrassing trying to explain to the Yanks that we hadn't informed our own troops of their movements. It was yet again another example of exactly why you should pass information onto people; it could prevent a potential blue on blue (friendly on friendly) fire fight that could get people unnecessarily killed.

We passed a few Patriot batteries on the way. Since we had no officers on board, and I really wanted to see one of these things up close, we stopped to have a quick chat and a look at one. They told us that they had shot down two Scuds a few hours ago, given the flight path of the missiles they thought they were inbound for the airbase to the south of us again. They were fired from a place just 15 kilometres to the north of where we were now. They asked where we were heading, so we told them roughly where we were going as a Regiment. They said any short-range missiles that were intended for places or targets in front of the Patriot battery, they would find it very difficult, if not impossible, to intercept. That was comforting to know, because we didn't have any type of air defence at all with us and there was none where we were going. As a unit, we certainly didn't have anything that could take out missiles. We said our farewells, and they wished us luck before we left.

When we arrived at our new location, we set RHQ back up, including the big tent and the green carpet again, but this time without a berm for protection. AJ and I got chatting and we both agreed; we doubted very much that we were just going to sit here for weeks on end and run the risk of getting attacked; we thought what the guys had been told the other day about G Days was true and we would be going in very soon.

Later on, I sat and watched a few Daisy Cutters getting dropped. Wow, did they light the sky up or what? The explosion was massive, and you could actually feel the shockwave off them now when they exploded. The biggest thing I had seen and felt before these was our own Giant Viper in Canada. It was nothing compared to this thing going off. Sod being under or anywhere near that. If they functioned as advertised, then we would have nothing to fight to our front come the time to go in.

The CO and Ops Officer were being really nice to me today; I wondered why? Even Steve and AJ commented on it. It was a little unnerving to say the least, and it was making me feel very uncomfortable, because it was not in their nature to act like this. I was waiting for the bad news to drop my way.

Int Update:

On the news Iraq had said it would withdraw its troops, but because it had conditions attached with it, the proposal had been rejected by the US. It was a start, I suppose, but it was too little too late. It was no doubt being driven by the fact they were getting a pounding now and either wanted to buy more time to get better prepared, or to save their military so they could still hold the power in the Middle East and do exactly what they wanted. Either one would not be good for us. We shouldn't let them off the hook again; otherwise, we would be back here doing this all again in the future. His forces were now believed to be at 50%, so let's get in and finish what we came here to do.

Chapter 11

G Days

The CO wanted to give everyone a briefing first thing, as he put it, "To bring us all into the picture."

He stated we were now on **G-5** and explained what it stood for. Once more reaffirming that the Int we were getting off the Yanks, because our own bosses were not telling us anything, was correct yet again. It was now official from the top; Iraqi forces were down to 66%, so all plans for any type of withdrawal were going to be rejected. MLRS missions were being planned; both US and UK, and we were going to be used as the Recce for both of them. Once we gave them the OK that all was clear, they would race up to the border, fire off all their rockets, then return for a re-bomb. If anything returned fire or tried to pursue the MLRS, we were to deal with it using the assets we had on call (Arty, AH and US MBTs). The first one was being planned for tonight; another was being planned for two days' time.

The breach for us was being planned for the 21st straight into Iraq; it would hopefully be a total surprise. We would be going through it on the 22nd. Our mission was to find the Iraqi 12th Armoured Division which had moved into positions just to the north of our current position. It should happen quite quickly; our role then was to ensure it got destroyed. After that, we would be given further orders. That was all he briefed and he took no questions.

On BBC news it said people were celebrating in the streets in Iraq, thinking the war was over due to Saddam's announcement about the peace plans. The Soviets and Iranians were still trying to push the peace plan and were asking us not to go in before Monday. They should have an answer before then off the Iraqis. That all sounded fine and something the coalition could do, as unbeknown to them, it was not planned for us to go in before Monday anyway.

All mail has now been stopped; it was too dangerous to transport it to where we were. We could still send stuff back as long as it was our guys taking it. Hopefully, those that do take letters back will spark and collect any incoming mail before returning.

The Engineers turned up again later on, so all the kit was once more packed away and the vehicles moved whilst they made another berm for us to get inside. Then as we did before, up went the tent before driving the vehicles in one at a time to position them correctly. Once RHQ was set up and the bosses were happy with the inside of the tent, it then became the usual tasks of digging trenches for our pink bodies, sorting admin and sleeping areas out, and then the wagons before getting food and hot water on. Ours had developed a gearbox leak. AJ was only driving for us; he was still remaining part of the crew of OD because he was their radio operator. With Steve not being trained on CVR (T)s, it fell down to me to get it fixed. To help make matters worse, a sandstorm appeared.

Once all the work was complete and everyone fed, stag lists were made up to relieve the officers who had been doing them, so they could get some sleep. Adam (I) and myself drew first stag. During our stag, we were given a secret trace, dated the 8th of Feb, to plot onto our maps. I signed it into the log and whilst the guys updated the maps in the other CVs, Adam and I made the traces and maps for the SHQs. That was how these things got quickly disseminated. A single trace would come into RHQ first, we would than make copies that were then passed to the OCs when they attended the O group at RHQ. Squadrons could then do it how they liked to get the information to their own troops; it very much depended on the Squadron OC at the time. The operators in SHQ would either make extra copies to give the troop leaders on a Squadron O group, or the OC would get the troop leaders to make their own copies after he had briefed them on the news from the O group at RHQ. Both ways had pros and cons.

After I plotted the enemy positions on the main map, I worked out the distance from them to us. We were now only 33 kilometres from their front line of troops, and well within range of the Iraqi's multi-rocket systems and Frog missiles. There were six Infantry Divisions dug in immediately to our front with two in reserve, most of whom have had 30 days of bombing from the air, and now the 'arty' was about to start on them. Dug in Infantry would be a massive problem for us to get through, or past in light armour, so they needed to be hit quite hard. We would have to ensure we either killed them or made them lose the will to want to fight. Six Divisions was a hell of a lot of men and firepower, and they could easily be reinforced by the reserves or the Iraqi 12th Armoured Division that was also somewhere behind them.

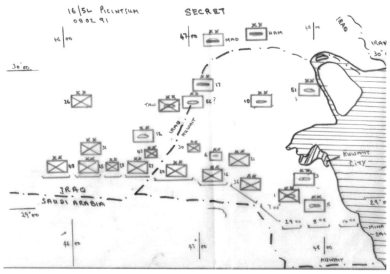

A trace showing enemy positions. XX above is indicating Divisional strength

145

There was another signals exercise planned for tomorrow, let's just hope the enemy didn't have any listening equipment or worse still, directional finding kit; otherwise, all our positions were going to be given away. Why we were doing this with days to go until we attacked was beyond us, and as usual, you got no answers from the top lot as to the logic of it. Did they want them to find us? Not only was the lack of information just causing people to speculate and get worried. It was really pissing people right off.

Even though I was tired, after stag I went and watched the MLRS firing. I loved these things; each launcher held 12 rockets, and each rocket contained submunitions. Depending on the variant of rocket, they could be fired up to 120 kilometres away. The 12 rockets could all be fired in less than a minute. One launcher firing all 12 rockets could completely blanket one square kilometre with submunitions. Hence, the MLRS was referred to as the 'Grid Square Removal System'.

A Squadron QDG was tasked to do the Recce for them. When the OK was given, the Yanks tipped up first with about 20 MLRS. They lined them all up and once in position they then let rip with all of the rockets in one go; took about 40 seconds in all. It was totally unexpected but what an awesome sight it was to behold, very impressive, and God help whoever was on the receiving end of that lot. I wish I could have filmed it somehow as I doubt I will ever see a sight like that again in my lifetime. Once complete, they departed to bomb back up and the four British MLRS that were attached to us turned up. They fired their rockets one at a time like they were on a firing range back in the UK. No doubt they were using it as a training exercise. It felt like 20 minutes in total and was very dull. It was kind of embarrassing to watch after the Yanks. With regards to the US and UK, we really looked like the poor relations in this war.

Video link to watch MLRS firing on YouTube: http://youtu.be/x7fj97-UckI

MLRS firing

SUNDAY, 17th FEBRUARY, 1991

G-4

On stag 0330 until 0530. I was getting quite used to the early hours now, or should I say only getting a few hours kip each night. It was still freezing cold with the large drop in temperature at night. Sitting inside a metal wagon, not being able to move very much, felt like being inside a fridge. Due to the vehicle being under cover and not getting any sunlight during the day, it stayed very cold throughout most of the day as well. It just varied exactly how cold it was depending on what time you were on stag. The only blessing came when you had to start the vehicle up to charge the batteries, because you could then put the heaters on for a while. This, of course, was hardly ever done though because we had generators to run things at night, they were far quieter than a vehicle engine on high revs.

Beno arrived today and he brought the rain with him; he actually volunteered to be the CO's new driver on the Spartan, which surprised quite a few people including me. On a good note though, he was very good with mechanical things and really knew his stuff when it came to vehicles, especially engines and gearboxes.

I gave him a hand while he got straight on with repairing the gearbox leak. He was in his element having something to fix. Me, I just watched and learned. After we had fixed the wagon and the REME had checked it, we took it for a run to make sure it was ok. Once Beno was content it was fixed, we returned. The Ops Officer told us to take it back out again and do an even longer run for a few hours to make sure nothing else was going to break on it, even though we had just driven 80 kilometres to get here. So, off we went for a few hours driving around in the rain. It seemed very weird and a little uncomfortable driving around alone in a war zone where you ran the risk of getting engaged, either by the enemy or friendlies who had no idea you were there.

Once we returned, we were met by some very annoyed guys from the REME. The Ops Officer had arranged for them to check the wagon out again. After they had finished, and we had finished apologising to them, we put the wagon back into its position in RHQ and covered it back up.

My post office book returned today; one of the lads went for a trip and had collected things on route before returning. I had been putting most of my water money into it rather than carrying it around in my pockets. It also stopped me wasting it playing cards, I now had £128 in it. It might not seem a lot, but it would get a few beers in back home.

The Ops Officer came and found me later on; he explained that the CO and 2IC had been chatting about the colours used on the maps to highlight the grid square numbers. We highlighted them to make them stand out so it was easier and quicker to read the map and find things. It was therapeutic at times but became a right pain when it involved several maps. We normally used a yellow highlighter and that was exactly what Adam and I had used when we spent all day yesterday marking the map sets out. He said the 2IC had agreed with the CO that yellow did look brighter, but pink looked far neater. The CO now wanted all the maps redone with all the grid numbers in pink, with a smile on his face he left. So, another bone task came my way. I went and burnt all the other maps before starting on the new ones. A few of the guys came and gave me a hand, all equally dismayed at what was 'wrong' with the last lot of maps.

On the news Iraq was saying the US had misunderstood its proposals. It would withdraw its troops first, and then discuss other conditions. The US was still turning it down though because Iraq had fired two more Scud missiles at Israel last night. For us, our attack (G Day) was going to be put on hold for the time being, but the air strikes were going to continue. The stance by the US was still very clear: either they pulled out with no conditions attached, or we were going in.

Played cards then had an early night. Besides being tired, it was either that or run the risk of getting another bone task given to me if I hung around inside the main tent. One of the guys put a comment in the piss-me-off book, 'orders from above, fuck the guys about all hours of the day'. With comments like that, I don't think the book will last much longer before ending up on the next burn pile. A fate I do not wish for my diary.

MONDAY, 18th FEBRUARY, 1991

G-3

Up at 0730, which really surprised everyone. There was no reason given at all, and it was not because the sentry had forgotten or slept in, it was actually written on the board in the CV for reveille to be at 0730. After grub, I cleaned the guns again and washed all my kit, the sun was up, so I decided to use it for drying the stuff out.

We were now being put on hold at G-3 until further notice, something to do with the politicians needing to make their minds up. Nobody quite knew for sure but the bombing was going to continue. They must think we are machines that can simply be turned on and off when told to do so. We were all ready and hyped up to go, but now we were being told to relax and standby ready to go through all the emotions again when they say so.

New NBC bags for our respirators turned up today. The old ones just couldn't hold half the kit inside that we were now supposed to carry in them. These were a much better design, and the stuff actually all fitted inside the small compartments. I managed to finish another camera film off so sent it home to my sister again. I hope she gets it; there should be some good photos on there. Flies were now starting to be a bit of a problem here; the things were everywhere. They were worse than in Cyprus, and that was pretty bad out on the UN line. I hated flies with a passion, all the disease they carried and how they ate their food, I always referred to them as the devil's creatures.

Int Update:

There were various reports in, and they appeared to differ on the exact strength of the Iraqi forces, depending on whom you listened to and its source. It was hard to tell who was actually telling the truth and who wasn't. In training, we were always told to be very careful about Int and its source, but this was ridiculous. When questions were asked, excuses were given as to why it was so far off, and this was just adding to the problem, not the solution. If Int was being passed to be used for planning purposes, it needed to be reliable and accurate, otherwise there was no point in it; anybody could guess or estimate things. The latest Int was stating that the enemy force was still strong and functioning correctly, or put another way, very combat effective. New map grids in suggested that they also seemed to be moving south, getting even closer to us, even though they were getting a pounding off the air forces. It made no sense.

The Yanks were reporting that they were running out of Daisy Cutters, and they have had two more firefights with the Iraqis crossing over the border just to our right flank. They have also managed to shoot and destroy two of their own vehicles with Apache helicopters. There were casualties but no other information. Other reports in suggested it was Bradley APCs that got hit. This was the second time now, and it was very worrying as we would be operating behind enemy lines and calling these guys up for fire support. If they couldn't recognise their own vehicles from the enemy, what hope had they got of identifying ours when they all looked so very different? We had a solution of sorts to help out during the daytime fighting but nothing for night time, we were totally reliant on them and their own ability to identify friend from foe.

Reports were coming in of the Iraqis moving biological and chemical stuff from factories into religious areas within the towns. This was a bit of a dilemma, if we left them then that would be a problem that would need sorting out later on. If we hit them now and caused civilian deaths, then we could cause massive problems with the Muslim world, which at this moment in time was not a good idea where Iran and Jordan were concerned. They certainly did not require further provoking.

Ten Scud launchers and 300 missiles were still unaccounted for; no doubt being kept hidden until we go in, then they will suddenly appear and be used. Reports also suggested that all the enemy concentration on the border area was because they were hoping to inflict massive casualties on us during the push, so that political pressure would mount back home for us all to stop and then withdraw. Given the political and military appetite up to now, I think that would only ever happen if they somehow managed to wipe out over half our forces, and they couldn't do that…or could they?

With this hold on, it gave more time for us to bomb the shit out of their forces, which could only be great for us, assuming it was having an effect and actually hitting intended targets. The downside was there being more time to think about things. A lot of the guys are very concerned about Iran and Jordan and their intentions; we all just hope they stay out of it, otherwise it will get very messy, very quickly.

Our drinking water has now been put on rations; they would not say why, but we were told it has nothing to do with the oil slick that the Iraqis have dumped in the sea by the Saudi water purification plant! Someone asked why they felt the need to tell us just that bit of information, either don't tell us anything as normal, or tell us why and what they were going to do to resolve the situation.

TUESDAY, 19th FEBRUARY, 1991

G-3

On stag 0330 until 0530, it was freezing cold as usual and all was quiet, which was expected given the hold that was going on. After stag, it was a pretty boring morning really. I spent it making new maps and a few traces for the Squadrons whilst listening to the CO talking to a few officers about the new orders that had just come in. Looking at the traces I was making and listening to what he was saying, it appears we were now going to be used for flank protection instead of going straight in at the front. The CO told the officers he was going to see if he could get it changed; he wanted the Regiment to be the first into Iraq. That is what will be recorded in the newspapers and the history books and no doubt the reason why other units were pushing to do it.

One of the guys had managed to get hold of a baseball bat and ball from the Yanks when doing some exchanges. He suggested we put it to use and have a game. Most of us were up for it, if for nothing else but to get some sun and have a bit of fun. None of the seniors objected, so we grabbed all our kit, as in weapons and NBC stuff and left the berm. We used our kit to mark out all the bases and then played baseball; we were having so much fun nobody noticed two hours went by.

RHQ playing baseball in the desert, the author showing just how to do it

Still not heard any news yet on the local radio. We wanted to hear what Iraq's proposals were given they were supposed to be making an announcement today.

We were told that G-day was marked for the 25th now. The Yanks wanted to get Saddam while the cards were in our favour and he was down, so we would not have to come back in a few years from now to do it all again. I was in two moods here. I agreed that we should get it sorted once and for all; after all, this was not the first time we, as in the West, have had large disagreements with Saddam. But there again, a part of me just wanted to go home and forget all about this crap. Whichever way we went, I just wished we would do something rather than just sitting in this shithole day in day out, twiddling our thumbs getting needlessly fucked about.

Int Update:

Our artillery (UK) fired last night over the border at Iraqi artillery. They apparently didn't inform anyone they were going to do it, and Yank helicopters engaged them for some reason. Luckily, nobody got injured. No other information came with it and nobody was asking. Without the whole story, you don't really know exactly what went on, but it would be interesting to find out if that was poor gunnery and/or poor judgement from the helicopter crews. This 'blue on blue' crap was getting out of hand. The artillery have decided to leave it until daylight hours to do any more firing across the border, that way everyone can see who was who.

WEDNESDAY, 20th FEBRUARY, 1991

G-3

Up at the normal time. I was feeling a bit knackered due to being kept awake all night with a commotion going on. To add to that it was pissing down and there was a gale blowing. At breakfast, we found out what the commotion was all about. The tent that the 2IC had taken off us to work in got blown away last night in the storm. The Ops Officer and he were sleeping in it at the time, resulting in themselves and all of their kit getting soaked through. The news cheered us up no end. Everyone took the piss, even the CO, who said it served them right for not securing it down correctly. They protested that they had secured it, but the change in wind direction had caused it to become insecure. Someone pointed out that by default and design, a military style tent secured correctly accepts wind from any direction.

Did another stag over lunchtime and managed to get some letters written to Lori. Afterwards I washed my kit again, then played cards while it dried. I managed to win over 100 dollars. The betting on the card games was now starting to get stupid, quite possibly due to what we were about to embark on in the future but also mainly due to the amount of money some of the guys were carrying around with them. I now had 400 dollars on me and nowhere for it to go.

Body armour turned up at last; well, when I say body armour I meant a waistcoat thing that had no sleeves or neck protection, at least it was desert coloured. Nobody had a clue what it was capable of stopping; only that it was called body armour. Some guys believed it could stop anything from any weapon carried by a person; others thought it was simply worn to hold your organs together until you got to surgery. I was not so sure.

One thing I was very good at, and also enjoyed, was 'people watching'. I immediately noticed things such as people's gaits, styles and how they walked. Also, their body language and facial expressions; were they sad, angry, frustrated etc.? Not only did I find it very fascinating but it had actually aided me in quite a few awkward situations. I was quickly able to work out what a person was about to do before they did it and pre-empt them. It comes in very handy at times e.g. when you're in a pub full of drunk people. It was noticeable to me in RHQ, mainly because it appeared to be an unnatural position to have your arms in when walking, that all our officers seemed to walk around with their hands on their hips, which for me made them look like they were 'camp'. I think it was the fact I had always kind of pictured a soldier with his hands either down by his sides or firmly on a gun. I actually tried it for myself and found it so uncomfortable. I was spotted by some of the guys who, after taking the piss, asked what the hell I was doing? Clearly, it did not look right to them either. When I explained and pointed out a few of the officers in the nearby vicinity, they burst out laughing. They insisted I recorded it in the diary, had the guys not have seen me, this would not have been written in here.

On the BBC news it said that the Americans had conducted an attack just to the right of us. Reports stated they had injured 700 soldiers and captured a further 500 during an assault on a complex which they had captured. We were not sure where the BBC were getting their stories from but an Op that size and being that close to us, we would have heard and definitely seen the firefights. There were no reports from any of the outstations at all about any fighting whatsoever.

On stag again later I read the latest Op order in the file. Once the Iraqi 12th Armoured Division was out the way, our new mission was to 'Find and destroy the RGF at all costs', this was from the top and was being deemed a top priority. Roughly translated, that meant they were not interested in any excuses or your losses, just get it done.

I spent the rest of the night watching the US MLRS firing over the border; hopefully, they were giving the Iraqis in front of us a good hammering. I never thought I would get another chance to see this impressive sight, but here I was doing just that. I just couldn't put into words how I felt watching these things fire. The sight was simply awesome! It could be I was a little sick in the head, but it was the immense power they unleashed that had me in awe.

THURSAY, 21st FEBRUARY, 1991

G-3

On stag 0130–0330, the wind was getting up again like last night but no rain this time, thank God. We drove the wagon first thing to A2 to get filled up and put some battle stocks on it, extra kit really. Had a chat with the lads there not only to say hello but also to find things out. They get their information from other sources, not just the Regiment, so they got to find out a lot more information than we did. From what they had been told, it did not look like the Iraqis were going to pull out at all. US troops came under fire last night by what was believed to be a battalion-sized artillery unit. They had three pronounced dead and two APCs destroyed. This clearly showed the Iraqis still had the intent and capability to reach across the border and kill us whenever they liked; scary thing was, we were all sitting within range of their artillery now.

When we got back, we told the lads what we had found out, especially about the artillery. We also checked the logs to see if the information had been passed to us in RHQ; it had not. Another O group took place in the afternoon; I was on stag again with Adam so we listened in on it. The CO stated that he was worried the discipline within British units was slipping, men were developing attitudes that because they were at war they just had to do their jobs and no more, some had even told officers to "fuck off". He wanted discipline jumped on in our unit. The men would be washed and shaved each and every morning. Boots would be polished, weapons would be cleaned, and dress was to be immaculate at all times. Anyone not complying was to be charged, there were to be no exceptions.

Adam and I just looked at each other. I said to him that it reminded me of that film *Zulu,* where they were defending the outpost awaiting an imminent attack and one of the guys calls out to the Colour Sergeant, "Sir, Zulus, thousands of them." His reply was, "Yes, lad, but important things first, do your button up." Adam just laughed.

Int Update:

Six Scud missiles were fired at 1720, two managed to hit the airbase just to the south of us. There were no reports of any casualties. Iraq had rejected the peace offers from Russia. The US were now fully determined to go in, no matter what Iraq came up with now, it would be dismissed. I guessed the time for talking was all but done now. Unless a miracle happened, we could expect the ground war to begin on Monday.

FRIDAY, 22nd FEBRUARY, 1991

G-2

On stag 0530–0730. I read the logs, it was official, the countdown had started again and it all looked set for the 25th. The berm and minefields would be breached on the 24th; crossing them would start from 0600 the next morning. President Bush has given them until midday tomorrow to get out of Kuwait or we are going in. I think that is going to happen regardless of what they do now. Given the size of the force they had put into Kuwait, it would take days to get them all out.

Just after breakfast, a warning came over the radio of a possible air/heli-borne attack inbound to our positions. Since we had absolutely no air defence and we were sitting out in the open, it would be a nice turkey shoot for the pilots; that was for sure. Whilst the officers decided to man the radios, we grabbed all the weapons off the tops of the wagons and headed for the edge of the berm again. There was no point being anywhere near the wagons, especially with all the flags still flying giving our position away from miles around. If I was a pilot, that would be the first thing I would go for. If it was helicopters inbound for us, we stood a bit of a fighting chance; fast jets on the other hand, we would have no chance at all with the weapons we had. After waiting for nearly an hour, the all clear was called. Turned out to be nothing in the end, thank God.

Artillery and air strikes seemed to have increased, and they were really giving the guys in front of us a pounding now the peace talks had been rejected. American and British artillery moved up with us next to the border, no doubt to give them a better reach into Iraq. Our Recce troops were informed to be on a careful lookout for any counter-attacks so they could direct fire support to help the artillery bug out if required. Interesting tactic really as it was normally the artillery that we would use for fire support. Guess we would be totally reliant on our US air assets if the shit hit the fan and we were attacked again.

AS 90 (Artillery) with a M548 resupply wagon behind it setting up a gun position. Others can be seen in the background

US heavy artillery moving up

The sky was so clear today that you could see B52 bombers and fighter escorts in the air constantly dropping bomb loads on enemy positions to our front. There were other planes that kept flying back and forth, doing something or other, no doubt protecting the bombers and watching out for any enemy fighter jets. Directly overhead we could see an air-to-air re-fueller with what looked like a fighter escort for its protection. Planes kept coming back and grabbing juice every now and again, then disappearing to our front. Looked like we had total control of the skies.

Spent most of the day making new maps again and putting the up-to-date traces on them. Once that was finished we then started on the wagon. I managed to get hold of some more spare track, which was bolted onto the outside. Beno and Steve changed the idlers for new ones, (metal wheels at the rear of the wagon on either side), whilst I cleaned and sorted the back of the wagon out. Extra food was shoved where I could get it to fit. If there was a gap, then an MRE got squeezed into it. We were given a shitload more ammo to take with us, mainly 20 boxes of 7.62mm for the GPMG (Machine gun). They think where we will be going once we go through the breach resupply will be a little slow or might not happen at all.

Given the fact I already had 6 boxes opened for use, and 15 further ones easily accessible, the 20 extra boxes got spread and buried under piles of other crap, like water. I was trying to think of if we got hit and it caught fire, how could I try and prevent most of it from going up and killing us? My logic being, place bottled water on top of it and metal spares around it for a bit of protection. I very much doubted it would work, but we had to carry it all and there was nowhere for it to go inside, so this was the best solution given the situation. Besides all the extra weight which was a concern, the wagon had now grown two feet taller and looks and feels like a gypsy's caravan; it had gone from being small and relatively hard to target to being an eyesore that could be seen from miles away.

Tomorrow the troop is splitting into 'Main' and 'Step Up', and the CO and Ops Officer are coming onto the wagon. Steve, not being combat trained, will be leaving us to go to A2. I was dreading having them two on the wagon on my own.

AJ and me on my wagon, which has grown two feet with all the extra kit now stowed on board

Tomorrow I planned on cleaning all the guns again and checking them one last time to ensure that they were still working correctly, then I would have a last-minute look at the signals kit to make sure nothing had been missed or overlooked. Everything was working fine now, but I know if it stopped working when we went in, it would be my fault even if I had no control over it.

Once I was happy the wagon was ready to go, I would check all my NBC kit one last time and give my respirator a good clean. All indications were, and we were constantly being reminded, he would use chemical weapons when we went in, so I wanted to be 100% prepared for it. You wouldn't get a second chance where chemical weapons are involved.

Once it all started and we went in, it was all bets off being told how to fight, especially with us being split up. There wouldn't be anybody around telling you when to load and when and what to fire at, it would all be down to your own judgement, which was probably not a bad thing in this troop. Training should kick in and hopefully would keep you alive.

Wrote some last letters as mail would not be coming in or out for a quite a while.

SATURDAY, 23rd FEBRUARY, 1991

G-1

It's the day before we go in and instead of thinking about what's going to happen to us as we approach, or when we try to cross the breach, or indeed what's waiting for us on the other side, all I keep thinking about is that these next few days are going to be the worst days of my life. I wasn't talking about the war either; it was all the running around that I would have to do for the CO and Ops Officer, who were now both on the wagon. I had already had a taste of what life was like when they were on board, and with us going into battle, it was not looking good for me.

After breakfast, Step Up (OC) left to join the Yanks at the breach. The big tent was taken down and went back with Steve and Visser in the cruiser to join A2, where they and quite a few others would remain until it was all over. With Steve gone, besides being a crew member down, it meant I picked his jobs up. I now had to command the vehicle as well as be the CO's operator. Two very distinct and completely different roles and responsibilities on any armoured fighting vehicle, and hence why you always had two people do them. To add to that, and I don't know how it had happened, but we were now left with just four radio operators in Main and most of the officers. All the operators now also either drove or commanded a vehicle as well. Given how little sleep we had when we were all together, I could now see us getting even less.

The remaining vehicles were all rearranged once RHQ had split to form a crucifix again. While we were busy sorting all the kit out, the CO came over and asked who was making him a coffee. Because Visser was no longer with us, as the CO's operator all of his tasks also defaulted to me to pick up. I informed him that once we were all squared away and up and running, I would get the brews on for all of us; it would only be about 20 more minutes. He said nothing and walked away. Two minutes later I was told by another officer to stop what I was doing and get the CO a brew; he hadn't had one since breakfast which was two hours ago. Obviously, I had misunderstood that when he asked, "Who was making him a brew," it actually meant, "Where is my brew?" The other guys said not to bother with them, they would grab one later once we had all finished. I left what I was doing and went and made him one. I would have offered to make the other three officers sitting in the back of the CV one as well but on seeing them I started to get enraged with anger. There was nothing more detrimental to morale than to watch people sit about refusing to lend a hand while you worked your ass off. Then when they wanted something like a brew or something to eat, they would just order you to make it before they went back to doing nothing again. And worse still, you never got any thanks because it was just expected as part of your job.

I vowed to myself there and then that after this was all over, I would be changing units or leaving the Army if they were all the same. I just couldn't and wouldn't put up with this type of behaviour; this was not the eighteenth century, it was so degrading and soul-destroying.

Chapter 12

Ground Assault

SUNDAY, 24th FEBRUARY, 1991

On stag at 0330–0530. I got to listen to all the attacks going in. They were happening simultaneously all along the border of both countries.

0400: 18 US Corps started to go into Iraq on our left flank whilst most of the Arab nations went into Kuwait on our right. Our breach had also been started. Fighting had broken out all over the place. The US Marines were doing an amphibious landing at 0538 into Kuwait; that was when the tide was at its highest, which would allow them to get further inland.

0600: 101st Airborne Division parachuted behind enemy lines to take over the main highway, thus cutting off supply routes and anything that started to retreat rearwards. Iraqi troops were surrendering in their thousands. This was expected though as it was reservists at the front line, and they had no wish to fight, not given what they have been subjected to these last few months.

1150: Told we were now on two hours' notice to go through the berm, amazing since it stated in our orders that we were not going anywhere until 0500 tomorrow morning. They reckoned the breach was going in much faster than expected because instead of having to protect and fight during the breach, nothing was happening at all. Therefore, they were now using those extra fighting troops to help clear the breach quicker.

There was no reported use of any chemical weapons so far despite the fact the US Marines were claiming that mustard gas was showing up on their Chemical Agent Monitor (CAM). The Int guys think it was from a chemical dump that was destroyed earlier in the week. As a result, and to be on the safe side, everyone was to wear NBC suits from the staging area forward, just in case. That information was quickly passed to one and all.

1200: Reports came in that a new trace of enemy positions was inbound and needed to be done and distributed as soon as possible; we were also going on 15 minutes NTM at 1415. We would be moving out at 1500 if we had not received orders to do so beforehand. We quickly got all the kit packed away, putting anything that was important on last so we could get to it first. With the amount of extra kit we were now carrying on the wagons, I wouldn't be surprised if we started to break down given all the extra weight. The CO told me to pack the 9 x 9 tent up and take it with us for him and the Ops Officer; they would be requiring it to sleep in. I couldn't believe it! We were going into enemy territory, fighting was breaking out all over the place, and he is thinking about where he is going to sleep later on!

The trace arrived. It basically had ten grouped Objectives on it. Number one being a valley forge just north of the breach, this was the Form Up Point (FUP). You always had a FUP after a crossing to gather everyone together before setting off again. Objectives two to ten were enemy positions marked in a north-easterly direction towards Kuwait. These were named after metals. BRONZE, COPPER, BRASS, ZINC, STEEL, PLATINUM, TUNGSTEN and LEAD. Ten had no name but was a concentration of enemy artillery sitting on the Iraq-Kuwait border. The trace was quickly copied and distributed.

Once everything was squared away, I went and had a word with the RSO since it appeared nobody else would. He was with the crew of OB and a few others. I asked about the lack of operators and manpower and how were we going to get around it. Had it already been discussed but not passed onto us yet as we had been told nothing about how we were going to operate as Main once we went across the breach. We all knew how Main worked on exercise, this however was not exercise. Most of us were fatigued enough as it was with the build up to now, and we were starting to make mistakes. Given the fact it's imperative that we now operate at 100 percent efficiency and we will be expected to operate both day and night at full operational capacity, how were we going to do everything, including things like the protection of the troop and if need be, fight, when the manpower had been vastly reduced? He told us all he wasn't interested because there were more pressing matters at hand now. A few of the guys pressed the issue, but he was not getting drawn into a discussion. He ended it by saying we would play it by ear as we went along; we would just need to keep an eye on each other and help out where needed.

1500 we moved out. Pre-planned routes had been prepared by the Yanks for units to travel down into staging areas. We went down route GREEN. Met quite a few Yanks on route, who all waved us good luck. I thought that was really nice and a bit of a morale booster. We may have worn different uniforms but we accepted that we were all on the same team out here, fighting side by side, trying to achieve the same goal. A sandstorm started to blow again and it was picking up pace. Other than the Yanks on route to our staging area, there really wasn't anything else to see; it was just flat open desert with a little bit of vegetation about. Not sure what else I expected to see at the edge of a battle area in the middle of nowhere.

We stopped for a rest about halfway along the route. When I dropped down inside the vehicle from the commander's seat to get the brews on, the CO blew his top at me, shouting that the comms were crap and that he couldn't speak to certain call signs. Given where we were going and what we were about to do, and the fact I'd had enough of him shouting at me like I was something on the bottom of his shoe, totally enraged, I yelled back at him saying all the crap on top of the wagon, which he had insisted on us carrying, like the tent for example, was interfering with the comms. Due to a lack of room, items were leaning on the antennas, and there was absolutely nothing I could do about it. I had already pointed this out to him days ago and explained that the result would be at least two out of the four radios would not be working correctly. I then gave him the solution, but he had told me I didn't know what I was on about, and we were to take all the extra kit as directed.

To prove the point, I got up on top of the wagon and switched the wires from the antenna he was currently using to an antenna on the outside of the wagon away from all the kit. I then told him to make a call. It boomed through to the furthest call sign, who was over 30 kilometres away. Now I had calmed down a bit, I explained once more to him that we either binned some of the crap on top of the wagon, or we had to keep stopping each time he encountered difficulty in contacting certain call signs so I could change the antennas over to use the masts on the outside of the wagon. He always had the other option of relaying it by getting another call sign to pass the message on. It was either that, or he accepted that some call signs he simply would not be able to reach from time to time. As a class one signaller who came top on the course, I did know what I was talking about with regards to how radios worked.

I was not sure if he was simply stunned at me shouting at him or the fact I had made the point. Either way he calmed down and said nothing more about it, except the fact he still wanted to take all the kit. On route to the staging area, we did not stop once to change wires over.

Approaching the staging area

Getting NBC suits on in the staging area

A2 Echelon in the staging area

Challenger 1 MBTs as far as the eye could see

Front of the Division forming up

When we were all formed up inside the staging area, we were told that we would be holding here for a while until the breach was complete. Everyone was to stay close to their own vehicles and not gather in large groups. I went for a quick walk and a chat with some of the guys; you never know, it might be the last time I would be seeing some of them. I took some photos as I went along. It was such a strange atmosphere. On looking around, most of the guys simply stayed within their crews on their own wagons. Some ventured a few wagons' distance away from their own vehicle; a few like me had wandered about to chat to friends. On chatting I found the guys had mixed feelings about what was coming next and what was expected from us. Finding fixed enemy positions and doing what we did best was fine, it was all the other unknowns. For example, what was going to happen once we went through; would we be engaged straightaway like we did to them when they crossed the border and attacked us? What about the enemy armour in reserve? With it moving about there was the risk of us bumping into it, or worse still, it actually looking for us. This was after all, perfect tank country with little or no place for CVR (T)s to hide. Tanks would have a field day against us lot. And of course, there was the ultimate question of *'how long was this war going to go on for?'* Sitting here waiting and contemplating was not good for anyone, we needed to get going and get on with our jobs.

MONDAY, 25th FEBRUARY, 1991

G+1

Still in the staging area and on stag 0100–0300. The wind was still blowing quite badly outside, kicking all the sand up and reducing the visibility…at least the NBC suits kept you warm.

Reading the Int logs:

Attacks so far were all being reported as going well and as planned. The US Marines were now south of Kuwait City and have had one counter-attack, which they fought off. The 101st Airborne managed to get a Brigade-size force parachuted in, all in one go with no casualties at all. I bet that surprised the shit out of the Iraqis seeing that lot drop from the skies. Were it not for the fact it was coming for you, it would have been quite impressive watching all the aircraft involved flying and the actual drop itself. From the list I saw of who took part in it, it was the size equivalent to all our flying assets in the British military combined.

The Egyptians, 7 (US) Corps and I (UK) Division would all be going in later today across a massive frontage. This would really fuck them up as it was all armoured and as I said before, this was perfect terrain for MBTs. Their RGF (so called elite) was in front of us and on the move somewhere, getting bombed to hell again. With these gone the top lot reckon that Iraq would surrender quite quickly. There was still no reported use of any chemical weapons so far, which was really good news.

We all got called forward at 0700 to start making our way towards the breach as a Division, so we all set off in a very similar fashion to the route march we did after the Divisional practice. When we arrived at the Iraqi border, orders came from Divisional HQ to halt us all. The whole Division sat in one big long line from the staging area to the breach, which was about 30 kilometres apart.

What a target we now made, talk about sitting ducks. It was a good job the enemy were not using air or artillery. Enemy pilots would have been in their element given this line of vehicles. A few of the lads got out of the wagons and started to take pictures, mainly of the signs on the ground. The Yanks at the breach went nuts, because there were still anti-personnel mines about which they had not cleared due to the need to get the vehicles through it a lot faster than expected. They also did not expect anyone to be stopping and taking photographs either.

Listening to the radio: The prisoner of war count was now between 8,000–9,000 and rapidly rising. The Iraqis were doing a counter attack down a wadi to our left flank. Air strikes have just been called in at 1045 to assist friendly forces.

We found out the hold-up was because Divisional HQ now wanted 7 Bde to go through first and do the break out from the breach. 4 Bde would then follow on. We as the Divisional Recce would go afterwards and make our way directly north of the first Objectives (COPPER and BRONZE), where we would set a screen up to ensure that they could not be reinforced when they were attacked by the Brigades. That meant we would have to get a shift on, since MBTs travelled a lot quicker across desert than CVR (T)s. This was now completely different to our earlier mission of finding the 12th Armoured Division before moving onto the RGF at all costs.

RSO at the breach crossing

With both Brigades now all through and well ahead of us, we were given the order to move out at 1155, using lanes C and D to cross. B Squadron led the way, followed by C Squadron, then RHQ, both A Squadrons and bringing up the rear was a mixed packet of vehicles. This was made up of the RAP, REME and a few others to help with resupply due to us losing all our SQMS packets to A2 Echelon.

Normally when conducting any type of obstacle crossing, a minefield or bridge being examples, you would be closed down. That meant all crews had to be inside the vehicles with hatches closed and locked, because the chances were that you would come under some sort of bombardment either from aircraft, artillery or both. Only when the enemy side was captured to beyond where they could successfully engage the crossing point with artillery were wheeled vehicles allowed to cross, since they could not close down and had little to no protection.

This crossing was quite uneventful, especially after all the hype and tension. Nobody was required to close down at all, although some did either through pure drills or just using it as practice. There were about 12 lanes in all and a lot of mixed vehicles, all crossing at the same time. Each lane was clearly marked with a rather large red-letter board.

Lanes cleared through the minefields

After departing the FUP, we came across American MBTs and APCs dotted all over the place. These no doubt were the force assigned to secure and protect the enemy side of the crossing. They had pushed further on and had secured an area plus of the FUP to a phase line called NEW JERSEY. They had cleared it of any enemy who could possibly attack the guys conducting the breach. This was another reason why the breach had gained momentum and been completed far quicker than expected. Their role was clearly accomplished now and no doubt they would be receiving further orders pretty soon once enough forces had passed through the breach and pushed on.

Passing American M1A1 Abrams and Bradley APCs after the breach crossing.
My GPMG on top loaded and ready for us

Five hours later we caught 7 Bde up. 4 Bde seemed to have gone in another direction, because we did not see them at all and they were supposed to be behind 7 Bde. Considering Divisional Recce was supposed to be in front of them all and not behind, we didn't appear to be conducting the conventional role of Divisional Recce at all. More orders came across the radio, we were still to head north and bypass the first Objectives (BRONZE and COPPER) but instead of setting a screen to the north of them and waiting until they were attacked, we were now to continue on at best speed to the north of Objective ZINC and set a screen up there before attacking it from the north ourselves. Objective ZINC was about 15 kilometres to the east/north-east of BRONZE. It looked like the Brigades were splitting and attacking the Objectives independently without the use of us. No doubt their own recce had found the enemy positions and they were small enough that they could pretty much just get on with an attack exactly how they had been trained in BATUS.

We passed quite a few burnt-out vehicles and old enemy positions, all abandoned. We saw 10 Iraqi soldiers walking towards us, arms up in a surrendering posture with no weapons. Just past them another 15 appeared and immediately surrendered to us as we approached. They had weapons so we stopped and disarmed them. One understood a little bit of English, so we told him to catch the others up, and keeping their arms up, walk the way we had just come from and someone would pick them all up very soon. They seemed happy enough given the circumstances; they were alive and as far as they were concerned, no more fighting for them.

Abandoned enemy positions

Abandoned 23/4 Iraqi Air defence position

Visibility was starting to reduce now, not only was it getting dark but the wind was picking up and it started to rain. I was listening to the comms of the Brigades, mainly because I wanted to hear how well the attack was going in at Objective BRONZE. This was the closest Objective from the FUP so should be the first one to be encountered. It was no different to what I did when I was in BATUS on the range safety staff. The comms were starting to break up, possibly

167

due to the distance between us and them, but the weather certainly was not helping the situation. I heard some of their own call signs struggling and asking for messages to be repeated or relayed; clearly, they were also having issues. It came across the radio net that the Staffords couldn't tell who was who in the poor visibility, so they all had to stop and confirm positions to prevent a blue on blue occurring. It was a very bold, but absolutely the right call to make, even if it did slow the momentum of the Brigade down. That could soon be picked back up again very quickly.

We were also having problems of our own. Vehicles were breaking down with us trying to go flat out to get into position. Everyone was briefed before we set off that if your vehicle broke down, try to self-fix; if that failed, the wagon in front was to tow you and it would get fixed later on. If that was not possible for whatever reason, then A Squadron had the task of collecting you since they were last in line and had the REME with them to assist. Getting into position north of the Objectives was the priority. Two of RHQ's CVs had already broken down. OB being the most important since that meant we could no longer talk to Divisional HQ; only they and OC had the correct radio fit to do that and OC had been left at the breach to count the Regiment through. Because OB required towing, the CO said to leave them and he would command the Regiment from the Spartan. He and the Ops Officer were now on board.

2000 hrs and we were now 50 kilometres north into Iraq. It was now raining heavily, and we had still not fired a single shot yet. Interesting was the fact there were no reports of anyone encountering minefields yet. Not even by or anywhere near any of the enemy positions we drove past. The Int reports in the build-up to this suggested all their defensive positions had minefields around them. Reports of enemy positions to our front started to come in from our forward Squadrons. We slowed down to get confirmation of exactly what was there. Armour and dug-in infantry were confirmed at the grids given earlier for Objective ZINC. The information was passed and the MLRS and A10s instructed to fix them until the Brigades caught up.

2230, reports started coming in of vehicles moving in-between and through our Squadrons heading north, and they were believed to be British. This was confirmed from C Squadron, who had a Challenger MBT drive across the front decks of one of their wagons. Confusion was starting to set in. Who were they, what were they doing this far north and where were they going? Given the heads up from the Staffords earlier and the fact the comms and visibility were so poor and getting worse, the MLRS and A10s were told to check fire and stand down. The CO tasked Liaison Officers (LOs) to go back and intercept the Brigade before we had a blue on blue. I think the LOs did a fantastic job here as I don't think they realised just how dangerous the task actually was. It might have dawned on them when they eventually found some of 7 Bde and managed to have a chat because they found out that 7 Bde had no idea we were up north of ZINC and that they had also been given the same orders as us to position and attack it from the north. Either by good training and judgement of all involved, or just by sheer luck, nobody had fired a single shot. Whilst this was being sorted at higher, the Regiment was pulled together into a very small concentration area to try and keep out of 7 Bde's way. Everyone was instructed to be very careful before pulling a trigger against anything they believed to be enemy.

Via the LOs, 7 Bde HQ informed us they were taking on the task; we would be receiving new orders from higher. All information collected so far about the enemy at ZINC was handed over to the Recce troop of 7 Bde. On reporting to Division HQ that we were going to clear to the north to get away from an attack that was being planned, we got orders to hold and wait until the attack was underway before moving off again. They never explained why even though we were informed the attack was not going in for a few hours yet. The message was passed and the Regiment went firm with everyone just sitting in their vehicles. So once more the whole Regiment was sitting in the open again with thumbs up our bums waiting, the only saving grace being the visibility was so poor now that the enemy would have to physically bump into us to find us. Considering there was supposed to be a full moon tonight, it was absolutely pitch black due to the rain clouds.

Whilst we were waiting to move out, it got me thinking about the situation that had developed. After our little bombardment, the enemy would clearly know we were in the area and about to attack them. It could prove a little costly affording them time to reorganise themselves before conducting an attack. However, as an advantage we were trained in night fighting and did have all the required kit. The Iraqis weren't and they didn't have any at all according to the Int, so hopefully it would just be one-sided and should be over very quickly. It was a good job we were not up against a more modernised fighting army. Thinking of my time spent in BATUS and how to counteract something like this happening to us, no way would I just sit there and allow the enemy hours to prepare for an attack onto my positions. I would hit them with a counter-attack whilst they were forming up. During that time, if they were trained anything like us lot, their main focus would be on just getting to the FUP and then waiting for the attack time before going in. During this whole event, they would all be closed down and thus have restricted views, they would have no idea who was who, especially if dust, rain or fog was also reducing visibility. When they were attacked, and even if assuming they became aware they were being attacked, everyone normally waited for the person who issued the orders in the first place to take control and give new orders before reacting. If that person had been taken out (killed), it all went to rat shit. I had seen this tactic played many a time during my stay in BATUS, when a Battlegroup stopped using the artillery to fix the enemy and then took ages to form up. It worked every single time, especially when the enemy came from the sides or behind and joined in with the direction of travel either to the FUP or from it. This tactic highlighted many dangers such as no flank (sides) or rear protection, the lack of momentum and being slaves to orders and Doctrine; hence, whilst I was posted out there, every now and again it was allowed to play out for people to learn from it.

Whilst we were waiting we all got told to take our NBC suits off as we no longer needed to wear them, having passed through the breach. Saved us sticking out like lemons wearing green/black NBC suits in a desert tomorrow morning.

TUESDAY, 26th FEBRUARY, 1991

G+2

0105 the sky lit up as artillery started hitting the ground to our front; everyone that was outside the vehicles instinctively hit the deck thinking we were under attack. Thoughts of an imminent adjustment followed by rounds landing directly on top of our heads went through my mind. My heart was pounding now because there's not a lot you can do under an artillery bombardment other than sit it out and hope you don't get hit. Besides absolutely frightening, it reminded me of extremely close violent rolling thunder; you saw and felt the explosions first, swiftly followed by the noise. At night, everything is so much louder and appears closer. The whole wagon shook with the severe force of it, that was how close it was to us. I have seen and felt artillery many times before in Canada, but not this close and not when I was standing out in the open.

Turned out to be friendly artillery engaging Objective ZINC, we hoped they knew exactly where we were and that whoever was calling in the fire mission didn't mistake us for the enemy. It was a very frightening experience to be this close to an artillery barrage, especially when you were not warned about it, God knows what it would have been like if it was actually coming down on your head. If anyone was feeling tired before, we were now all very much awake and alert.

Once the attack started we were told to push on to Objective LEAD, the furthest one away on our maps. We were to bypass the smaller Objectives on route and anything else we encountered. Orders were passed across the radio net for everyone to move out. Same order of march as before, B Squadron, followed by C Squadron, with both A Squadrons bringing up the rear.

The visibility was slowly starting to improve as the rain eased off. Gaps now started appearing in the clouds above, and the moon could be seen every now and again.

Chapter 13
Objective LEAD

Lead elements of the Regiment got to Objective LEAD and found pretty much the same enemy set-up as the last encounter at ZINC. The Regiment formed a sort of box formation as a screen went in straight away on the western side of the objective. B Squadron was positioned on the north-western side of the objective, with A Squadron QDG taking the south-western side. Our own A Squadron was tasked to protect our southern/right flank; C Squadron was tasked to screen the north/left flank for any reinforcements to LEAD. RHQ, with all the logistics, went roughly into the middle with the MLRS holding off in an area at the rear set-up and ready to be used. OB and OC were now fixed and had joined back up with us.

As daylight emerged and enemy targets were positively identified, MLRS and air was called in to start hitting them. A number of dug-in MBTs and APCs were hit and destroyed on the first salvo down. Some of the infantry immediately surrendered from the dug-in positions nearest to B Squadron. They just got up and started walking towards them with their hands in the air. The Squadron was told to hold back as another fire mission had already been called in and was on its way from the MLRS. I felt sorry for them as there was absolutely nothing we could do about it.

After the fourth MLRS fire mission, they launched a counter-attack. A Squadron QDG and B Squadron stood their ground and took on the advancing MBTs and APCs. Both Squadrons used their Guided Weapons (GW) troop to take on the tanks with Swingfire missiles whilst the CVR (T)s took on the APCs and the infantry. B Squadron GW troop alone managed to hit two tanks and an MT-LB (a Soviet APC) by mistake. They had fired at a T55, but the distance was over 4100m, so the wire at the back of the missile, which was used to send commands down it for guiding it, had snapped. The missile by pure luck went past the tank and hit the MT-LB, killing all the infantry on board. A Squadron QDG also reported equal successes, destroying numerous tanks and APCs. The counter-attack was short lived and they withdrew back to LEAD.

Whilst everyone got their breath back from that little surprise, RHQ frantically tried to call Divisional HQ for support but nobody was answering. As Recce our job was to FIND and FIX the enemy until the Battlegroups caught up. These in theory should never be that far away because not only do we not have an endless supply of ammunition to FIX the enemy, but there is only a fine amount of time before the element of shock and surprise are lost, then the enemy will react, as we had just witnessed.

A Striker of GW troop firing a Swingfire missile

A Colonel and a Major from the Iraqi infantry had been captured. They were brought to RHQ for questioning since we had the Int Officer with us. Another of his roles was that of a trained interrogator. The captured men were made to sit about 50 feet apart with their hands on their heads. The Int Officer asked AJ, Dave B and myself to guard them whilst he had an individual chat with each of them. The Major looked hurt and really scared, while the Colonel looked what I could only best describe as being right pissed off, no doubt wondering why he was being treated like a POW and not a high-ranking officer being whisked off to the mess. I felt really sorry for them, strange really, but I just couldn't stop picturing how I'd feel if I was in their shoes. When you get captured, you have absolutely no idea how you are going to be treated at all, you just hope that the enemy will treat you as would treat them, but it's not always the case.

The Colonel refused to talk to the Int Officer. The Major, on the other hand, told him they had come from one of the positions behind us, and not Objective LEAD. The Colonel gave him some verbal abuse for talking, so he decided not to say anything else. The Int Officer asked me in my role as a medic to ensure they were not hurt or injured. Since the Major looked hurt, I went to him first. He no longer wanted to talk so I explained that I was a medic and I only wanted to help him, which no doubt was not very convincing given the fact I did not wear an armband with a red cross on it. The reason being, only personnel whose primary role was medical were allowed to wear them. After giving them both a quick check over and satisfied that they had no major injuries and could travel for a bit, we gave them some bottled water, then sent them west with an escort towards our logistics guys.

Afterwards, I chatted to the Int Officer. He said these two had obviously come from either ZINC or PLATINUM since the Brigades were attacking them. That meant we now had added problems. Objective LEAD was to our east, PLATINUM to our south and ZINC to our west. All of which could be reinforced from the north, meaning they would have to come through our positions to do it. Any forces retreating from ZINC or PLATINUM would produce the same results, and then there was our own Objective, who could attack us again at any time.

To add to the problems, a sandstorm started to pick up again and the weather started to worsen; visibility quickly reduced and soon got down to about 200 metres in the blowing sand. It now meant we would not be able to use air support, so no A10s or Apaches. Using MLRS or Swingfire was also going to be a problem. I grabbed the GPMG and the LAW off the top of the wagon and prepped them in a position near to where I could use them if needed.

Reports were coming in from C Squadron using a Man-portable Surveillance and Target Acquisition Radar (MSTAR) that over 200 vehicles were heading towards us from the north; the lead elements were only 8 kilometres away. It was either the RGF or the Tawakalna Force (TKF). This was not looking too good, because there was nowhere for us to go and if they got here, we were all dead. The enemy would not only outman us, they would also outgun us. They had T72 MBTs and CVR (T)s were no match against those babies. It really would be one-shot one-kill from those things against us. There were no reinforcements for us to call upon. The Division was still 35 kilometres away fighting battles, and we now had no air or artillery support. The MLRS attached to us was far too close to be used for fire missions now. Even if they did manage to get firing, you would not be able to see where the rounds were landing, so trying to correct it would be a complete waste of time. Everyone was told to hold their positions and keep their eyes open.

0845 and they attacked us again from Objective LEAD, no doubt taking full advantage of the poor weather and the news of the reinforcements coming from the north. A Squadron reported T62 MBTs and MT-LBs coming up from the south, they were engaging as and when they could see. All four CVR (T)s from one of their troops had fired at an enemy MBT, after about 40 rounds, the crew just got out and abandoned it. Nobody had a clue why it had not fired at them, which was a blessing because a single round from that thing would have destroyed a CVR (T).

The sound of vehicles driving about very close to us could be heard above the noise of the sandstorm. Those of us standing about hit the sand and listened out, they sounded like CVR (T)s. We then saw two CVR (T)s driving past us in the dust, which was strange because each Squadron should be holding a line. Geordie told me that A Squadron QDG had asked to withdraw earlier but the 2IC had refused them. We got to our feet and went to OB, where one of the guys informed the CO of what we had just seen. He immediately got on the radio net and tried to find out who was driving where. All Squadrons reported back that they were still holding their lines. After a few heated radio calls and confirmations, it became clear it was A Squadron QDG who had withdrawn due to the fact they had come up against T62s attacking them and couldn't hold them. They were told to hold their positions where they were because there was nowhere for them to go; the Regiment was in a box formation and each Squadron was fighting its own battle.

Reports came in that Iraqi tanks were firing at troops from behind them, in other words they were inside our formation now. A CVR (T) from C Squadron had been hit with machine gun fire from a T59. Due to a round penetrating the wagon and ending up in their ammo, and the crew believing it would all explode, they abandoned the wagon. They managed to return later when it did not go up. Why the tank had not chosen to fire a main round at the CVR (T) was a complete mystery. This was now the second reported case of an enemy MBT not using its main gun. Maybe they had no main armament ammo, which would be a bonus for us if it was true.

I then saw a T59 about 50 metres from us. I yelled for everyone to get out the wagons as they would be sitting targets inside. If they did see us, it would be the vehicles they went for first. I ran over to my vehicle and grabbed the LAW from where I had previously left it. Possibly due to the poor visibility, or for some other reason, the tank didn't see us; it drove right past and disappeared into the storm before I could open up on it from behind. I was gutted, that would have made a nice kill. I was so hyped up now I just wanted to shoot something, or someone. We lay in the sand for a while with the LAW prepared and ready to fire; actually hoping another tank would roll by! We were unable to see or hear jack shit, all we could hear was the noise the storm was generating.

Reports started coming in thick and fast from all the Squadrons. The enemy column was now five kilometres from our positions, moving in for the kill from the north. The logistics vehicles had also been attacked and bugged out to get away. Crews in two separate wagons that were being towed had fired on enemy MBTs that were attacking them. One of our M548 had been engaged by a T62, it was destroyed and the crew were missing. We were now being fully attacked on two fronts, enemy tanks were inside our formation and large reinforcements were on route. A withdrawal was called to move back to the north-west to a safe area that we had come through the other day. We could not fight a force that was three times the size of our Division equipped with T72s, amongst other things. We started to withdraw in contact with tanks on our asses. It was not looking great; this was not how we practised this type of withdrawing, no air or artillery support, no pre-planned traps, ideas or killing areas. There was no back up for us to run to because it was 35 kilometres away tied up in another fight, which no doubt was the reason the Divisional HQ was off the radio so we couldn't even tell them what was going on. All our training had been geared around the rolling wooded countryside of Europe, which was great for small lightweight CVR (T)s, which could zip along using speed and concealment to hide and hit the enemy in order to slow them down. Out here it was a whole new ball game; it was flat open desert, ideal for manoeuvre warfare using tanks with big guns and heavy armour. This was where maybe certain other nations had it right when they embedded

MBTs within their Recce units in order to fight for the information and to protect when needed.

The guys told me later on that we had received a radio call out of the blue from an American call sign; they were slightly off-track due to the weather and had seen some of our vehicles. Like us, they were sweeping in an easterly direction just to the north of us with orders to hunt down and destroy an Iraqi armoured Division equipped with T72s. They were equipped with M1 A1 Abrams. They were given our rough locations and told that we had no MBTs at all. If they drove east through us, in about three kilometres max they would encounter enemy tanks consisting mainly of T55s and T62s. After them, head slightly north-east and they might then find the TKF or RGF with T72s. The grids were passed of the rough location the MSTAR had detected them. Everyone was told to go firm and expect M1s to drive through coming from the west. Not that they might get to see them, given the poor visibility. It was a beautiful sight to see Abrams go through your position instead of Russian vehicles, not to mention the flapping was now over as we had tank support.

Once they had passed through, the Regiment moved back to a concentration area to regroup and restock. The storm started to die down, and it looked like it was going to be a nice day. 7 Bde eventually caught us back up again after finishing off Objective ZINC. They were tasked with finishing off Objective LEAD. The boot was now firmly back on the other foot, with them now being outmanned and outgunned. They quickly surrendered on seeing the Challengers and Warriors appear.

Collecting POWs from Objective LEAD

For some reason, we were still unable to contact Divisional HQ so stayed put awaiting orders whilst keeping an eye on all the POWs that were coming our way. Everyone managed to get a quick bite to eat and a brew whilst all the wagons got refuelled. It was reported that all eight Objectives given to the Division had now been taken and secured. The Squadrons were told to quickly get sorted and await new orders; it would give them time to find out the state of all their vehicles and the men.

RHQ having a pause at Objective LEAD after the battle. A Squadron in the distance

The bosses at A2 called us on the net. They said what a brilliant job we were doing and that everyone was so proud of us. A few of the guys commented that they thought they were just snivelling up to the CO. Either way, I didn't think they knew the whole story: yes, we had done a brilliant job, but we got surrounded, attacked and nearly got completely cut off from our own forces and had to withdraw. Even RHQ had enemy on it. Not exactly the plan according to how we had trained and exercised for many years as Recce. For me, it all boiled down to one thing: the enemy was real and it had a vote. Had it not have been for someone else taking that enemy column out, I wonder how many of us would have been killed. 'Lucky' might be a better word to use, and we were indeed, very lucky. Still, we got out alive, so thank God for small mercies as they say.

The two REME lads who were on the M548 that got engaged were confirmed as killed in action. The names were being withheld at the moment. L/Cpl Evans from the QDGs was still reported as missing.

Orders came in at 2100. Our mission still stood with regards to the RGF. We were to pursue using artillery and air until they surrendered or re-attacked us. If possible, we were to get behind them and stop them retreating. These were quickly passed onto everyone and we were all told to get ready to move out. They really wanted the Iraqi armour destroyed at all costs, especially the modern T72 tanks. Clearly, those up top were unaware of what had just happened to us when we tried taking MBTs on, and it appeared nobody in our command was going to tell them either.

Not counting the lack of sleep beforehand, most of us have not slept for over two days solid now; I was really starting to feel tired. The adrenaline in and out every two minutes probably wasn't helping the situation either. The officers were becoming edgy and snapping at the lower ranks for the slightest thing. Seems the lack of sleep was affecting them as well now. The CO and Ops Officer went back onto OB for the advance, which was good news for me. Because of the problems the Regiment was having with the radios, it was decided my vehicle was now going to be used as a comms rebro and a go between to 7 US Corps, Wolfpack (Apache) and Wolf Eagle (A10s), despite the fact we had OE, which was equipped for those exact roles and had the crew to facilitate them. Rebro was short for rebroadcasting. You basically set the radios up so that they received a message in on one radio, normally as far away as possible from the sender, where the signal was now getting very weak. It was then automatically sent out on the other radio at full strength again, thus increasing the distance the messages could be sent over.

Chapter 14
Into Kuwait

The Regiment set off; crossing Wadi Al Batin back into Kuwait and then we started to head north. On route, we encountered small pockets of dug-in enemy all over the place, most had little to no tank support at all. Now this was more like it, and we did what we did best as Recce. Once found and identified to be enemy, we hit them, and hit them hard with everything we had. Those who did decide to put up a fight were continually engaged until they surrendered or were killed. Those that did surrender to us had their weapons taken off them, given a little food and water and instructed to stay put until someone else arrived to take care of them. We then continued on with our task.

It got to the stage we stopped taking the weapons off the troops; we had that many and nowhere to put them. I decided to strip down and hide an AK machine gun in the vehicle for myself as a souvenir; I'm sure it will be asked for later on.

It was a good job that we kept stopping every now and again to collect weapons because it was the only way I managed to find out what was going on, the rest of the time was simply just follow OB as per usual. Orders from the top kept changing for some reason, and we were now chasing 17 and 52 Armoured Brigades (enemy) as well as carrying out our main mission; it was all getting a bit messy now. They wanted all the armour found and destroyed; that was the priority. Two Warrior vehicles were reportedly shot up by A10s during one of the attacks on an Objective; 9 were dead with up to 20 injured. It pissed the guys right off, one said, "The Yanks may be good at other things but their recognition seemed to be fucking appalling. A Warrior APC looked absolutely nothing like a BMP or a MT-LB; if anything, it looks more like their own Bradley APC." Some other call sign, believed to be an American M1 A1, had engaged the Queens Royal Irish Hussars Recce troop, no info on casualties as yet. Fucking unreal, more and more blue on blue, and it was starting to enrage people. It seemed everyone just wanted to shoot something now and the trigger was getting pulled before taking a quick moment to pause to be absolutely sure it was enemy first. It's difficult enough in the heat of battle as it is, which is exactly why your vehicle recognition needs to be shit hot.

Some of the weapons and a captured vehicle taken from Iraqi soldiers

WEDNESDAY, 27th FEBUARY, 1991

G+3

Given that I had been told nothing other than to follow OB as normal, I kept track of where we were going on the map. We were still moving northwards, staying very close to the Iraq border inside Kuwait. The border pretty much went in a north-easterly direction. All the enemy we now started to come up against started a small firefight then quickly surrendered, it was almost like it was a token effort either to test us and see if it was worth having a real go, or simply to say they had done their part in the war. Whatever the reason, the exchange of fire was short and sweet. We came across loads of dug-in destroyed Iraqi tanks all over the place. Somebody or something, no doubt the Yanks we had encountered earlier in their MBTs, is ahead of us doing this since only a few seem to have been destroyed by aircraft bombs. You could tell the difference between when a tank had destroyed another tank, compared to one that had been hit by either a bomb or a missile from an aircraft.

Destroyed dug-in Iraqi tank

Other than a small place on the map called Al Abraq, we encountered no civilians or populated areas at all; it was just pure desert again. About halfway up the border, we received orders that we were to halt again. We were instructed that 7 Bde would go forward ahead of us. Again, no reason was given, 4 Bde was not mentioned and there was nothing reported to our front at all. Either Divisional HQ knew something we didn't, or more likely, as one of the guys suggested, they were after some glory now things seemed to be quietening down. To be fair the Challengers and Warriors were travelling a lot faster across this terrain compared to CVR (T)s and if it was the main armour they were after, it made total sense to put tank against tank in open desert.

Destroyed 2S1 Artillery piece

A report from higher said that all exit points from Kuwait into Iraq have been blocked, so we could now concentrate all efforts on finding and destroying the RGF who were still on the move somewhere inside Kuwait. Listening to the BBC news it appears that Iraq was complaining like hell, saying it was our fault that they couldn't withdraw their forces out of Kuwait due to us preventing them from doing so. They clearly wanted to keep the RGF and as much of their armed forces as possible intact. Taking everything into account that has happened so far and the progress everyone has made with little to no resistance, it's obvious that we will win this war now; everyone had their tails up. We just needed to keep the momentum going and overrun them as quickly as possible to stop them reorganising or being able to come up with any plans for counter-attacking. The bosses were pushing us to smash as much of his army as we possibly could, especially the armour, to force a total surrender rather than one with conditions attached to it. Given what we were hearing on the BBC news, this appeared not to be a popular decision held by some politicians back home. It was no doubt another reason why we were being pushed to move as fast as we could to get it done before they got a chance to say anything about it. That was why quite a few of us did not understand why we kept getting told to halt every now and again with no explanations as to why, it was very annoying. Everyone just wanted to get on with what we were trained to do, especially now that we had the upper hand and were winning.

Passing by a destroyed Iraqi tank

What was left of an MT-LB (Iraqi APC)

The US Marines have captured Kuwait Airport, and the Egyptians were now entering the city. The main highways out of the city were secured, especially the A80 and the A801, which went north to Busayyah, Safwan and Um Qasr. Hopefully, the RGF was now totally cut off out in the open and had nowhere to go, which made bombing the shit out of them very easy, that way we should get a surrender really quickly and this would all be over a lot sooner.

1310: Still held halfway up the western border of Kuwait, awaiting further orders from higher. A few of the guys had come over for a brew and a chat whilst I was scribbling in this diary. It was the only way to try and keep each other awake. I was feeling pretty knackered now and was quite sure I was doing an impression of a nodding dog, and I wasn't the only one either. The CO and Ops Officer came over to the Spartan and told us all to get out so they could get into the back and go to sleep. I was required over at OB as I was going onto stag for a few hours. Once we had cleared out, they got into the back and just seemed to pass out. It was really strange, I know we were all tired but the speed in which they both just fell asleep was amazing. We later found out from chatting with the guys at the RAP, it was because the doctor had been prescribing them caffeine tablets to keep them awake. Once they had taken their toll fatiguing the body to hell (and they eventually would), the body would simply just crash; that was what we had witnessed. On receiving that news, it angered quite a few of the guys, especially given the fact they had constantly been having a go at people for being tired when they were taking tablets to help themselves stay awake. Had this been a protracted war it was scary to think of what could have happened. Everyone cannot simply just be on tablets all the time, which is exactly why you need to adapt and lose the UK camp mentality when at war or on Ops. Troops need to be organised so the guys are allowed to rest when required in order to sustain a 24-hour capability.

1500: Reports came in that three Spartans in the Divisional Admin Area (DAA), ones that had no protection at all, had been engaged by T72s belonging to the Egyptians, yet another blue on blue. No casualties reported, so hopefully they were all okay. Commander Royal Artillery (CRA) has tasked the Regiment to go back and protect the DAA. The CO was woken up and given the news, he dispatched C Squadron complete to go back to do the job.

After stag, whilst making a brew and some grub, a few of us sat having a chat about the DAA. The usual piss-taking started about how they weren't real soldiers, and that's exactly why they were positioned that far back. This was followed on by frustration and anger about how they always managed to get and wear the latest gear before any of the combat troops got any of it. Eventually, the conversation turned to their so-called protection, or lack of it. Even though the DAA was supposed to be positioned far enough back and out of harm's way, none of us could get our heads around the fact that it had no protection at all. Especially since it was where all the supplies were, as in food, fuel, ammo, water and spares for the whole Division. Even in our role we were taught, when war fighting, always go for the command and control first, followed by something like this and remove it off the face of the battlefield. Get that, the supply chain stops and eventually, the Division it was supporting will grind to a halt. It can save you from having to go toe to toe with a fully equipped fighting force, especially if it is greater and more powerful than yourself. It is just barking not to have any air and ground defence on such an important asset. It was yet another example of the Army thinking, or maybe not, that they were untouchable and that what we will try to do to the enemy will never ever be done to us.

1600: Orders from top came in that we were all to deploy as a Regiment and go back 80 kilometres from where we have just come from and set a protective screen up for the DAA. We were to start moving No Later Than (NLT) 1700. The CO was mad as hell on hearing that, he said we were now getting palmed off with a job that would effectively take us completely out of the fighting for good while the rest of the Division moved east towards the coast (60 kilometres) to try and catch what was left of the RGF and destroy it. A lot of the guys were not too bothered about the news. The job was virtually over now and his army was on the run. We had destroyed most of his equipment, taken God knows how many POWs and nearly all of Kuwait was back in our hands. Other than the RGF, which now had most of the coalition looking for it, all that was left to do was mopping up operations to clear what little resistance maybe encountered, and that was getting few and far between now. There were no more dug-in main defensive positions, so there would be no more battles, that was for sure. As for the MBTs of the RGF that were out in the open, and assuming that they didn't surrender, then they would conduct manoeuvre warfare so you really did need other MBTs, not CVR (T)s, to take them on. We just needed the good news to get the hell out of this shit-hole once and for all before someone ends up volunteering us for something that will get us killed.

1730: We set off back towards Iraq in the dark, where the DAA was. We thought that the decision to delay everyone for 30 minutes past the NLT 1700 part was to make a point about something. It was the usual route march back; however, everyone was told to remain vigilant though just in case. Two call signs went into ditches on the way back; one casualty was reported to have broken ribs. Other than the burnt-out hulks and old enemy positions that we had encountered days ago, we saw nothing else. There was no fighting to be had at all on route and the radio nets were very quiet. It appeared like it really was all over. We arrived at the DAA at 2358.

Chapter 15
Ceasefire

THURSDAY, 28th FEBRUARY, 1991

Everyone was called together for a brief first thing. We were told we would be staying for a few days and even though there was no enemy threat deemed to be here, which was no doubt why the DAA had no trenches dug etc., the CO wanted us looking like combat troops to show the difference between them and us. All vehicles were to have cam nets up, trenches were to be dug, sentries out etc., the whole nine yards.

After getting the vehicle squared away and cammed up with Beno, the CO went on radio stag whilst he had me set his 9 x 9 tent up, roll his sleeping bag out, make him a brew and something to eat before I then started to dig a few shell scrapes for self-protection. Once finished, AJ and I were required on stag to relieve the CO so he could get his head down. It was now 0400 in the morning. Before he left he told us to pass onto the sentry that he wanted reveille for everyone at 0600. No sleep for us again then!

At 0500 it came across the radio that a ceasefire had been declared and until further notice, there was to be absolutely no unessential movement anywhere by anyone at all. Iraq had apparently agreed to all the UN's resolutions, not that they really had any choice now. Kuwait was now totally sealed off. So far 50,000 Iraqi soldiers had surrendered. All Iraqi troops remaining inside Kuwait had 24 hours in which to surrender, otherwise we were going to start the bombing again and the tanks would go back in. It was only the Iraqi Armoured Corps that were still fighting. They were not too much of a problem really; most of the tanks they had were the old Soviet type, as soon as they saw our tanks, they surrendered. The crews were removed from the tanks and they were then destroyed. It was a direct order from the top to carry that out. They estimated three quarters of all Iraqi tanks were now destroyed or in bits.

I wrote it all in the Int log and passed it on to Adam when he came on stag to relieve me. He remarked that not being allowed to move anywhere would result in just one thing for us lot. We could not after all have the guys sitting about doing nothing now, could we?

Come daylight we touched base with our Regimental guys that were in the DAA. Most already knew that we had been tasked to come back and join them. However, they were not sure if or when they were coming back to join us as nobody had said anything to them. Now we were in the DAA, mail and newspapers started to arrive again. I got four letters. One was from a very ugly and unknown pen pal, who just wanted a soldier to write to her. Why it had come to me I had no idea; I offered it around but had no takers, it went straight into the bin.

At 1020 we received more orders. We were to escort the DAA to a new location within Kuwait; it was about 150 kilometres away, pretty much where we had just come from last night. So much for the order about no vehicle movement whatsoever. It would take about a day to get there given the size of the DAA, there must have been well over 4,000 vehicles in it. We were absolutely amazed they had no protection at all.

A sandstorm started blowing again; we were due another one sooner or later. The guys in Provost troop returned to us and took great delight in telling us that they had had a whale of time being away from RHQ and all the bullshit. They told us that the CRA was very impressed with the Regiment, even more so because we were the first British soldiers to enter Iraq and Kuwait. It was all that the officers were talking about now, who was 'the first' to do this and that. All the guys had mixed feelings about this; some totally agreed and added other things that they thought we should be given credit for because we were the first to accomplish them as well. Some thought that out of everything we had accomplished, being the first into Iraq and Kuwait was not the most impressive. A few, including myself, were not bothered at all about who was first to do anything. Not only would it be fiercely contested and argued by all that had taken part, but this was supposed to be a team effort with coalition partners to get a job done against a common enemy. It was not about bragging rights over one and other. It actually angered me because it was that type of mentality that was to blame for people being unhelpful and why we struggled before and after we arrived out here.

We had a few hours before moving out, so I got all the guns off the wagon to clean. The GPMG barrel was rusty as hell again due to the weather. Once they were all cleaned and replaced, we packed up and filled in all the trenches that we had dug for our long stay here. We were all hoping that A2 would meet back up with us soon so we could get the manpower back to help out. We then started back towards Kuwait with the DAA vehicles. This time, all the DAA vehicles had their headlights on, mainly so no friendly forces opened up on us.

The place was crawling with coalition military now. We drove back through a few of the Iraqi fighting positions again. I think the route was deliberately chosen so guys in the DAA could have a look at things. There were bunkers, tanks, bodies and kit all destroyed just laying everywhere. It was like a turkey shoot had happened, especially since there were no casualties seen from our side. I bet the Iraqis couldn't believe what was thrown against them. They were told we had worse kit than theirs and that it was old and out of date. Then came the air strikes, MLRS, followed by modern MBTs like Challenger and Abrams backed up with APCs like the Warrior; they just got massacred. Int reported that the POW count was now up to 175,000. The dead have not been counted as there were just too many; most were still lying where they had been killed. The war was over, although Iraq was claiming it could still fight. I think that was more face saving than anything else. Kuwait was totally under our control now.

Destroyed Iraqi tank

Destroyed artillery piece

Another destroyed artillery piece

Throughout the night as we were travelling you could see fires burning all over the place in the distance. The small ones were either being put out or were slowly dying out, but some of the oil ones were huge. God knows how they intend to put them out; it was not like we had some trained oil rig firefighters out here.

Oil fields burning in the distance

FRIDAY, 1st MARCH, 1991

As light came up and started to remove the blackness of night, you really got a sense of the whole picture. Enemy battle positions scarred the landscape everywhere that the eye could see. Some bunkers had just been abandoned, even if they had not been touched with any firepower at all. Others had been pounded to pieces. There were dead bodies, ammo, guns and explosives lying everywhere, as if there was little or just no fight put up whatsoever. You had to feel sorry for these people. They probably didn't want to be here, let alone fight, and they were totally misinformed what was coming their way. But on the other hand, they were willing to fight us when they thought we were a weaker nation knowing we had older kit, and had it been true, they would have. After all, they were soldiers under orders just like us lot. All the information building up to this, both military and in the press, was that they had raped Kuwait and done some really shitty things here. It was pure dark ages shit and wasn't exactly what we would call being a soldier or part of your duty. The Iraqi soldiers in Iraq did none of this, so we had little quarrel with them, where possible we just captured them and destroyed their kit as per our orders. The ones in Kuwait, however, where possible we have tried to kill as many as we could before they surrendered; they deserved it given what they have done here.

We eventually arrived at our new location. Once set-up was all complete again, we were volunteered for some bunker clearing. That was where you went in checking for enemy first, then anything of Int value once clear. The golden rule was to always be mindful of booby traps. Not that we were trained in searching for or dealing with them. That role fell to specialist teams in other units who had the correct training and equipment. Every bunker I went into caused the hairs on the back of my neck to stand up. I was absolutely positive there was no enemy inside, but thinking about, and trying to look for where booby traps might be, was a right pain. We just prayed for a bit of luck.

Bunker clearing

There were dead bodies everywhere, both inside and outside the bunkers. The ones inside always gave me a little jump at first sight. I think I was half expecting them to move or something whilst I was looking around the place. I couldn't really explain it, too many horror films as a child, I thought. Most of them looked like plastic dolls to me, even the ones who were burnt to hell. Some were in such positions I wondered how it was possible for a human body to end up like that. I was not sure if that was my mind playing tricks on me, but it was not registering that these were actual dead human beings. I guess I just wasn't thinking about it or if I was, I was blocking the thought from my mind. Some of the guys took pictures, I didn't see the point, what were they going to do with them? Try to come across as being a man by showing other people what a dead human being looks like, or simply brag that was what they had done during the war? I thought it was totally disrespectful. I was just getting on with the task in hand and ensuring I got no nasty surprises that would bite my head off. The last thing I wanted was to get seriously injured checking for bits of paper.

Most of us found no Int at all. Those that did, because the war was over, it was of little significance. The only plus was the fact nobody managed to detonate or find a booby trap. We marked the bunkers that had ammo or explosives in for the Engineers to blow up later on. Fuck touching any of that stuff, you had no idea if it was safe or even booby trapped. I had seen enough films to make me think twice, training or no training. I did, however, see an AK 47 bayonet lying in the open, so after careful examination I took it as a souvenir. That would go nicely with the AK 47 that I already had.

When we got back, I received some more mail, all dated Feb 14th. After reading them, it got me thinking about the things I needed to do when I got back. Firstly, I needed to definitely sort the women in my life out, starting with completely getting away from Silke once and for all, so I didn't end up back with her again. I kept thinking about how to get my car and kit back that was with her. Then there was Lori, I wondered how we were going to get on as I was determined to visit her after this was all over. And, of course, there was Michelle. She wanted to visit me, not sure how that would go down with Lori and how she'd react. I might have to forget that idea.

And then there was the Army and a million and one questions. Did I stay, did I go, did I try and transfer to another unit, would it be different or were all units like the cavalry? If I left, where would I stay and what would I do? I needed a plan, I needed to think of and weigh up all the pros and cons before making a decision rather than just jumping into anything, and then I needed to stick to it and not get talked out of it.

We had a briefing later on after lunch by the RSO. He informed us that now we were settled again and a ceasefire imposed, the CO wanted things back to how it was before the war kicked off. The big tent had reappeared again, and it was to be put up with cam nets, cooks tent, the whole lot. Reveille was to be imposed again, and everyone was to be up, washed and shaved first thing, no excuses at all. As for dress standards, boots were to be cleaned, headdress on and combats looking smart, all the crappy attention to detail again. And, of course, he wanted his Land Cruiser back for him to get out and about in, the latter statement was said as a joke but unfortunately nobody laughed.

So, the war was officially over. Only two dead, a few injured and most people a lot wiser to how the Regiment operated in a war. I was quite sure that after this experience, when we returned home, we would get a lot of guys leaving, and it would not just be from our unit either. I always wondered the reasons why after conflicts the military always got a mass exodus of people. I am quite sure there were a lot of individual reasons, but now having been through this, I could really appreciate and understand why guys would leave, and the sad fact was, it was totally preventable.

Visser and Steve turned up at 1800 with the news we were moving again tomorrow, two kilometres up the road. That went down like a lead balloon with everyone, especially when we all found out it was not a joke and they were not trying to wind us up. The reason given was the place we were moving to was apparently more suitable.

Beno told me the gearbox on the wagon had gone again, he had already spoken to the REME and a new one would be fitted tomorrow. He said to be fair it had done wonders, given what it had been put through these last few days, it didn't exactly have a smooth bedding-in period. I was on stag 1830–2230, I decided to do Mick's as well as I wanted to write a few letters. I was briefed on the handover from Dave, and some of it was in the log, that the CO was off to see the General tomorrow morning. Apparently, the command group couldn't brief the General on exactly what the Regiment had been doing over the last five days, because they didn't know. They had informed him that the reason they were unsure was because the comms had been continually dropping out, so the General now wanted a debrief from the CO. Dave also pointed out that it was both amazing, and scary, that a whole Regiment could be out of comms with its command group for five days and yet they did nothing about it. He added that the CO had also said he was going to ask for the Regiment to do another job rather than everyone sit about until we go home.

SATURDAY, 2nd MARCH, 1991

Either someone had said something to the CO or he had heard the mutterings from the guys, because before he set off to see the General, he explained that the reason that he wanted us to move was because we were far too close to bunkers that had unexploded ordnance inside. So, after we had all finished grub, we packed everything away ready for the move. Due to our gearbox being bust, our wagon stayed where it was. The rest literally moved 500 yards before starting to set it all back up again.

Beno stayed with our wagon and started to prep it ready for the new gearbox to be fitted when it arrived. Steve, Visser and I all walked across the sand to give the others a hand with setting RHQ back up. After six hours, we had managed to move RHQ 500 yards closer to 7 Bde main HQ and were once more situated right next to more bunkers. The guys were not happy!

Once RHQ was up and running again, we returned to our wagon. The REME didn't show until gone 1600. They told us there was no way that they would get it fixed tonight, which was good news because it saved us trying to fit into the RHQ set-up in the dark. I decided to get all the guns down and started to clean them again. I also stripped and cleaned the AK47 as well. I'm determined to get it back home; everyone I know in the troop has got something or other now. The Regiment has already asked if anyone has any kit to hand it in for the Regimental museum when we return. A few officers have also been tasked to go and find certain bits of kit; I think they were talking about vehicles though rather than weapons.

Being only 500 yards away, our crew was still rostered into the stags. The CO returned from seeing the General and on stag we overheard him talking to the 2IC. He told him that we would be leaving here and going home in 35 days. He also said that because he didn't want people sitting around getting bored during that time, he was trying to get the Regiment on the body clearing details (tag and bag). Someone would inform him later on of the decision made.

SUNDAY, 3rd MARCH, 1991

The wagon was fixed in the morning and we drove up to RHQ. Some of the guys had been out and about and had managed to tow a BMP back to the location. Beno was in his element upon seeing it and after a few hours of working on the engine and gearbox, he actually got it up and running again.

Broken down BMP

BMP being repaired and cleaned by the troop outside RHQ

Having done all the training with Red Star Company, we pretty much knew all about the vehicle and how it worked, so most of the troop lent a hand and we soon had it in good working order. Whilst Beno was working on the BMP, Steve and I sorted our wagon and our sleeping area out. We took our time, as we wanted to make it as big and as comfortable as possible, since we had no idea how long we were going to be staying here. We were quite chuffed with the finished product, so I took a few pictures.

Steve and I outside our admin area

Once complete, we got all the kit sorted then decided to get some sunbathing in hidden at the side of the wagon. It was starting to get really hot out here now during the day. Whilst the CO's overheard conversation from last night had been passed around, there was still no official news on the exact date we would be leaving or what we were going to be doing between now and then.

Reports came in of people getting injured and one confirmed dead whilst looking for and picking up kit to take back home. It was always the same during and after a conflict, people went souvenir hunting. Something that you were warned never to do. The main reason being, you always ran the risk of either setting off a booby trap or inadvertently setting off unstable explosives. Some people just didn't think about this, others simply took the chance because they wanted a souvenir to take back home. It would not surprise me if more people were injured or killed before we left here.

Looking around the area you could still see some small and three massive fires burning at night, they must be oil refineries or something to do with it. One on the horizon was absolutely huge and at night it lit the whole sky up orange. It would take ages to get that put out and no doubt require some specialist teams as I couldn't see how the hell you could even get close to it in the first place.

Some of the guys from A2 turned up. With them they brought the container which we had loaded all those months ago and sent back to the docks. I got my box returned with my personal belongings and $395. The pay guys informed us that unlike other nations out here, it looked like we would not be getting war money after all. The government had now stated that it was not keen on the idea at all, despite what they had said when we first arrived out here. It was getting very political; the government was now saying it didn't want us to be seen as mercenaries by paying us to go to war. One of the guys commented that it made no sense, given we already got paid to do what we do; therefore, the logic of us being seen as mercenaries if we accepted a bonus was flawed. The change in stance was more like an excuse not to pay the troops and save money instead. They agreed and told us that on a plus note, they should be able to pay us all some more water tomorrow.

Later on, we had a parade and the CO blew a fit on everyone for sunbathing, stating that we were not on holiday and just because 7 Bde were sunbathing didn't give us the right to do it. As per his last instructions, everyone would wear full uniform at all times, carrying their weapons; nobody was to wear shorts at all. The next person seen disobeying his order would be charged.

MONDAY, 4th MARCH, 1991

On stag midnight until 0230. Nothing was happening at all, so it was really quiet. That gave me the opportunity to catch up and get some letters written in peace.

After breakfast, we were briefed that the General and Tom King (Secretary of State for Defence) were visiting tomorrow; therefore, everyone has been allocated some tasks to do. Beno and I were told to clean the BMP up, especially the inside, as they intended to give the visitors a ride in it. We went across to the REME to get some cleaning fluid and rags so we could get the job done. Whilst we were cleaning it I asked Beno if they had asked him to drive the BMP tomorrow, he replied no and asked why. I explained that during all the other preceding visits RHQ had had, the lower ranks had been shunned away; therefore, I thought this was an interesting dilemma, because I doubted any of the officers in RHQ could drive a BMP.

After lunch, we found out that someone had arranged a baseball game followed by a football match with 22 Signals Regiment who were close by with 7 Bde, so I went up and played in both games. We won both games, which was great, but more importantly, it was just good fun and we all had a laugh. It was brilliant to actually play some sport again and meet up with guys from another Regiment for a chat. Pity there was no beer about for a social get-together afterwards.

A report came in about guys driving around in enemy vehicles and the dangers of doing it unannounced. One of them had been engaged by friendlies for driving close to their positions. It appears that there were still a few itchy trigger fingers about that wanted to chalk up a kill before going home. I wondered how they would feel if they actually ended up killing a friendly; especially given the fact there was a ceasefire on, so there should be a lot more restraint on guys firing now.

No mail today but we did get our water money paid right up until the 15th of this month. Since we have still not received any official news on a date when we were getting out of here, from the water money given it could be inferred that we will be here until at least the 15th as a minimum.

Another soldier got killed today picking something up. It was just not worth it; we were almost home and dry now.

There was a brief later on to inform everyone that orders had come through from Division that nobody from the Regiment was allowed to take back any firearms or ammunition whatsoever. If you had anything at all, you were to hand it in. Our leave when we get back from this is being reduced to two weeks so we can get on with the preparation for the handover, it has been confirmed we are now moving to England in August. The fact we have all been out here, including all the vehicles and equipment, it is going to take a lot of work, involving long days and weekends, to get everything up to the required standard ready for the handover. The news really cheered everyone up no end. Guys moaned stating that after all we have been through, all the effort, not to mention stress and messing the families about before and during this conflict, they could not believe that they would not cut anyone any slack at all. The vehicles and most of the equipment would surely go back by ship again so would take months to arrive. Having three or four weeks off for leave would be of little consequence in the overall bigger picture.

TUESDAY, 5th MARCH, 1991

Up at reveille, it was pissing down. The start of returning the POWs back to Iraq had begun; the control centres were having problems because a lot didn't want to go back with Saddam still in power. They felt they would be punished for not fighting against us. Unfortunately, we had no choice but to send them back.

POWs being processed to go back home

We spent the morning finishing off other last-minute tasks that came our way in preparation for the visit. When the General did visit, we were all told we needed to form up because he wanted to make a speech. We were expecting something like an inspiring speech about our overall contribution, but instead, all he went on about was what we had done during the war. He literally just recounted the facts about our days from forming up, going through the breach, the attack on Objective LEAD, into Kuwait and then to here. The guys were just looking at each other with surprised faces. Besides the fact we were all standing in the rain, none of us really cared. We knew exactly what we had done; we were there. After the speech, he had a quick chat with the CO and some of the officers before leaving shortly afterwards.

Hit the sack at 2030, nothing much else to do in the rain but stand around and wait.

WEDNESDAY, 6th MARCH, 1991

Up at the normal time and had breakfast. Afterwards, we went on a scrounging mission around the area with SSgt Mick (B) to see what kit we could get hold of to make life more comfortable for everyone. Mick was a very friendly and resourceful guy. He was like Arthur Daley: he had his fingers in so many pies and somehow people always seemed to owe him favours. If you wanted something and couldn't get hold of it, the chances were he was the man to see.

Got chatting to some Yanks we bumped into trying to do some exchanges, they told us they were starting to leave for home as of tomorrow. They asked when we were going home, and we said we hadn't got a clue, we had been told nothing from our bosses but we were working on a rumour we'd heard, which currently had us on 34 days from now, but that was not official. We did the usual thing of exchanging kit; they were more than happy to hand over quite a lot of theirs given the fact they were leaving and felt sorry for us that we had no idea when we were going home. We thanked them and wished them a safe flight home before departing towards A2.

I bumped into Robbo at A2 and because the pay people were out and about, I gave him $200 to put into my post book to stop me spending it. We managed to get a few board games, a TV, a video recorder and some videos from HQ Squadron. When we got back to RHQ, we set the TV and video up in the big tent, and then watched *Pretty Woman*. Not really a film of my choice but seeing a TV after so long was a sight for sore eyes. It's amazing all the stuff in your life that you actually take for granted because either you see or use it on a daily basis and so therefore, don't even think twice about it. It was only when you were completely without those things for quite some time that you could appreciate them in life when they reappeared. Whilst we were all watching the film, the 2IC came in. He stood for a while and then before leaving mentioned the fact he didn't like the idea of a TV and a video being here in the tent. Everyone looked at Mick, he just smiled and said carry on it will be fine, he would sort it.

After the film had finished, I went and washed my clothes and hung them up; it didn't take them too long to dry given the heat.

Wrote some more letters and received some more in the mail run. Now the mail system was up and running again, it seemed as fast as I was writing letters I was getting more. Served me right for having so many people to write to I guess. Silke wrote, she was moaning about the bank taking my bank card off her when she tried to use it. I couldn't believe she actually tried to use it in the first place, it's not like we had a joint account!

After dinner, we went back to the tent to see if anyone was putting another film on. Everyone decided that given the comment made earlier by the 2IC, it was probably not a good idea until we got the all clear from the RSO. We decided to vacate the tent and retire to our admin area, where we played cards out of sight. I lost some money this time but wasn't too fussed about it as it was only riyals. As long as I had money in the bank that was all that mattered, this was just pocket money out here.

Saudi riyals

Chapter 16
R Days

THURSDAY, 7ᵗʰ MARCH, 1991

Because we were co-located close to 7 Bde HQ, they insisted that we took a turn in cleaning their makeshift toilets out, even though we were using our own ones that we had built. Of all the people in the troop, Dave C and I were volunteered to do the shit burning fatigue first thing. It was no doubt a punishment for something we had yet to be debriefed about. It was OK so long as you were not squeamish; besides, someone had to do it, so I just focused on it being our turn and got on with it. It was a simple case of dragging the ten shit bins, which were cut-down oil drums, out from under the makeshift cubicles, pouring some petrol into them, and then setting them alight. Golden rules, one, never pour too much petrol into them as they could explode, burning you, or worse still, covering you in shit. And two, always make sure you stand upwind of the things: shit stinks. Standing there watching them burn, it reminded me of films I had seen of the US in Vietnam; only difference, we had no weed.

When we got back, we found the guys all really depressed, then we noticed the TV and video were gone. Dave with his dry sense of humour commented, "Well, that certainly didn't take long." I went to our tent to have a strip wash before playing cards and a game of Risk, a board game we had procured. We had built the tent large enough that we had an area for admin as well as a sleeping area. The guys all kept coming around, as it was somewhere to hide out of the way. It was kind of nice that they came to our tent feeling they could relax and chat. It also allowed me to carry on getting information for this diary and the guys could read it in safety without someone getting upset. After listening to the guys moaning about the TV and video, we decided we would pay Robbo a visit and see if we could get them back and then somehow set them up in our tent.

On stag at 1830, a message came through from Division HQ. Today was now being called **R DAY.** It did not explain what the 'R' stood for and on asking around none of us actually knew. We thought maybe it stood for **R**eturn home day, since it was the start of the countdown to going home. It also stated it would be 36 days until everyone (British) was out of here, assuming all went to plan. Someone immediately pointed out there was the flaw straightaway, we had already experienced their 'so-called plans' out here when it came to moving people about. The message went on to say that all attached personnel were to leave tomorrow and return to their parent units. The German Government has stated that they did not want any British soldiers returning to Germany without having had leave in the UK first. Guess they were worried about us getting drunk, letting off steam and smashing the place up.

I received a parcel off a pen pal called Carole. She had put all sorts of things in it, really nice of her and it cheered me up that she had gone to all the effort of doing this. I wrote a few letters, including a big thank you one to Carole for sending the parcel.

FRIDAY, 8th MARCH, 1991

R+1 (-35 days)

Divisional HQ has now asked for all the spoils of war that should have been collected by the Regiments to be sent directly to them. They wanted to centralise it all before shipping it back. Each unit has been allocated a limit and told exactly what they could and couldn't take back home. We were very sure that once it was all collected, it would have other limits applied and then reallocated to where they thought it should best go.

The Regiment, as always, had gone totally overboard. Each Squadron had been out collecting. So far, we had a T59 (Tank), a BMP1 (APC), a D30 (Artillery piece), a SA9 Gaskin (Air defence) with missiles, a ZSU 23/4 (Air defence), and loads of small arms, not to mention ammo and mines, both anti-tank and anti-personnel. I will be amazed if we are somehow allowed to get those live missiles back home. It would, on the other hand, be very useful to take it all back purely for training purposes. Instead of us having to go and train with the kit Red Star Company has in Southern Germany, we could set up and have our very own Company for all British units to utilise. It made absolute total sense to utilise this kit and the opportunity, and that's exactly why it will never happen.

Captured SA9, minus missiles, with some of the lads from C Squadron

Captured T59 by B Squadron

Inspecting a captured ZSU 23/4 air defence vehicle

Baz (C) and Bunny (W) sitting in the back of a BMP 1

The dreaded mobile Scud launchers

Captured kit, starting to stack up

We said farewell to the US and RAF guys who had been attached to us. The artillery guys were staying for one more day before returning to their parent unit. The RSO said he wanted all the secure radio kit to be handed back in before it has a chance to be lost. OB would remain on secure comms for the time being, but there was no need for everyone else to be on it, given we were all together now. He wanted it to happen by no later than dinner time. I went to our wagon and erased all the crypto data from the bricks and the guns. I then checked to ensure it had happened, and when I was absolutely sure they were all empty, I took them all to the collection point at the back of OB, where Geordie was taking them in. He signed them all off me and placed them into the safe. That was one major big burden off my shoulders now.

C Squadron challenged RHQ to a game of baseball, so that afternoon we took the challenge up. It was great just to meet back up and have a chat with the guys again from my old Squadron. After the game, it was back to the tent for a quick body wash. Robbo came by later and gave me my post book back; I now have £239 in it, not bad for just being out here. We had a few games of risk but soon ended up playing cards again. Mick (B) had started to join in on our card games and he quickly introduced us to a new betting game that was very tempting, simple to play and very addictive. The dealer places a pile of money (called a pot) onto the table and then deals you three cards, which you can look at. Each player then bets on the chance of beating the next card turned over from the pack, it has to be in the same suit. Whatever the bet size, if you lose, it is added to the pot, if you win, you take that amount out of the pot. This is done twice; the third time the cards are dealt face down and the top card is now turned over to view.

Clearly, if a two of something is turned over, you only need to have a card in that suit and you win, therefore the temptation to bet the whole pot is very high. The betting started to get stupid now with over-confidence and Nicko lost over 1000 riyals (about £150). Thank God most of mine was in my post book, so I couldn't touch it.

Wrote another letter to Lori and Sarah (another pen pal). Mail arrived but I received none, there was still no sign of any of the photos I had sent off to my sister, she did tell me that once they were developed she would send them out to me. There were rumours going around that inbound photos were being inspected and those deemed inappropriate were being removed; this was further fuelled by letters and parcels reaching people that had already been opened up. None of this was being confirmed or commented upon from our bosses but we had been told right from the off that any mail suspected of containing alcohol would be opened and searched. Anything found would be removed and if it was later proven that the individual had requested it, they would be charged. I didn't think any of the photos I had taken were inappropriate, but there again, I wasn't making that judgement call. Went to bed at 2200 as I was on stag in the morning again.

SATURDAY, 9th MARCH, 1991

R+2 (-34 days)

On stag 0230–0430. Read in the logs that the US was going to leave 25,000 troops here and they were asking the Brits to also leave some. Divisional HQ has planned to hold a discussion on R+10 (17th) as to whether 4 Bde would stay or not, the logic being 7 Bde had been out here longer than 4 Bde. They would let everyone know on R+21 (28th). Why it was going to take 11 days to pass the message was not explained. If the decision was a yes, then the whole of 4 Bde would all be moving to where we were located now. Reading between the lines, that must mean the Regiment would not be moving from here then until the decision was made. However, it also stated further on in the log that low loaders were booked to transport all our vehicles to somewhere on the 17th, the destination was not mentioned. Mixed messages as usual. Unfortunately, the job of the radio operator was just to record the message and not to ask questions or try to decipher what the hell they meant. I guess if the low loaders show up, we are moving and if they don't, we are staying.

Another field hospital packed up today and left for Saudi. There was probably a very good reason why units came and went as they did, but it was never explained to us. It really got guys' backs up because all that the combat troops saw was the REMFs turn up late, have a relaxed way of life (slipper city as we called it), not get involved in any fighting at all, and then be the first to get the hell out of the place, having been awarded exactly the same medal. REMFs was the piss-take name attached and stood for Rear Echelon Mother Fuckers.

The RSO was changed over again, and once more we were not given a reason why. We now had Captain N-E. He was another really good bloke that was down to earth, well-liked and respected by the guys. The kind of officer you'd do anything for. First thing he did once he was settled in was to give us all an individual career interview. He told me I would be staying in the troop for a long time yet given my performance out here. They were going to bid for me to do the Regimental Signals Instructors (RSI) and the First Aid Instructors (FAI) courses when we get back to Germany. When he asked how I felt about what he had just told me, I replied that I would believe it when I saw it since you had to be a full Corporal even to apply to get on the RSI course in the first place. That was what had prevented me from doing the course these last three years. It had not been because I was not good enough to do the course, simply that I was not at the required rank. Also, we are told you require three good reports in a row for promotion. On my last yearly report, not only did it not recommend me for promotion, but it placed me nowhere near good enough simply because I was working in the gym and not on the tank park. That was current Regimental policy, so whilst I was disappointed and did not necessarily agree with it, the report did not come as a surprise to me. He just smiled and said to wait out.

SUNDAY, 10th MARCH, 1991

R+3 (-33 days)

Everyone was up and told to parade at 0730 for Physical Training (PT) dressed in combats. Despite half the troop not being on parade, the 2IC stated that we were all going to be doing it every morning from now on until we leave. We then went for a two-mile run. Although I absolutely love PT, I was not sure that filling your lungs first thing each morning with the fumes from burning oil was going to be good for your health.

When we returned, we found out that five of the guys had departed us to be flown out this morning: the Ops Officer, the old RSO, Mr Stokes, Podge (G) and Russ one of the cooks. Either that was a last-minute thing or they actually knew they were departing but said nothing to anyone about it. It also explained why the RSO had been replaced yesterday without any explanation. Seems things were actually starting to happen then with regards to us leaving.

Guys from the QMs tipped up. They collected all the leftover BATS, NAPS, Combo pens and morphine injections. That was all the chemical warfare stuff handed back in now. They also issued us with our desert boots and scarfs, which had finally arrived; only in the Army could that happen! They brought mail with them and I got three parcels, one each from Lori, Michelle and another pen pal.

The RSO gave us an O group later since a few of the guys had given him grief for not telling us anything that was going on. It wasn't about guys venting or deliberately trying to give him grief, it was more like he was the only officer in RHQ who would listen and actually do something about what we said. He told us it was official now and had been confirmed: the Regiment was moving to England in June. It would all be complete and the rear party would leave Germany in August. Flight dates out of here for the Regiment were between the 26th and 31st of this month. As always, those dates were subject to change. The low loaders were still booked for the 17th to take the vehicles and all the equipment back to the docks; nobody yet was saying anything about what would happen to us lot once they went. That was currently being chased up, once he knew he would pass the information on straightaway.

After the O group, we asked him if he would have a word with the CO about the TV and video. We played on the point that not only was it good for morale, but it kept people a little pre-occupied, not to mention out of the way. He went and had a word. On return he told us all that the CO had agreed we could have them back, but on condition that they were not to use any of the CV's power, and they could only be used after 1800. We thought this was his attempt at trying to discourage us from getting them back because we had no other means of wiring them up to electricity. I told the guys I would ask around when we next went to A2. There was bound to be some REME or signals blokes who could help us out, either by wiring them up directly or coming up with a solution to the problem.

A Regimental manning conference took place later on in the tent. Dave and I just happened to be on stag at the same time and overheard them saying I was staying in the gym for the handover/takeover to sort things out. Great news for me really as that would give me some time to get fit with selection for 22 in my mind; I could also get on some courses that I had in mind to help me out.

MONDAY, 11th MARCH, 1991

R+4 (-32 days)

On stag 0230–0430. I was slowly turning into a nocturnal animal. Still, days to go out here were getting shorter; there was light at the end of the tunnel. PT at 0730 turned out to be yet another run. Steve and I approached the 2IC afterwards and brought the subject up of doing something else like sport to get the guys fit, if that indeed was the aim of doing all the PT in the mornings. It was firmly rejected; he said most of the officers did not want sport being played. Their argument, which he agreed with, was that sport was for fun not fitness, running was how you got soldiers fit. Steve asked if it was fact or simply the direction from the CO, because given his qualifications he could prove that argument was totally flawed and added that all fitness if done correctly, should be fun. No matter what we said, it was ignored. So, running it was.

On a brief, we were informed that RHQ was going to host an inter Squadron *It's a Knockout* competition based on the TV series. It was going to be held in three days' time, and Mick (B) had been tasked with the overall organisation of it. Given Steve's background and my qualifications, we were tasked with going around canvassing ideas and players from other units near to us. After discussing some ideas, we drew up some plans of things and then got a few of the guys in the troop to start to build them. We asked them for their thoughts and ideas but got the distinct impression they would rather just not do it. They just wanted to be left alone as this just seemed like another whole pile of work. We explained that not only was it something to do but it would be fun if we had anything to do with it. Only downside, no beer or women…yet. Mick (B) said he had a plan to ask the Navy guys to fly down south and find some.

206

News got around about the flights. 50 guys were to leave today as part of the advance party; they would be flying out tomorrow. AJ, Dava and Nico have been selected from RHQ to go. The main party would be leaving this location on the 20th and would be flying out of the country on the 25th. It was great news because that's nearly three weeks earlier than we were expecting. It never ceased to amaze me how things changed so fast in the Army. I wondered if it was just down to poor planning or poor communications right from the start. The bad news was, all the cooks and facilities were going with the advance party tomorrow morning. We were to start cooking from the vehicles from now on until they get loaded up on the 17th; after that, nobody has a clue how we are getting fed.

A few of us managed to get away from RHQ for a while and up to A2. We used the excuse we were canvassing for the *It's a Knockout* competition. I found Robbo and told him of our TV and video problem. He said he would ask around for us as a few people owed him some favours, he was confident he could get it sorted. We bumped into a few of the guys from A Squadron and had a chat. One of the guys told them about my diary, so they told us all about their exploits hoping for me to write them all into it. It sounded like a lot more went on than what was actually reported to RHQ, so much so that there was no way I could write it all into here. They told us about another incident where artillery was used on guys who had surrendered, again believed to be another late call, but the sceptics were out. It was always the same when someone else heard something; they immediately jumped to conclusions and damned the guy first without having heard all the evidence. For all we knew, it never happened like that at all. The one fact that was certain was that once the rockets had been fired, there was absolutely nothing you could do to stop them. Given that most people calling in a fire missions would have done it from distance, you don't even have the opportunity to warn or tell them to get down. In the future, they may make guided ammo that you can steer off a target, or ammo that you can self-detonate on route should the need arise, but until then, unfortunately it was what it was.

They said an officer from their Squadron was up in front of the CO tomorrow for threatening to write to the papers and tell them exactly what went on out here, not what the press had been told by the Regiment. He apparently was totally sickened by the artillery coming down on Iraqis who had surrendered and that was the last straw for him. Guys within their Squadron all had varied opinions and something to say about his actions. They went from total support to downright loathing. I guess this was always the issues with war, both before, during and after. You would get those for it and those against it, and people would view it and events within it differently. It was like a car crash being witnessed by ten people. They would all have seen the same thing happen, but the stories they told could then all be different. Why? Because depending on how their own mind worked and what was important to them at the time, it would influence their interpretation of events. I guess some people morally felt that the truth was more important than trying to cover things up, even if it cost them their Army career, and believe you me, it would. I very much doubted anything would come of this once the CO had had a chat with him and none of it would be recorded.

When we returned to RHQ, the RSO informed us that the changes from the manning conference held yesterday were now official and have been sent out to the Squadrons for everyone to be told. I was staying in Command troop for two years minimum, and to keep me happy they were allowing me to stay in the gym for that period. He told us all as a heads up, but it sounded more like a warning not to moan or complain, that D Squadron were off to Cyprus for a six-month tour when we got back to the UK. That meant guard duties for guarding the camp in Wimbish would be thick and fast for the rest of us left behind. It roughly worked out that we would be doing a minimum of one a week.

On a good note, the CO wanted a cook to stay and keep central cooking going within RHQ. So, whilst we were all extremely pleased about that decision because it saved us all a lot of effort and heartache, some poor cook just had his flight pulled from under him and was now returning back home later than expected. Whoever it was, unfortunately, wasn't the only one receiving that bad news, the three guys from our troop who were also on the advance party had just returned. They had been taken off it for someone else to take their places. Being unimpressed was probably an understatement of how these guys felt right now. We cheered them up by taking the piss, it's what soldiers do best.

Now that I knew what the Regiment intended for me, I could start making my own plans work. First things first, I needed to get much fitter, so I went for a three-mile run with a 30-pound bergen on (military term for a rucksack). Felt quite good really considering it was across sand, might be all the frustration and stress being burnt off. The aim now was to try and religiously do it on a daily basis and slowly build it up.

After washing my kit, we decided to play some cards in our admin tent before calling it a night and hitting the sack.

Chapter 17
The Burning Oil Fields

TUESDAY, 12th MARCH, 1991

R+5 (-31 days)

Got up early and went for my run with the bergen on again. Doing all those early stags have made getting up really easy to do now. When I got back, the RSM had a word with me. He said whilst it was great that I was doing it, I still needed to attend and do the PT in the mornings like everyone else; it was a parade after all. Either I went a lot earlier or I did my training after the PT, it was my choice. It was a dilemma because the bergen running was going to be far more beneficial for me and my training than the PT; I didn't understand why the rules were so hard and fast. For example, why couldn't I attend the parade then do my own PT? It wasn't as if I was trying to skive out of doing a bit of PT, what I was doing happened to be about ten times harder. I spoke to Steve to see if he could have a word and try to get a compromise, he tried and failed. His advice was to use the PT as a warm-up session and then do a bergen run afterwards. It was sound advice and any other time I would have taken it up, assuming I had the luxury of being allowed to (time off work etc.). The problem I was facing was that I needed to do PT to get fitter, but I was concerned about the air quality I was doing it in. The shorter I could keep the amount of time I spent deep breathing due to PT, the better. I needed to come up with a plan.

There was a rumour going around that the advance party had been delayed by 24 hours and would now fly from here on the 14th and then out of Al Jubail on the 18th. We wondered if the same fate awaited the rest of us with regards to flights.

Visser and I went and picked up a few Engineers, who had kindly offered to help us out with the setting up of the *It's a Knockout* competition up. They brought some heavy equipment along to build a few berms so people could sit and watch the games, and dig some ditches that we required for the individual events. Most of the guys were now working on the different games/ideas, having been sold on the idea that it would be fun. We were trying to come up with as many different ideas as possible given the resources available out here. The major stumbling block was water. We needed lots of it and not only was it in short supply, but there was the problem of how to get it here. The Engineers again offered to get on the case and see if they could assist.

All around us the sky was now pitch black, almost like it was going to rain, but they were not rain clouds; it was the smoke from the burning oil fields. This cannot be good for your health and yet there is no advice coming from the top and none of the bosses will say anything, not even about the fact the 2IC wants everyone running first thing each morning. A lot of us now have flu-like symptoms: runny noses with headaches and bodies aching all over. Being a qualified medic, I knew it wasn't flu or symptoms of fatigue, not given the numbers that were all complaining of the same symptoms in such as a short period of time. All my paracetamol was depleted and it had not helped either. As an educated guess, I would say it was being caused by breathing this polluted air in.

Like a few others in the troop, I have started to produce some nice big black slimy bogies from my nose just lately. It was kind of alarming and I was hoping and praying that this was my nose working correctly and the shit was not going into my lungs. I have had enough crap put into my body already since being out here. From now on, when I go running, it will be with a handkerchief around my face to try and help reduce it.

Oil fields still burning away all around us

Every direction you look oil fires burning away

We were all told to stop doing the events for the competition for a while because we have more visits coming up and as before RHQ needs to be immaculate for them. I never knew the Army had so many Brigadiers out here, especially considering there were only two Brigades out here. We spent a few hours titivating the set-up before being released to carry on preparing the events.

Thick black smoke in the sky

By the end of the day, we had managed to get most of the stuff completed for the competition; we could finish the rest off tomorrow. Robbo tipped up, and with him he brought the TV, video and a few guys from the Royal Signals. We set it all back up in the big tent whilst the signal guys wired in some electricity from an Iraqi generator that they had brought with them for us to have. Robbo had also brought some whisky with him for us to share. His mum had put it in a shampoo bottle to try and prevent it from being intercepted and had sent it in a parcel. I didn't even like whisky; mind you, this tasted more like *shampoo,* not whisky. His mum, bless her, either needed to have washed it out more, or used a different bottle, because it was simply just the wrong choice of bottle to use with whisky. Since it was the first drop of alcohol we had in a long time, we drank it anyway. I was sure my insides would pay for it later on. He told me that from higher they were looking for people to give medals to. Each unit was to nominate a few guys and write citations up. He was wondering if we had wind of it and if we knew who had been selected since this was passed a few days ago to all the COs. I told him nobody had heard or mentioned anything about it at all, but now that he had, he had me intrigued. I would dig around and see what people said. We had the competition in two days' time so we would meet loads of the guys, I could ask about then.

WEDNESDAY, 13th MARCH, 1991

R+6 (-30 days)

On stag 0430–0630. The Divisional radio net had now closed down, no doubt in preparation to go home on the advance party. So, all that was left to do now on stag was to listen to the Squadron radio nets, and these were really quiet since nothing was going on. It gave me a chance to write some more letters and the diary.

After breakfast, we finished off most of the stands and games for the competition. The Engineers turned out a blinder and water arrived in a big truck, so all the dug ditches got filled with it. We had lined the bottoms of most of the ditches with anything we could get our hands on to stop it draining into the sand. Content with it not draining away, we were all pleased that this was now going to be a really good laugh. Once we were happy that all the stands looked complete, Mick (B) said we needed someone to do a run through of them all to ensure they worked. We used a few, shall we just say, less fit and sport-orientated guys to ensure they were both challenging and above all else, fun. We were fairly happy that most stood up to the test. Some needed a few modifications, adjustments and rebuilds, but above all else, the guys who did the run through were able to complete the events and they said they really enjoyed them and had fun, which was our ultimate main aim.

Because the top lot had had no involvement in the designing, organising or building of the competition, after lunch they wanted to see another run through so they could give their input. Once that was done and they had left, most of the games were to be changed and altered again, quite simply because they could be.

Whilst it annoyed the guys to hell, given all the hard work and effort that had been put in to get it to this stage, it was nothing new, and we were totally expecting it to happen, because it always happened. Quite a few of the changes that were requested Mick decided to ignore as he felt it would remove the fun element out of it, but the major ones we had to do. Hopefully, it would all work out fine and would still be a good laugh for everyone on the day. It was after all, a hell of a lot of work and graft put in by us lot for what was going to be just a few hours' worth of fun for everyone else.

A sandstorm started to blow again, missed those little gits. It might just get rid of some of the crap in the air, that or mix it all up. It absolutely stank of burning oil now and was getting worse each day. I have started wearing a rag around my nose and mouth, especially when doing anything physical. I had been told to take it off by three different people today whilst building some of the events. Each time when I explained why I was wearing it, I was told completely different things back. Firstly, that I didn't know what I was talking about and to remove it. Another said he didn't care if it was bad for your health, it was not soldier-like, therefore remove it. And lastly, I was allowed to wear it, but only when doing PT and that was it. I am sure it won't be the last I hear about it either.

I received two parcels today; one was off my sister who had sent lots of foodstuff including spices and flavourings. I gave it all to the cook. I was sure he would find it useful, and I would rather it benefit all than just myself.

I was thinking of stopping writing this diary now that the war was over but decided against it after reading back over these last few days. I think this will enlighten people to what really actually goes on in a war, rightly or wrongly. I have tried to capture what was going on around us and how people felt and acted, all the small details that play a massive part for those individuals involved but that you never see in a film or read about in a book. History, certainly military history, will either not record or will alter most of the things that I have written about in here for various reasons, the main one being to protect and/or enhance the reputation of the British Army. Because of that, I will keep writing until we leave here.

Time felt like it was really dragging now; I guess it was because we had gone from flat out working before and during the war, to now really struggling to find constructive things to do. What was also probably not helping was everyone knew we were going home soon and just wanted to get out of here now. It was all that the guys were talking or thinking about.

Before hitting the sack, we had a brief. The advance party leave tomorrow. Once they have gone, we can start to pack away things that we don't use and add to the oil smoke-filled air by burning all the maps, traces, papers, logs and records, etc. Nothing was coming back with us, and it was not to remain because it was classified, some even secret. We had to ensure it was destroyed, so burying it was out of the question. My diary was mentioned with a strong 'suggestion' that it also end up on the burn pile. I chose to ignore the comment.

Another Brigadier, TV and BFBS (British Forces Broadcasting Services) are coming to visit us tomorrow, so everyone is to watch what they are saying and doing. They believe the media is following and filming the Brigadier for some sort of documentary and not coming just to see our Regiment.

THURSDAY, 14th MARCH, 1991

R+7 (-29 days)

It's a Knockout competition:

Up at 0630 and after grub we finished off all the tasks, once that was done we built the ladies' toilets. We had some good Int that women were going to turn up courtesy of our Royal Navy helicopter friends.

The sandstorm had died out last night, and it appeared to have removed all the black clouds that were over us. Whilst you could still smell oil in the air, it was not as bad as yesterday, and the sun was coming up so it looked like it was going to be a good day for the competition. The advance party left first thing, taking the Int Officer, Adjutant, RSM and his driver. We took the piss saying they had taken the places of AJ, Dava and Nico just to try and wind them up.

News reached us that none of the press or high-ranking officials were turning up now, so everyone could relax. It was a pity about the press; it would have been good for them to see what we could produce in the middle of nowhere given a few squaddies and some willingness to enjoy ourselves. It was that ability of the British soldier to get almost anything done, anywhere, anytime with absolutely nothing, that made us who we are.

Teams from all the Squadrons and units nearby turned up all eager and keen to have a go. There were nine events in all, including a mascot makeshift game and a singing competition. Most required a team of at least six to compete in it and each of our Squadrons had to enter a ladies' team. Needless to say, we didn't have women in our Regiment, so it was up to the guys to use their imagination.

The events:

We had managed to get hold of an Iraqi air defence gun. It was one that required two guys to sit and operate it to rotate the guns through 360 degrees. The REME had welded a seat onto the end of the guns. The idea was a team had three guys on this and three guys around it. The guys positioned around the gun were blindfolded and had to throw potatoes and fruit towards the team member sitting on the chair. His job was to try and catch the stuff in a pan as he was being rotated around by the other two guys operating the gun. The crowd could help or hinder by directing the blindfolded guys with their throwing and picking up of fallen stuff, or by putting them off with makeshift water bombs we had created from cutting foam up into large pieces and placing them into nearby barrels full of water.

Silly walk: A straightforward race that involved two people at a time, but they were back-to-back on planks of wood. We had got hold of some planks of wood and nailed some NBC boots to them. It required a lot of skill and co-ordination to race the very small distance set across a few obstacles, and of course the sand.

Assault course: A mini assault course was set up but to make it harder, all participants were wrapped in 10-inch foam from head to foot so they could not see where they were going. They had to be directed by other team mates.

Waiter dash/piggy back race: Only to make it harder, the guy doing the carrying had to wear his gas mask to restrict his view (and his breathing). The guy being carried had to carry fruit on a tray; each piece had a time penalty if it failed to arrive at the finish line. The crowd were encouraged to use the water bombs to knock it all off.

Walk the plank: Set over a very large ditch filled with water. The team had to get across the plank to the other side, retrieve a piece of kit and bring it back. A large swinging sand bag was attached to a crane, which the opposition could use to knock them off as they ran the plank. Everyone else had water bombs.

Slippery walk: This was set on a large piece of NBC CALM (plastic sheet) that was continually kept wet with flowing water and washing up liquid. Makeshift elastic bands had been made from tyre inner tubes and attached to a vehicle; the other end went around the contestants. The idea was to try and take a bucket full of water and empty it into a barrel positioned at the other end of the CALM, return and then go again. The team which had collected the most water by the end of a set time was the winner. Again, the crowd had water bombs.

Grab an apple: A straightforward relay, through a water-filled ditch, then a final sprint to a barrel at the end. The barrel was only half filled with water and completely dug into the ground. You were not allowed to use your hands so you practically had to get upside down into it to retrieve an apple. Grab an apple, back through the ditch and the next team member goes.

The singing was straightforward. The team just had to sing a song of their own choice for at least three minutes and they could get as many other Squadron members as they liked to join in. Points would be awarded for various things, such as loudness, having female singers (members of the ladies' team) and the funnier it was the more points you got awarded.

We nearly thought the women from the hospital were never going to show, but eventually, a Sea King helicopter landed. The ladies appeared to a rather load cheer. They were invited to take part and after getting soaked by the guys with the water bombs, they decided to join in on the grab an apple game. This really cheered everyone up.

I personally thought the whole thing went really well, even though RHQ never got to participate ourselves due to having to run the competition. Nobody got hurt, which was amazing considering the effort (enthusiasm) being put in by some people. And as for the women turning up…wow. They were really good sports by joining in and without a doubt they were the highlight of the competition.

Video – It's a Knockout Competition:
https://www.youtube.com/watch?v=5q9vHNoKqvc

During the competition, I bumped into loads of mates again. It was really great to not only see them again, but to have a chat and catch up in such a relaxing atmosphere. At the end of the day, we had all just come out the other side of a war in one piece. Whilst it will no doubt go down in the history books as a short war with all the stress and fear being forgotten, nobody at the beginning of all this could have predicted that it would turn out like this. I was told quite a few more stories for my diary. Of the many things we chatted about, I asked about the rumour I had heard about medals going to be given out and that they were looking for nominations. Some did not know anything at all about it, but others not only knew about the rumour but they actually knew who had been nominated in their Squadron and why. Quite a few people were not happy, and this was what had prompted the rumour to spread. Reasons varied from simply jealousy to people feeling that other individuals were far more deserving than those that had been selected. Other people were not happy with the actual stories that had been written, because they felt they had either been over exaggerated/embellished or simply just made up. It sparked some interesting and heated debates about the whole medal issue thing.

The competition finished at 1700. The women had to depart to mixed booing and cheering off the guys. Whilst our officers went for a chat, we set about clearing it all up. Anything that could be burnt was put into one big pit and set alight. Given everything else that was burning about the place, nobody batted an eyelid. All the metal stuff we just put into another pile and left. The berms and trenches were also just left, the water would eventually evaporate and the sand would fill the holes in.

Had dinner then went and watched some vids in the tent; it had been a very long, hard day for us lot. No mail again today.

We got told later on that we might have to move location on the 16th. The Artillery wanted to conduct some live firings and of all the entire desert out here, they have chosen a template right by us. In case they were not quite as accurate as we would like, it had been decided we would move if they went ahead and fired.

FRIDAY, 15th MARCH, 1991

R+8 (-28 days)

On stag 0400–0600, afterwards there was no point going to bed as we were all up for PT at 0730. On parade, the guys were moaning about the fact they couldn't believe we did not get a lie in after all the hard work done by the blokes yesterday to ensure the Regiment had a brilliant time. Deliberately ensuring it was loud enough to be heard made no odds because it was simply just ignored.

PT was a slow run again, just short of four-miles this time. I decided to wear my bergen rather than do this then go for another run afterwards. The 2IC made a comment about the silly rag on my face and called me an impetuous fool for doing PT with my bergen on. Not sure what that was about or even what it implied. I was going to say something back to him about him insisting on us all running in this shitty air quality, and then having the neck to have a go at me for wearing a rag over my face. But I thought better of it. It started to rain just as we finished.

After PT, we decided to rebuild our tent because it was starting to rain and the tent was already showing signs of collapse from the storm the other day. A truck loaded with parcels turned up, they were placed in the big tent and we were encouraged to have a few each. We had that many now we didn't know what to do with them and guys were refusing to open them. Apparently, parcels had been arriving since we got out here but were only going to people in the rear echelons, before and during the actual fighting. Someone now thought we should get extra parcels because we had missed out over that period. No letters arrived, which was a bit disappointing.

1500 and it was still raining. Weather was all to cock just lately. I think weather history had been made since we have been here, that or it had always been misreported in the past. One of my mates said it was God just being annoyed with us all and wanting us to stop. I wondered if it was just Mother Nature's way of telling us all to pack it in wrecking the landscape, killing the animals, etc.

We had another O group before dinner. We were told that when we eventually leave here, we would be flying back to Germany. We would spend 48 hours in camp before going on leave, and that was only to sort admin out. Seemed the push from the German government was having an impact. The plan was still for the Regiment to leave here on the 20th. There was no news of any changes yet, but we were all to be prepared to be royally fucked about 20th/21st during our move as it was totally unclear on exactly how we were going to be moved.

Due to it still raining, we decided to play some more cards in our admin tent until it went past 1900, then we all went into the main one and watched a video (*Cocktail*). The CO came in, had a word with the RSO and then left. The RSO then told us to turn the video off and to completely tidy the main tent up, including giving it a really good sweep out. Once done he advised us not to turn it back on again but to find something else to do tonight. His pleading look said it all so most of the guys headed back to our tent to play some more cards.

I was on stag again at 2200 so just pottered about finding crap to do to keep me occupied until then. To add to the rain, a storm started up when I was on stag and it was growing in strength. The force of the wind was physically shaking the wagon; I was glad we had decided to rebuild the tent this morning.

SATURDAY, 16th MARCH, 1991

R+9 (-27 days)

Up at 0715 for PT and it was still raining. Completely out of the blue, Steve decided to run a circuit training session instead of doing a run. He was not his usual calm mannered self and really beasted everyone, ensuring they were putting maximum effort in all the time and getting a sweat on. It made a nice change from a boring run that was for sure. I asked him afterwards in our tent what had prompted the change, he replied that he wanted to make a point and prove running was not everything when it came to PT, and that was all he wanted to say on the matter. He clearly was still pissed off about something and given his placid nature, it must have been really bad to have got to him.

Received a letter from Lori dated the 7th. Seems things were backlogged due to the REMFs leaving the place. WO2 Paul C turned up at RHQ, and he told us that he was going to run a marathon out here in aid of the guys who had died from our unit. He was coming around getting sponsorship; everyone so far has donated at least 25 riyals or more, which was really great to see. We all chipped in. It was a sad reminder of the loss of Sgt D and L/Cpl E.

The rain stopped which was great, but no sooner had it stopped than a sandstorm started to blow again, visibility quickly dropped to less than ten feet. At least now I could wear a scarf around my face without incurring anyone's wrath.

We spent most of the day collecting and piling kit together before it was taken off us by members of the QMs staff. Hopefully, the ammo would go soon as we still had loads of it left. Whilst collecting the kit they told/warned us that bottled water would no longer be arriving, so once we had drunk what we had, that was it. In other words, start watching what you were drinking. This news immediately sparked anger off with the guys, and they vented it at the QM blokes. Comments were made such as: "Talk about another brilliant piece of planning, someone must have known about this ages ago," and "Why was this information not passed sooner, so people could stock up and be prepared?" If we didn't leave in five days' time, we were screwed because some of the crews only had enough water to last them for two days. The reason for that was because they believed we would be getting a restock as per our last replen instructions. The QM guys said they would see what they could do but couldn't promise anything as others were in exactly the same boat. This comment didn't help the situation and resulted in more anger being directed at them. It just highlighted what the guys were trying to say, as far as they were concerned it was the fault of the QM guys, who should have sorted this out much earlier. I told the guys I had nine boxes of the stuff on top of my vehicle and 60 bottles inside (hoarded before we went into Iraq). I could dish some of it out to the crews that were low. Someone asked if PT would stop in order to conserve water and was immediately told that it goes ahead as usual, clearly they did not grasp the gravity of the situation!

Since the sandstorm was blowing, it didn't leave us a lot to do. It was either the main tent, or our tent, so we all played some cards and board games again in our tent to stay out of sight.

Orders came in; they reckoned our flight wouldn't be delayed and we would be on leave by 28th March. Our ammo was getting collected tomorrow but not the GPMG or 9mm, just the bigger stuff off the vehicles and tanks. I still had 16 boxes of GPMG on the wagon.

SUNDAY, 17th MARCH, 1991

R+10 (-26 days)

Up at 0715 as normal for PT. The 2IC told everyone it would be our last one here due to the move, not the water situation, and we would continue it when we got back to Al Jubail. Just to remind us all about getting back to the old ways again, he emphasised fitness and how you would never be promoted in this unit if you were unfit. Later on, in our tent, the old debate came up again about what he had said. We had seen so many guys in the past get promoted that couldn't even pass the Basic Fitness Test (BFT). The long and short of it was, if they wanted you promoted, you got promoted no matter what. Likewise, if your face didn't fit, they would find any excuse not to promote you. The factual evidence was there for all to see, regardless of what they said. If you tried to reason or debate the issue with your boss during your yearly report, it only got their back up. I didn't know which was worse, the fact they lied to your face, or the fact they thought you was an idiot and believed what they were saying.

Steve came back later from going around the place. He said one of the Squadrons has decided to organise a team events tomorrow, so he entered a football and volleyball team from RHQ. Details would be in later but they were looking at doing it sometime after lunch.

The trucks turned up to take the ammo. They collected all the 84s, LAWs, spare ammo and the grenades.

Our pay people came around later, giving everyone a phone card and £30 in cash. The money was in place of other phone cards (one per month) that we should have received whilst we had been out here. They did not know why we had not received them, or the cash before, and they were not sure if we would ever get the chance to use this one. Given the fact we had not received the last three, we had the option of handing this one back in and taking another £10 instead. I said I would rather keep mine, they were made by British Aerospace, so it might make a nice collector's item in the future one day.

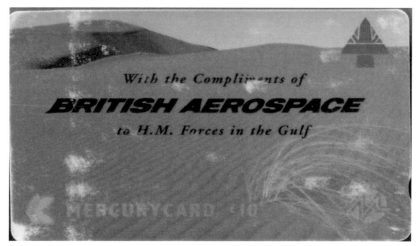

A phone card given to all who served in the Gulf

Another truckload of parcels turned up. They were placed in the main tent again, and this time we were all told that we 'had' to take a few because most of the guys had said they did not want or need any more with us about to go home. We were told that the CO has insisted he wanted us to open them, and then write letters back to the people who sent them for making the effort. Billy explained that most of us totally got this and understood exactly where he was coming from. It was just really annoying to know that these parcels had been arriving in theatre from day one of us getting here, and rather than them being dished out, they had been stored in the rear lines for the REMFs to use when and as they needed them. The post dates on the parcels clearly proved this. Now they were leaving they were dishing them out when they were of no use to anyone at all and would not be appreciated, hardly what the sender had in mind.

I asked why they could not be sent to the hospitals in Kuwait; surely, they needed them far more than we did and they would be better received? I was told the reason they were not being sent there was because nobody had the time or resources to do it. Besides which, the whole campaign had been about sending stuff for soldiers to receive, not civilians. If civilians did receive them, they would not be able to write letters back to the senders with a thank you note. I suggested that 'we', and I didn't just mean our Regiment, open them all up, take the letters out and then send the parcels to the hospitals. 'We' then write a thank you letter back, at least that way the parcels would be used and far more appreciated. I was told that was impracticable because it would take too much time and effort. We were again all told to take at least three parcels each before the officer left.

Some of the guys said they were going to take them as ordered but throw them straight into the bin because there was nothing in them that they wanted or needed. After being given shit by the rest of the guys for saying that, everyone joined in to open up all the parcels and remove the letters, these were then dished out until they were all gone. We then all pulled up a chair and began writing thank you letters.

Whilst we were writing the letters in the main tent, the CO came in. To nobody in particular, he said that the RHQ set-up was starting to look like a camping site now, and instead of blowing his top like he normally did, he went and made himself a cup of coffee. Everyone stopped writing and just stared. That was the first one I had actually seen him make since we had been here. Not sure if it was shock or disbelief but nobody moved to lend a hand. I did have to tell him though, since nobody else would, that the Land Rover, unlike a CVR (T), didn't require the engine to be revving at greater than a 1000 rpm to provide electricity in order to get the water to boil in the boiling vessel. A few of the guys started taking the piss but it was totally wasted on the CO, that or he had chosen to ignore their comments. They insisted it got recorded into the diary.

Chapter 18
Basra Road

MONDAY, 18th MARCH, 1991

R+11 (-25 days)

I woke up with one major pounding headache for my stag 0400–0600. Took some tablets but they didn't do anything to alleviate the pain. When I got off stag, I went for a walk as my head was still killing me. It was still pitch-black outside, which was unusual as it normally started to get light by now. Found out why later on when it did get lighter, thick black smoke was all around us now and didn't start clearing until 1400, leaving a dull grey sky. There must have been a change in the wind direction last night because there were plenty of stars out when I went to bed.

At 1400, we went to play in the team events. What a total waste of time it turned out to be! Due to the number of teams and the brilliant organisation, the games were limited to five minutes each, and all games had to be finished in time to see the end of Paul's marathon. As RHQ, we managed to play just one game of football and that was it. On the plus side we got to have a chat with the guys again away from RHQ.

At 1600 we all had a fright. A humongous explosion, no more than about a kilometre away, went off. It was that powerful that the shockwave blew people off their feet. The whole ground around us just seem to lift and drop in an instant, producing a small dust cloud about one foot off the ground. It was a right surreal moment. It turned out to be the Royal Artillery blowing up nearby ammo stocks.

When we returned to RHQ, I received some good news, of sorts. Although someone else was taking the credit for it, someone had listened to my idea. It had been arranged for us to take piles of food parcels by helicopter and road to the hospital in Kuwait. Also, the postal guys from now on were going to readdress all parcels with a BFPO 3000 to go there. They just wanted to let me know. I was just pleased that it was happening. We certainly didn't need them, and I was sure the people in the hospital, or who lived close by, would be very grateful.

It was passed around the guys that they could also go if they wanted to, they might get a chance to see the city and Basra Road. For those that were unable to go today, there would be another trip organised in a few days' time. The vehicles were leaving straightaway but if anyone fancied a helicopter ride they would have to wait awhile, maybe even until the next trip. I asked one of the lads who wanted to go in the helicopter if he would take some pictures from the air for me as I wanted to go by road, just in case the helicopter did not show for whatever reason. Having heard so many rumours about all the bombing on Basra Road, I wanted to see it for myself and not miss out.

It took a while to get there and I don't know quite what I was expecting to see, but on approach the road itself was totally clear and traffic was flowing in both directions. We drove down Basra Road; wow, what a sight! I can only describe it as if you were driving through one big long scrap yard. It didn't strike you as shocking at all. That was until you noticed the military vehicles everywhere and then the carnage inflicted on it all. The Air Force had bombed to shit a convoy that had left the city; clearly, it had no protection against aircraft. I guess the Iraqis probably thought that nobody would notice if they mixed military and civilian vehicles up together. Big fucking mistake. It must have been a dream come true to the Air Force, just one big long strafing run followed by another. We were told that it had been cleared of bodies and weapons so we stayed to take some photos, the trucks continued on into the city. There was still a lot of ammo, especially tank ammo, all over the place so we took our time and treaded very carefully.

Basra Road

Tank upside down on Basra Road

Destroyed T55 on Basra Road

Another destroyed Iraqi tank

Basra Road from the air

Pilot's view of flying down Basra Road

Basra Road from the air

As soon as we got back, we were told to take all the cam nets down off the vehicles and pack them away ready for shipping back home. There went the shade, not that you needed it with all the crap in the air blocking the sun anyway. Once that was done, we were told to take the cooks' tent down and pack that away. Tomorrow we would have to self-cook from the vehicles. It looked like we were actually going then, no way would the CO see that get packed away if we were staying.

An operational analysis team tipped up later. They gave us all a quick chat about why they were here and the purpose of their visit. They basically wanted to know how we did during the war, our tactics, procedures, and how the equipment performed. They had already visited some of the troops, collecting data before coming to us. Interesting was that after the chat to us all, they only handed questioners out to the officers to fill in.

Since I had no forms to fill in and was really interested in the work they were conducting, I got chatting to one of the team. He told me about the Swingfire evaluation that they had conducted a few days ago. He said the team got the impression that it hadn't performed as well as expected, which surprised them. Besides the expected normal misfires and missiles going rogue, some of the crews experienced the weapon system completely shutting down on them and they were unable to fire. That was the first time the team had come across that issue before. That aside, he said that tactically one of the main problems highlighted to them was the close distance between the enemy and our own troops when they attacked. The Swingfire in this scenario was useless due to the range required to gather and control the missile before being able to hit a target. The team believed the vital use of Swingfire was a practised scenario as part of our tactics and procedures that we conducted when back home playing war games. Therefore, how was it possible in reality that when deploying the Swingfire in its role in the open desert, it differed from playing the exercises? From the results and data collected in training exercises back home, the team had expected a very high-kill ratio out here given the fact it was open desert, ideal killing ground for such a weapon system compared to the wooded terrain of Europe, where things could hide or worse still, get in the way. Statistics and reality were showing a very poor, low-kill ratio compared to training and exercises. I told him it was probably because out here the enemy and the weather had a vote, on exercises they didn't. He enquired as to what I meant so I quickly explained about us always playing to win on exercise, then he understood it. I asked him who actually gets the reports once they are completed, and he told me they go to different departments who have different interests and needs. He had nothing to do with that, was not sure how, or if, we actually got the full report ourselves. I told him I thought that was a pity as I believed at our level we would not see it at all, even though it might contain some very important lessons which could be learnt from it. Being sceptical, I would bet a month's wages that there would be no lessons to learn, and because of the fact that Swingfire has been used out here in combat, it will only get praised and used as a selling point for the industry. He didn't challenge my comments.

Interesting to read was a report he showed me from one of our own troops. They had fired 40 rounds of 30mm, most of them armoured piercing, at a T55, using all four wagons from the troop. The thing just would not stop. Eventually, the tank stopped, the crew opened up and they surrendered. On inspection later on by the Ops analysis team, strike marks were clearly visible all over the tank from the rounds that had hit it, but it was found that the T55 had only actually been penetrated three times. It was presumed the crew gave up due to the firepower that was hitting them and they didn't want to push their luck anymore once a few rounds got in. Considering this was old-type armour on this tank, our 30mm didn't appear to be as armoured piercing as what we had been led to believe it was capable of.

I asked him about the Challengers and damaged Chobam armour that I had seen whilst out here. I was curious because we had been told it was the leading technology in the world on armour protection for tanks, yet some of the damage that we had seen was caused by tanks simply bumping into each other. He relayed that the whole team were under strict instructions not to say anything at all about Chobam to anyone, regardless of rank. It was left at that.

TUESDAY, 19th MARCH, 1991

R+12 (-24 days)

No PT this morning, or central breakfast so the sentry did not bother to wake people up. It meant we got a lie in. Steve was already up and had done the cooking for us. After breakfast, Beno drove the wagon around the front of the big tent, where we took everything off it and then began to pack it all away ready for the trip back to Germany. I stripped the secure radios and all the wiring back out of the wagon then handed it all back in. They were no longer required because everyone was now just using normal radios and speaking in plain clear speech, like you would on a telephone. Nobody really cared anymore, there were no secrets or sensitive information that required talking about and generally nothing was happening at all. Once the radios were squared away, all the weapons were stripped down and cleaned. Ammo was removed from all the magazines and stowed back into boxes, where we could easily get to it for handing it back in at some point. All maps, electronic instructions, traces, log books etc. were placed in a big pit that the Engineers had kindly dug for us, and burnt. Along with it all, the big stupid green carpet from the tent, which really cheered the guys up. On being asked for my diary to follow suit, quite a few of the guys immediately jumped to my aid saying it was personal and therefore they had no right asking for it. After a few veiled threats, when I refused to hand it over I was told/threatened that should I ever try to publish it, a world of hurt would descend upon my head and I would be sent to jail. The subject was then dropped. When there was nothing else left to throw into the pit to burn, the big tent was taken down and packed away.

We then all got together and had a troop brief. We were told that we would all be up early tomorrow morning and moving. Exactly how we were getting moved, timings etc., would all be confirmed later on. All that we required to take with us was a weapon, a sleeping bag and our respirator. Everything else was to stay in the wagons. The Regiment had been booked onto two separate flights out of the country, which were now 0400 and 1600 on the 23rd. They should arrive at Hannover in Germany at 0900 and 2100 local time. As always, all of this was subject to change but shouldn't move as they were now using civilian Boeing 747s to get us out of the country. The flight manifests were out, showing who and what was going on which flight. We were all to have a read and find out which flight we were going on. I found out I was on the second flight.

We were then briefed about a signal from DPR (A) in HQ 4 Armoured Division back in Herford, whoever that was, about the media. It was to be disseminated and briefed to all ranks. It was quite a wordy document, but it basically said, nobody was allowed to talk to, or have interviews with, anyone from the media at all without permission. Those that were given permission from higher would be briefed by a team on exactly what they could and could not say. For everyone, topics such as Special Forces, treatment of POWs, future defence reviews, war crimes and blue on blue were not to be discussed at all by anyone at any time. In public, everyone was to watch what he or she was saying, especially in bars or where alcohol was concerned. Bottom line, the general theme for everyone to take and to pass onto the public back home, was that we were all glad to be back home.

There was another trip being organised to go into Kuwait City via Basra Road, and they wanted to know who would like to go on it. Although I really wanted to see inside the city this time, I declined the offer because I had been the other day, so it seemed only fair to let someone else go. At the end of the brief we were told about L/Cpl J W. He had lost his thumb and finger when the detonator of a hand grenade went off whilst he was trying to de-prime it (remove the detonator from inside the grenade). God knows how that has happened, because everyone was told not to do that for that exact reason. We were all told just to hand the things in and someone else would de-prime them all.

No mail again. I think the postal system for us lot is well and truly over now given the fact we are off tomorrow. At 1800 all the wagons in RHQ were lined up in one straight line. They were all closed down with hatches secured. Everyone not in a wagon stood well to the rear of them whilst all the flares and smoke grenades were fired off. Looked really nice, like a firework display on New Year's Eve. The wagons were then just left where they were, all locked up ready for the low loaders arriving in the morning to take them away. A road party had already been selected to load them up and travel with them.

On stag later on, I had a chat with Capt. B about who was getting medals from our lot. He was surprised that I knew anything about it, because he believed all that information was being kept quiet. I took the piss and said, "You mean like everything else that went on during the war." He just laughed. I told him that not only did guys in the other Squadrons know about it, but they knew who was being nominated and why, and there were quite a few unhappy people about. He said that it had come down from the top that there was a quota per Regiment. Other Regiments had already put guys forward for medals so we had to do it as well, besides it would look good in the future for the Regimental name to have had guys receive medals in a war conflict. I said that I totally understood the reason and the logic, and agreed it would look good for the Regiment in the future. But surely the Regiment should have actively been putting its guys forward for medals in the first place, rather than being forced to do it with a quota because other units were doing it. Given everything that we had accomplished out here, I was sure that with a bit of research they would find guys who were well deserving of getting one, instead of plucking some of the names out of a hat and then having to invent a story. If after the research it turned out that there were quite a few candidates, then so be it; nobody who deserved a medal should not get one simply because someone set a quota. Having spoken to quite a few of the guys in the Squadrons, many of us thought that by having a quota of medals and picking names out of a hat, it just made a joke out of the whole prestige of awarding and wearing medals. Personally, I just couldn't accept, and wear with pride, a medal that I knew damned well I hadn't earned. It would be so embarrassing trying to tell someone what I had earned it for; it was just totally fucking wrong in my eyes. He agreed that in truth it could have been handled more professionally, especially on the part of the Regiment, but what was done was done; that was life.

When we got off stag at midnight, there were still no confirmed timings etc. about tomorrow's move other than the early start, so I just rolled my sleeping bag out on the ground and hit the sack.

Chapter 19
Going Home

WEDNESDAY, 20th MARCH, 1991

R+13 (-23 days)

Everyone was woken up at 0400, but all we did was sit about on the desert sand until 0600, then we were all told to move to A2's location, which was 500 metres away. We waited there for another hour before trucks turned up and transported us to a desert airstrip, where we waited around until 1300 in the desert with no food or water again. There was nothing here waiting for us and nobody had any because the last instruction given out was to 'just' have your weapon, sleeping bag and respirator. Everything else was to stay on the wagons. A few Hercules aircraft were inbound, so we were all told to sweep the airstrip for loose items, whatever the hell that meant given it was a sandy strip in a desert with stones, rocks and small bushes everywhere. We just formed lines and walked the entire length of the strip only, if a rock was on it we picked it up and threw it to the side. Once that was done, we formed up into lines about 100 metres away from the strip to await the inbound aircraft.

The birds came in, and boy, were they throwing them about! One looked about a 100 feet off the floor and did a sharp left turn; I could have sworn the wing tip was about ten feet off the deck in the turn. Looked really punchy and warlike. Ramps at the back were already down, with guys hanging out when they came into land. No doubt they were using the pick-ups for practice. One of the guys commented that they thought someone had forgotten to tell the pilots the war was all over. The aircraft just followed each other in, one at a time. Each aircraft on landing quickly turned about and taxied back down the airstrip to awaiting lines of soldiers. Guys standing on the ramps ushered us all on; there were no seats, so we just sat on top of our sleeping bags on the floor. They quickly crammed in as many as possible before turning around to get airborne again. We all felt like cattle. A few of the guys took pictures as they couldn't believe it. On a plus, we were getting out of here at last.

Hercules aircraft arriving to pick us up

Our bird coming to get us

One about to depart with some of the guys on board

Guys in the back of the aircraft

We flew to Al Jubail, where we all got to see exactly where all the mail was. Half the airport was full of sacks of the stuff just sitting there on the tarmac; it would take months to sort through that lot. We were quickly ushered off the plane and taken to a spot on the far side of the airfield, where we received a brief. We were told that dress regulations were in force here, and anyone breaking them would be punished. In other words, no sunbathing. We were to just chill out exactly where we were until the vehicles arrived as there were no tents and nowhere to grab shade or a drink. We also had to supply two men for guard duty and one for fatigues. They were quickly volunteered by a keen senior rank.

Later on, the RAF tipped up and set a makeshift cookhouse and shower tent up. After having a quick bite to eat and a drink, I went and grabbed a shower; it was cold but I didn't care: it was a shower, something I'd not had in months. They thanked us for our holding up of the flag and doing a great job in Kuwait. It was really touching. They told us the Yanks were still very much busy and had shot down an Iraqi fighter jet in Iraq today, nobody really cared. All that was on people's minds was the fact we were getting out of here now.

The road party tipped up at 1700 in some trucks. They had unloaded all the vehicles just down the road from us. We sat in the sand and watched a civilian 747 lift and depart, the RAF guys told us it was full of Yanks going home. What a sight that was and it cheered everyone up because now the realisation dawned on people that it was finally happening: we were on our way home. As the night drew in, everyone just got into their sleeping bags where they were and drifted off as best they could.

THURSDAY, 21st MARCH, 1991

R+14 (-22 days)

We all got woken at 0530 and informed breakfast was on at 0630. Nobody could have a wash and shave because the water had run out from everyone having a shower yesterday. After grub, coaches turned up and took us to the vehicles. First things first, we had to get all the ammo off the vehicles and hand it in to guys waiting on the backs of trucks. All our body armour and cam nets then followed on from this. Once the trucks departed, we crewed all the vehicles up and drove back to where we had just spent last night. Here more trucks were waiting to take all the left-over compo (food) and water from us. Once everything was off that they wanted handed back in, we were told to load the wagons with any and all kit going back to Germany. They would be driven to the docks in the morning, locked down once we were happy, and it would be the last we would see of them until they arrived at the port back in Germany. There really wasn't a lot for us to do other than remove all the loose kit from the outside of the wagons and stow it on the inside. The rest of it was already secure in either container bins on the wagons or it was securely bolted on the outside.

We had a troop brief later on. Some mail managed to get to us and was handed out. Lori was still in love with me, but I thought she was starting to sound different in the letters, no doubt it was just me and how I was feeling. We all had another gypsies' warning about taking souvenirs back with us. Anyone getting caught, from the top it was going to be a court martial and kicked out of the military. They were going to play hardball on this to stop any weapons getting onto the streets in the UK. I decided to keep the AK 47's bayonet as a souvenir but I would bury the weapon itself. A few of the guys said they were going to strip them down and hide them in places on the vehicles. I didn't see the point, it was not worth a court martial and they would do it just to prove a point. As for all our UK weapons, nobody seemed able to make a decision on what to do with them. All the other SQMS had taken them in after being cleaned and placed them into bundles before loading them onto a wagon. Our SQMS didn't want to do that for some reason, so we still had them with us.

Later on, an O group for the top lot was called and held within earshot of us all. It went on for hours. It appeared that now the Regiment was all back together again, everyone was dropping straight back into the old Regimental way of life and trying to get their oar in just to have a say, no doubt to try and look good in front of the CO. Most were just irrelevant points and niff naff and trivia just so someone could speak for the sake of speaking. Of note though was the following; the war was over so it was back to 'all the bullshit' as it was eloquently put. Everyone was to be dressed in full combats all the time now with headdress on paying the correct compliments (saluting officers). No more sunbathing, no T-shirts or shorts at all. The civilian planes apparently had beer on them, we could have a drink, but anyone getting drunk would lose their leave. Everyone was to have a clean pair of combats on for the trip home. Although the desert here looked like a rubbish tip, before we left we were going to clean it up. The CO didn't want other units commenting on what a shit state we left it in. Teams were to be organised straight after the O group to get on with it.

So, we spent the last few hours of daylight cleaning another piece of the desert up. The area here just looked like the population simply emptied their rubbish straight out into the desert; I'd say at least 99% of the rubbish here couldn't be attributed to the military at all. Judging by the state of decay of most things, it was no doubt here well before any of us even arrived in theatre.

Once dark, there really wasn't a lot else to do, so I once more rolled my sleeping bag out on the desert sand and hit the sack early.

FRIDAY, 22nd MARCH, 1991

R+15 (-21 days)

Everyone was woken up again at 0530. All the vehicles were crewed up with just a commander and a driver, Beno and I crewed ours. They were then driven the 10 kilometres to the Combat Manoeuvre Area (CMA) at the docks. Once parked up and all the weapons removed, they were locked down. We were all told to move to an area out of the way of other vehicles coming in and wait for transport to arrive to take us to Black Adder (BA) camp. 1130 it eventually arrived, talk about being pissed off or what, most of the guys were fuming. We had sat in the blazing sun for four hours doing fuck all but twiddling our thumbs. To really cheer everyone up, for whatever reason, some bright spark decided we should clean the CMA up before we left. Nobody was allowed onto the coaches until that task was completed. One of the guys commented that the 16/5th Lancers would be best known, and remembered, for area cleaning every bit of this country before we left it. Quite a few of the guys agreed with the statement as we set about picking all the rubbish up.

We arrived at BA camp, vehicles now firmly out of our hair until back in Germany. It was back to the massive tent city, and a case of finding a place to sleep. We hunted around until we found a few empty tents close together so that we could kip as a troop. Word got around to everyone that they wanted all the guns collected in, starting with our troop at 1300. Steve and I stripped ours all down and gave them a good clean before lightly oiling them up ready for the journey. As a troop, we went down together to the collecting point. When we got there, we found the SSM and SQMS having an argument. Despite it being his department's role, the SQMS didn't want to take the magazines in from the larger weapons; he was only prepared to take the magazines for the pistols and the submachine guns. He said it was too much hassle; the troops could take all the others back themselves. The SSM couldn't understand his logic and hence the argument. The SQMS was not budging. So now we had shitloads of magazines that we needed to look after and carry in bags all the time around with us. It was a chargeable offence to lose one of these. Once all our guns were handed in, we were told by the SSM that command troop were going to be supplying the guard force from now until we left since we had the biggest troop in BA camp. A Cpl tried to argue the fact that we had the biggest because of the number of officers and SNCOs in it, but they did not do guards. Therefore, we were no bigger than any other troop. He wasn't interested and said to get a stag list to him within the hour. I couldn't believe that we were supposed to be going home and yet everyone was looking depressed as hell. I knew they told us to be prepared to get fucked about, but I never thought they would actually go out of their way to ensure it happened.

Word quickly spread around that the first flight was now delayed for some reason by eight hours. That changed three more times over the next few hours, the end result being that it was delayed, but nobody actually knew for sure by how long. We were supposed to pride ourselves in the military on things like precision, accuracy, man management and organisational skills. The truth was, we were absolutely poor at it. Most things got done because of the 'wilko' attitude of the guys and them making it happen, something that was quite often taken for granted by the bosses. Sure, the guys had a moan, but then they got the job done, even if they didn't have the right equipment, qualified personnel and resources or had to work long hours. Whilst this was quite admirable, they basically were not helping the situation because as long as they were willing to just simply get on with it and get the job done, nothing would never ever get rectified or changed.

Guys in Command troop had obviously been telling mates in other Squadrons that I had written a diary out here because guys started to turn up and ask me to read it out to them, some even asked me to lend them the book. No way was I letting it out of my sight; I had already been asked to hand it over for destruction and warned about it ever being published as a book, so I was mindful of a plot to try and get by deception. It gave them a good laugh and brought back some memories, some bad, some good. Some that came even shared experiences about their own exploits. It seemed most of the guys in the troops never even knew what was going on throughout the war, which frustrated the hell out of them. Unlike all the training we conducted back home on exercises, they were constantly kept in the dark, with little to no information flowing to them. There were very few to no back briefs or feedback given to the guys, even after O groups had taken place, so most guys went throughout the whole war not having any idea of the main goals or the bigger picture at all. They just simply waited for the next set of orders to get on with the next task. This went against everything we were previously taught.

Most had no idea of what went on at Objective LEAD. The one thing they all knew about though was the QDG withdrawing. Most took the piss and really wanted to rub their noses in it, saying they also came across the enemy, but rather than run away, they stood their ground and fought. It was pointed out to them that we all had to withdraw in the end because of the overwhelming enemy strength. They were quite shocked when they were told by others in Command troop that we were totally surrounded, cut off with no help from our own UK forces and getting hit from all sides. Each Squadron was fighting its own individual battle, hence could not be helped out or reinforced. The QDG guys no doubt saw overwhelming forces in front of them and did what most Recce guys should do. You move, get safe, regroup then attack again. There was no way you could take MBTs on in a CVR (T), especially when they just appeared out of the dust right in front of you. Some of the guys were not interested; as far as they were concerned, the QDGs had run away and it was ammo to take the piss, now and forever in the future.

A lot of the guys asked me to add things to the diary, but I told them I really didn't want to do it because it had happened in the past now. It might also contradict what we had been told. That was not to say that I didn't believe the guys, but it would detract from the fact I had written mainly about daily life in Command troop and what we were and were not being informed, rightly or wrongly, of what was going on at the time. If I started to add other stories in from the guys, where would I stop?

The guys on the first flight all packed their kit away later on. The buses turned up late, so they didn't leave until gone midnight. That was them off to Darrah for their flight. Most of us did the usual thing of seeing them off, saying we would see them all back in Krautland and wishing them a safe flight home.

SATURDAY, 23rd MARCH, 1991

R+16 (-20 days)

Woke up at 0600 with the sun on my face coming in through holes in the tent. Guess the excitement was coming back in as loads of the guys were already up and moving about. Nobody had been told to wake anyone up as the top lot had all buggered off last night. It was almost like having grown-ups in charge for once. I managed to get the keys for the Land Cruiser so a few of us drove to Camp 4 for a shower. The place was deserted, but it did bring back some memories for me of when I first arrived in country. 33 Field Hospital had left ages ago and so all the women had left with them. The cookhouse was still open though, so after we all had a shower, we went and had a descent breakfast before returning to BA camp. I gave the keys to another guy, told him exactly how to get there and what was there if anyone else wanted to go.

If everything went to plan today, this would be my last entry in here from theatre. The flight should be out of here tonight. I might write a summary and then think about what to do with this when I get back. It would be nice to go into the Regimental museum along with all the articles I have from the newspapers, but I doubt they would accept it given what is written in here…as in the whole truth rather than a distorted one simply being full of praises to all those in command. That's what the Regimental diary is for.

Another Iraqi fighter jet got shot down today. The rules of the ceasefire were very clear: no enemy fighter aircraft were allowed off the ground at all, otherwise they would be engaged. It could not be any simpler than that so God knows what they were playing at. In the news, it seemed the Muslim community were starting to have a go at each other now, different factions, etc. in different countries, not just here. They appeared to be arguing about the invasion into Kuwait, some were for it and some were against it. And then there was another argument going on about how it was all handled when we arrived and who should have been in charge etc. It was all getting rather heated, and it appeared that most our efforts out here had gone in vain. I can honestly see us being back here again in a few years to sort it all out again.

0915: The trucks rolled up, we loaded all our crap onto them before getting onto the coaches. Once seated, everyone was once more warned about drinking on the plane. Get caught drunk, you were going to jail and leave would be removed. It always amazed me how many times they felt the need to tell you things, almost like you were a simpleton that didn't understand or something. Yes, you would always get someone who broke the rules, no matter how many times they were told, that happens in all walks of life, but it didn't justify treating everyone like they were idiots because of the actions of one individual.

We left BA camp at 1015 to go to the Military Controlled Check Point (MCCP) that had been set up in Camp 4. On collecting our bags off the trucks, we proceeded to the checkpoints. Before the checkpoints, there were amnesty boxes, where you could put stuff in with no questions asked whatsoever; almost comically, nearly every one of them was full and overflowing with guns, knives and ammo. At the checkpoints, all our kit was X-rayed and everyone was searched from head to toe, no exceptions. Guys in the queue saw this going on ahead and started to react. There were pistols, knives and even grenades being kicked down the line from the X-ray machine. It was so comical but obviously very serious. Who takes a fucking hand grenade onto an aeroplane for fuck sake? It was because of idiots like this that we were all treated like retards all the time.

On passing through the checkpoint we were given a piece of A4 paper to read in the departure lounge, it was entitled GOING HOME.

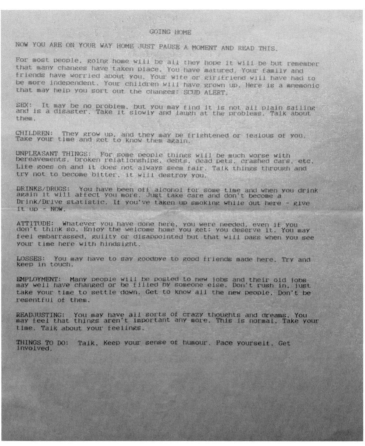

Going home SCUD ALERT

Most of the guys threw it straight into the bin without even reading it. Others simply read a few lines then muttered things like, "Tell me something I don't already know." I kept some because being an RMA I thought this was a very poor attempt by the military to show how it dealt with issues such as battle shock, stress, PTSD etc., for guys that had just been to war. Especially given the issues that had resulted from the Falklands War less than ten years ago.

At 1315 the coaches reappeared, and we were all told to get back on board. We would be travelling as a convoy straight to the airport. The drivers clearly didn't have any licences over here because they were speeding, overtaking at improper moments and racing each other side by side down the road, so much for the convoy. Unbeknown to the drivers, had we crashed, I was quite sure the guys would have lynched them. We arrived at the airport at 1440 to be told there was no plane, so we were to wait on the coaches until it arrived.

It landed 30 minutes later. Nobody really cared, at least it was here. We were told to remain in our seats due to one of the coaches getting lost on the way to the airport. For some reason, the military movers wanted everyone together before they were going to let anyone get on board. We eventually boarded at 1630. It was a 747 Kuwaiti airline. It felt really good to be sitting down in a nice,

238

comfortable seat, and no doubt it would be my first and last time flying with this airline company.

Our 747 to take us home

Waiting to be cleared on to get home

1700 the aircraft took off to a very loud cheer and we were finally getting out of here. It was 16 days after the war finished but 20 days earlier than originally planned.

The flight was uneventful and most guys just slept. When we landed at Hannover Airport, we were told to remain seated whilst the aircraft taxied to another part of the airfield away from the main terminal. Looking out the window we could see it was secured off with both our own military and German civilian police. Once we came to a standstill and the doors were opened, someone came aboard. He told everyone that there had been a change of plan because the press was in the main terminal, and it had come from the top that nobody was allowed to talk to them. Coaches were waiting to take us back to camp, we were to get straight onto them upon leaving the plane, all our baggage would be taken care of and catch us up later on. Nobody was to worry about wives, girlfriends, etc. they had all been previously warned that they would not be allowed to meet anyone at the airport and so were waiting at camp.

We got off the plane and onto the coaches. Once everyone was off the plane, the coaches left for Herford in a convoy escorted by German and military police. It was such a strange situation; we had never had this happen to us before.

Gates of our camp in Herford Germany

Just inside the main gates

We arrived back at camp in Herford and were driven straight up to a hangar next to the cookhouse to await the arrival of our baggage. Inside the hangar, the Families Officer had arranged a welcome party for all the wives and children to meet the husbands. No girlfriends had been invited at all, so it felt really awkward watching them all meet up. It was very emotional and there was lots of hugging, tears and children crying. Photographers were zipping about the place, trying to take pictures of the reunited families. Why we were all kept together like this was beyond me because all the single lads felt really out of place and didn't quite know what to do with themselves. All the attention was completely on the families. I guess had I been married, I might have appreciated all the effort that was put in it. Once my kit arrived, I quickly grabbed it and left for my room to have a few beers with Robbo and Zeb, who had flown out on an earlier flight. They had already filled our fridge with lots of beer in preparation for my arrival. Now that's what you call mates.

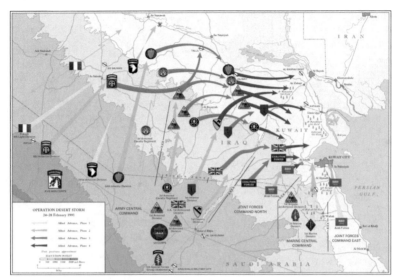

The bigger picture of who went where

RHQ in the Gulf

Chapter 20
After the War

Silke and I did split up, and whilst on leave I managed to get to London where I met up with Lori. We got along really well again and started seeing each other after that. A few months later after our return, I received a telephone call informing me that the HQ SSM wanted to see me. I made my way up to the Squadron offices and waited outside his door. He called me in, so I marched into his office and stood to attention. He said I was incorrectly dressed and allowed me a few seconds to try and work out what he was talking about before throwing a set of Corporal tapes across the desk to me. He then dismissed me, so I marched back out. Whilst I was happy about the promotion, and especially the pay rise, it wasn't what I would call something to be proud of. I assumed I was just being promoted so I could go onto my course because I was loaded onto a first aid instructors' course in June. Months later, an officer I knew really well quietly told me that my promotion might have had something to do with the fact the CO had been singing my praises to other officers, especially in the officer's mess. He had said I was brilliant and had him in check all the time out there, even though I was just an L/Cpl. He even told a select group of them that I had bollocked him a few times, and he took it because he knew I was correct. None of this was ever conveyed to me at all.

The Regiment on return just dropped straight back into the way it had been operating before the war; it was as if we had never been out there. The focus was all about the arms plot again. Nobody was going to be allowed to give the Regiment a bad name by not having something 100 percent ready for it. Guys worked long hours and even weekends to get everything immaculate and ready for the handover. It was inspection after inspection until it was perfect. I have to say, the work and effort all the guys put in, and the standard we achieved at the end, was something to behold. It was more than what could be said for what we took over. Rather than make a 'fuss' (as our bosses called it), we were told to just take it over and then get it up to the same standard we had just produced on our handover.

I stayed in the gym for the handover/takeover with the new unit. From our side of the house it all went smoothly, and I went into the gym at Wimbish. Once settled in at our new base, I asked about the signal instructors' course and explained what the RSO had briefed me on in the Gulf. I was told that they would not load me onto a course, because I was in the gym, I needed to get back onto the tank park if I wanted to do it. So much for the career interview. Well at least I was where I wanted to be for the time being and I had been promoted.

For me personally, the Gulf War had opened my eyes to quite a few things, especially how the Army, and in particular, the Regiment operated. The reality of war was totally different to everything I had been told, how I had been trained, and even what I had seen on TV. Besides the 'them and us' and the frustrations bore out of a lack of trust and information flow. I saw and experienced first-hand just how little your life actually meant to those in command. Most blindly just followed the person above without question, and they expected the same loyalty from the ranks below. It didn't matter which side you were on, we were all just pawns for someone else's agenda. Whilst I realise that there will be situations when you just have to blindly follow orders and someone has to do it no matter how ugly it is, I personally did not want to be killed by just being a 'yes man' and 'always' following what was being said without question. I wanted the information and the understanding. I wanted to know that the people above me were telling me the truth and that what I was fighting for was honest, just and for the right reasons, not personal agendas. We were exposed to so many things that just should not have happened in my eyes, e.g. going to war with no ammo, body armour or desert kit. And the scary thing was, people seemed to be more worried about their careers than saying something about it. Soldiers need leaders, not bosses, and this is even more so when at war.

Because we had won the war, I doubted very much that any fuck-ups, mistakes or errors would be recorded; so no lessons would be captured and passed onto all ranks to learn from them. If the British Army was to go to war again, and it surely would, the same mistakes would be made all over again. Like a lot of my friends, I never wanted to be put into that situation ever again.

Whilst quite a few of my mates decided to leave the Regiment, some even left the Army, I still had pride in being a soldier. I knew, however, that I need to get out of the Regiment. It was very clear to me that those in charge do not like intelligent soldiers in the lower ranks and are quite content for Regimental life to stay as it is, as it always has been. It is going to take years for them to accept the fact that times are changing and they need to change with them. Soldiers are educated now, some even more than the officers, and they are more than capable of thinking for themselves. They will not put up with being treated as if the Army was still in the seventeenth century. They will leave and when they tell their stories, recruitment will then also become a major issue.

My focus and goal now was selection for the SAS. I started by going on the prestigious NATO Long Range Reconnaissance Patrol Leaders Course in Weingarten in Bavaria.

…to be continued.

Glossary

A
Abrams – American Main Battle Tank (MBT)
AFV – Armoured Fighting Vehicle
AH – Attack Helicopter or Apache Helicopter
AK 47 – Old Soviet machine gun
Ammo – Short for Ammunition
APC – Armoured Personnel Carrier – A fighting vehicle that carries infantry
APTC – Army Physical Training Corps
A2 – Rear echelon – Has all the supplies, post office and larger workshops, etc.
A10 – American military fixed wing aircraft, also called a 'Warthog'

B
BATS – Biological Agent Treatment Sets – Tablets
Bde – Brigade – A military formation size, normally three or more Battlegroups
– see below for military structure at the time

C
Challenger 1 – British MBT
CO – Commanding Officer – The officer in charge of the Regiment or Battalion
Comms – Short for Communications
Compo – Composite Rations – British military food for the troops
CRA – Commander Royal Artillery
CV – Command Vehicle, can also be called a Control Vehicle
CVR (T) – Combat Vehicle Reconnaissance (Tracked) – A light mobile armoured fighting vehicle
C/S – Call sign – A prefix given to instantly identify something or someone, e.g. 22B

D
DAA – Divisional Admin Area – All the supplies and large workshops are located within this set-up
DS – Dressing Station – A medical facility smaller than a hospital

G
GPMG – General Purpose Machine Gun – Large belt-feed machine gun

I
Int Officer – The Intelligence Officer

L
LAW 80 – Light Anti-Tank Weapon
LMG – Light Machine Gun
LO – Liaison Officer

M
MBT – Main Battle Tank
MRE – Meal Ready to Eat. American military food for the troops
MT-LB – Abbreviated Russian name given to a Soviet multi-purpose fully amphibious armoured tracked vehicle, basically an APC
M1 AI Abrams – American MBT

N
NAPS – Nerve Agent Pre-Treatment Set – Tablets
NBC – Nuclear, Biological and Chemical
ND – Negligent Discharge – Unintentionally firing your weapon
NLT – No Later Than – A time by which you must do something by
NTM – Notice To Move – A time you will be given before you must move
NVD – Night Viewing Device
NVS – Night Viewing System

O
OC – Officer Commanding – The officer in charge of a Squadron or Company
O Group – Orders Group – A briefing or orders for selected personnel
Ops Officer – The Operations Officer

P
PT – Physical Training
PTI – Physical Training Instructor

Q
QM – Quarter Master – Normally a Major in charge of supplies
QMs – The stores where the QM and his staff worked

R
RAC – Royal Armoured Corps
RAP – Regimental Aid Post
Recce – Short for Reconnaissance
REME – Royal Electrical and Mechanical Engineers

RGF – Republican Guard Force – A formation in the Iraqi Army

RHQ – Regimental Headquarters – Workplace of the command group of the Regiment. E.g. CO, 2IC, Ops Officer etc.

RMA – Regimental Medical Assistant – A fully qualified and trained medic

RSM – Regimental Sergeant Major – The top Warrant Officer Class One in the Regiment

RSO – Regimental Signals Officer – The officer in charge of all signal/radio matters

RSWO – Regimental Signals Warrant Officer – The Warrant Officer who is second in charge of all signal matters to the RSO

S

SAS – Special Air Service – Special Forces

SHQ – Squadron Headquarters – Working place of the command group of a Squadron. E.g. OC, 2IC etc.

SNCO – Senior Non-Commissioned Officer, ranks above Corporal but below officer

SSM – Squadron Sergeant Major – The Warrant Officer Class Two in the Squadron

SQMS – Squadron Quartermaster Stores – Supplies for the Squadron. It is also a title given to the person in charge of the men who work in there.

T

TBC – To Be Confirmed

T55, 59, 62, 72 – Soviet tanks used by the Iraqi Army

W

WO – Warrant Officer

2IC – The person who is Second in Command

Military Structure at the Time

Troop – Squadron – Regiment – Battlegroup – Brigade – Division – Corps.

Troop – Normally 12 men and 4 vehicles
Squadron – Normally 5 troops to a Squadron (1–5 and SHQ) about 110 men in total
Regiment – Normally 5 Squadrons to a Regiment (A, B, C, D and HQ) about 650 men in total
Battlegroup – Normally 3 Regiments in size
Brigade – Normally 3 Battlegroups in size
Division – Normally 3 Brigades in size
Corps – This can comprise almost anything from one unique group, e.g. The Royal Armoured Corps, to a military fighting force of 3 or more Divisions.

Some Regiments were slightly different due to the number of vehicles they had, e.g. MBT Regiments. The size of units described above was for peacetime operations only; during times of war, the manpower and vehicle allocation was increased. It was known as a War Establishment.

Ranks in the Regiment

Lower Ranks
Trooper (Tpr) – The first title you are referred to as when you join the Regiment. Equivalents in other units would be Driver, Signaller, Gunner, Private, Sapper, Guardsman, Rifleman etc. depending on the Corp/Regiment.
Lance Corporal (L/Cpl) – First promotion after a minimum of 3–4 years' service. A single stripe was worn on the arm. Also referred to as a Non-Commissioned Officer (NCO).
Corporal (Cpl) – Second promotion, minimum of 3 years more service after the first promotion. Two stripes were now worn on the arm.

Senior Non-Commissioned Officers (SNCO)
Sergeant (Sgt) – Three stripes. Normally, a minimum of 12 years' service by now.
Staff Sergeant (S/Sgt) – Three stripes with a crown above. Normally, would hold a position such as SQMS.

Warrant Officers

Warrant Officer Class Two (WO2) – Normally holds a position such as SSM.
Warrant Officer Class One (WO1) – Normally holds a position such as RSM.

Officers

Second Lieutenant (2Lt) – First rank held on commissioning from Sandhurst. Single pip worn on the shoulder.
Lieutenant (Lt) – Two pips, normally after 2 years' service. Would normally be a troop leader in a Squadron.
Captain (Capt) – Three pips. Normally, a minimum of 5 years' service. Would hold a position such as Squadron 2IC, Ops Officer, etc.
Major (Maj) – A crown on the shoulder. Normally, a minimum of 8–10 years' service. Would hold a position of command such as OC of a Squadron.
Lieutenant Colonel (Lt Col) – A crown above a pip. Would be commanding the Regiment.

Military Clock

Military time is as per a 24-hour clock and so runs from 0001 to 2359. Times beyond midday simply have 12 added; for example, while 1am is simply 0100, 1 pm becomes 1300. Other examples are:

   0500 = 5 am
   0200–1100 = 2 am to 11am
   1200 = midday
   1900 = 7 pm
   1400–2359 = 2 pm to 1159 pm

   0000 = Although it indicates midnight, in the military we never use this; it's either 0001 or 2359 because of the potential for ambiguity. For example, an attack to be launched at 0000 on 3rd Feb could conceivably be launched at 0000 at the start of the third day in Feb, or 0000 at the end of the third day in Feb. There is only one 0001 or 2359 on a given day in the 24-hr clock, either of these would be used instead of 0000, thus avoiding any potential embarrassment.

A Very Special Thank You

For allowing the use and publication of photos:

'Podge' Goodeve (OD Int crew)
Dave Ireland (RSM)
Jason 'Visser' (CO's driver)
Pete Bradbury (B Squadron GW troop)
Sean Lysaght (OB crew)
Steve Baker (1st Troop C Squadron)
Ken Godfrey (2nd Troop C Squadron)
Johnathon Westwood 'Westy' (2nd Troop C Squadron)

For vetting/comments and top tips:

Sue Finch
Iain Johnston
Mel Bulpitt

For making and putting the videos on YouTube:

Richard Titchener

The Gulf War – The Soldiers Tale complete trilogy on YouTube:
https://www.youtube.com/watch?v=PTl4ACxn3T4

The memorial at the National Memorial Arboretum in Staffordshire, in memory of the 47 British service personnel who were killed during the war